THE BLACK BUTTERFLY

THE BLACK BUTTERFLY

An Invitation to Radical Aliveness

Richard Moss, M.D.

CELESTIAL ARTS
BERKELEY, CALIFORNIA

For one human being to love another, that is the ultimate, the last test and proof, the work for which all other work is but a preparation.

Rainer Maria Rilke

CONTENTS

PREFACE
AND
ACKNOWLEDGEMENTS

The language of transformation grows from dimensions of experience that by their very nature are highly subjective. Our greatest challenge is attempting to appreciate life and ourselves in wholeness, as indivisible parts of an unnameable totality. Our usual language is poorly qualified to do so; by its very nature it tends to fragment and contrast. I have attempted to create an objective description of dimensions that most of us intuitively sense, but have never known how to put into words. Such a language must unfold out of a spiraling process where ideas are presented in anecdotes, metaphors, and quasi-logical arguments that are repeated and overlapped until a whole new picture gradually takes shape, and the many themes converge in *heartfelt* understanding. Therefore, I would suggest that you read the book in sequence, as the more mystical and free-falling quality of the later chapters is only possible because of the scaffolding of images and concepts laid down in the earlier ones. To help you move into a fuller feeling for some of the concepts, a glossary has been included.

It is my deepest hope that together we can go beyond the words to the spaces and energies from which they flow where a quickening of the great adventure of transformation is not only possible but ever more likely.

The writing of any book is a major commitment, not only for

the author, but for many others who support and contribute to it. This is especially true for *The Black Butterfly*. I wish to thank my associates at Three Mountain Foundation: Jan Bright and Christina Poniecki for assistance in retyping and copying; Beatrice and Steven Ledyard, Mary Fisher, David Darrow, and Richard and Cathy Larson for generally supporting the space in which this work was undertaken.

I thank Lynne and Chris Muendel, Patricia Carney Moss, David Bushnell, Sharon Huffman, and Aster Barnwell who read the early drafts and offered valuable feedback. The initiative for a glossary and the first draft of its text was graciously contributed by Aster Barnwell. Joan MacIntyre, who edited *How Shall I Live*, also made contributions to the seed material for this volume. The final copyediting and refinements were expertly done by Judith Johnstone, whose enthusiasm provided a constant lift. I thank Shara Miller for her drawings of the spiral energy pattern and the Sacred Meditation. In addition, it was a pleasure working with David Hinds at Celestial Arts, who supported this book from its inception.

I am especially thankful to Anita Brown for major editorial assistance. She read this book again and again as it unfolded and, working side by side with me, drew upon her own depth of being to help clarify the expression of difficult non-linear concepts and significantly improve readability. Hers was a true labor of love.

And always, given freely and eloquently, was the love and friendship of my wife Patricia.

Finally, this book is a song of a great adventure in consciousness lived by many others. I honor the many people who have explored with me over the years and the work they continue to do to make life richer through their radiance.

Richard Moss
Hidden Valley Ranch
Lone Pine, California
July 1986

Introduction:
An Invitation to
Radical Change

*The most beautiful and profound emotion we can
experience is the sensation of the mystical. It is the
sower of all true science. He to whom this emotion
is a stranger, who can no longer wonder and stand
rapt in awe, is as good as dead. To know that what
is impenetrable to us really exists, manifesting itself
as the highest wisdom and the most radiant beauty
which our dull faculties can comprehend only in their
primitive forms, this knowledge, this feeling, is at
the center of true religiousness.*

ALBERT EINSTEIN

IT WAS THE SECOND DAY of the conference.
For several hours Laura had been singing a childhood hymn,
repeating it over and over. Suddenly the quality of her singing
changed. She felt as though she were no longer singing. She *was*
the song. She found herself lifted to her feet, her arms raised toward the sky, her head arched upward. She said her hands did
not end at her fingertips, but continued into the air and sky. The
air and sky were alive, and she and they were the same. Her feet
seemed to disappear into the earth. Earth, feet, body, arms, sky,

song, singer—all were one living being. Laura did not consider what was happening, it just took her. She was the experience.

The next day her terminal liver cancer was gone. The grapefruit sized bowel metastasis that she had supported with her hand was gone. Three days later she realized that for the first time in thirty-eight years she hadn't taken her daily insulin injections. In the ensuing weeks, all the secondary complications of her diabetes and cancer—kidney failure, fluid in her lungs, tumor-ridden lymph nodes, partial blindness, loss of sensation in her hands and feet, addiction to pain medication—healed. Even a few recently broken toes were completely mended within days. She was radiant; a palpable presence poured from her body like a gentle flame and the whole understanding of her life was radically transformed.

Radical means "root," the support or foundation, the fundamental, the basis or basic principle. Radical aliveness invites and challenges us to go to the root of aliveness, to the place from which our very sense of being emerges. It is a state that transcends any concept of ourselves. Laura spontaneously awakened to what might be called her fundamental nature, a condition in which her cancer and diabetes were not the final reality. For most of her life she had identified herself as diseased, and in recent years as a person dying of cancer. Suddenly she saw that this perception was a fiction. All her urgent efforts and her desire for health were outgrowths of that fiction. The woman who was dying was not who she really was. The woman who wanted to live was equally unreal. For a little while she experienced herself as pure Consciousness, and that realization transformed her.

This book is about the possibility and the process of change. It is not about miracles, nor is it about something that happens to only a few. It is about change that is happening to all of us as a transformation of consciousness and of what it means to be human. We will be talking here about how that change comes forward in our lives, sometimes radically, even frightfully, fast, but usually gradually, and always presenting us with new challenges about how to live and express our aliveness.

*

This book is an invitation to inquire more deeply into our own experience, especially into the difficult areas where we seem most uncertain. Here, before the great mysteries of life, in the darkness of ourselves, reside the doorways to new possibility. Here is the potential for the evolving intelligence and soul of mankind. Before we define our experience, before we accept the labels of our conditioned thoughts and feelings, we must learn to create a space of unknowing—a space of openness to new interpretation.

We do not step into the unknown without preparation. Like climbing a mountain without proper equipment or technique, that would be foolhardy. But, while preparation is essential, it is not the journey. In the journey of transformation, it is easy to confuse the preparatory steps—our imaginings about the journey, our techniques to alter consciousness and produce new insights—with actual change. Many people convince themselves that the new experiences, the partial modifications of awareness and behavior produced by these techniques, are the new possibility. And their inquiry slows or ceases. Many feel they have found a new identity and are content to call this transformation. Many then go on to become teachers and work to save the world without ever having passed through the period of fundamental restructuring necessary for the birth of a truly new aliveness. Some even go so far as to create a new fundamentalism out of these preparatory tools and practices.

But genuine transformation is much more demanding, and much more ambiguous in its implications for life. To begin with, it is a fundamental change in the quality of energy that animates our consciousness. If we imagine that our states of consciousness are notes in a scale, the first, a low note, represents our basic state and the second, a high, pure note, represents the new energy after the opening. The shift to the higher note is not to be equated with alterations in behavior, values or beliefs. While these alterations are inevitably the consequence of transformation, it is quite possible to change in these ways without ever undergoing a basic energetic shift.

Fundamental change is spiritual in nature. To even speak of it requires language usually reserved for the poet or mystic. And, always, the language is misleading when we interpret it through ordinary linear consciousness. At times in this book I speak from this mystical point of view; at other times I speak from the linear perspective. It is my hope that the contrast between the personal examples that are accompanied by philosophical and psychological discussion, and the more immediate mystical sharing, will augment the inductive quality of the book.

✳

We want knowledge to give us command over our world. Reason continually analyzes and defines positive change in terms of growth and results measured against predetermined goals. Yet we must ask the question: How can we measure the new? If something truly new appears, we have no familiar criteria to evaluate it and no immediate formula for its application to life. So how can it be measured by our usual yardsticks for change? To do so immediately disavows the newness. In fact, to approach the new we need a radically different way of considering change. We also need a very different way of life.

This book calls us to explore the new in ourselves, where living becomes revelation, a "yoga of the possible."[1] It is a space of realization when we are At-One with life's mystery. It is bequeathed equally by Grace as by effort. Here, in these moments of pure being, essential change occurs.

Such change is instantaneous; it does not occur in time, and it is without determinable cause. It is energetic in nature, as the basic note of our being moves to a new vibration. This brings about an important shift in our usual assumptions about change. Measurable evolution, the acquisition of knowledge, the application of such knowledge, and the concomitant emphasis on achievement, can no longer be regarded as genuine change. Instead, what looks like change to us is really the embodiment in time/space of a shift that has its roots in another dimension. We may refer

---

[1] For this term, I would like to thank my friend F. Aster Barnwell, the author of *The Meaning of Christ for Our Age* (Llewellyn Publications, 1984).

to this process of incarnation as Becoming, but it is not change. Real change occurs in the timeless dimension, the dimension of Being. Thus it seems instantaneous, encompassing all aspects of life at once. We, on the other hand, are continually altering our environment and our life style in the name of growth and evolution. But now we must ask ourselves whether this involves a fundamental change in consciousness, or simply a cumulative process of applied knowledge. A fundamental assumption of this book is: *Alterations of our inner or outer circumstances that do not involve a fundamental change in the energy or note of consciousness are not growth.* This implies a major shift in emphasis and attention as we approach new possibility.

And as long as we believe that the outer and observable phenomena of life represent the only true reality, we tend to think that by choosing to alter the apparent reality we can orchestrate change on our terms. In my experience this is a profound misunderstanding. For example, I regard the first thirty years of my life as a process of Becoming (or unfoldment) occurring at one level of energy. An experience on my thirtieth birthday, which I describe in the chapter entitled "The Black Butterfly," represented an instantaneous change of the most fundamental kind into a state of Being in which there was no time or space, no movement or causality. Yet it was precisely here in that timeless dimension that the note of my aliveness underwent fundamental change.

As individuals, we may have no memory of such a moment of realization, so it is hard to conceive that, underlying all we do and are, there is a timeless, causeless dimension. The degree to which we, and our collective society, have realized this dimension determines the possibilities for growth and embodiment in the ceaseless process of life's becoming. Nevertheless, like Laura, the moment we touch this dimension directly, the whole fabric of our existence is radically changed. We are forever participating in a larger sense of relationship to existence. Here and only here is change that reflects life's wholeness (rather than the reaction to life's appearance) possible.

✳

The energy of a moment of fundamental change is not merely personal in nature; that is, it is not something particular to one individual. The Realization of Jesus literally transformed and continues to transform all of humanity. Consider how Einstein's breakthrough continues to influence an enormous range of theoretical and technological possibility that is transforming every level of human affairs. There is something intrinsic to this higher energy that impels expression in a larger, more coherent, body of humanity. It calls each of us as we awaken to assume our place in the collective body in order that the energy be incarnated in daily life. Each new realization is incomplete until it is a living reality in every individual.

Thus, to me, transformation can never be regarded as a personal achievement or as a goal for one's own sake. The individual who still regards himself as a separate egoic being and is striving to change himself for the purpose of personal fulfillment will find that the transformational quest leads him into ever-deepening despair until he has seen through this fundamental error. *We must understand that all personal growth is intended for the awakening of the whole.* In reality, we are all, individually and collectively, involved in an unending process of embodying higher consciousness. As the consciousness becomes finer, there is a greater possibility for expression in all areas of life. And, as the diversity and variety of possible human expression grows, so too grows our appreciation of the underlying One. Human beings are forever modifying and infilling the energy levels that have already been realized, and thus carrying those energies into fuller and fuller incarnation. Simultaneously, in varying degrees and depths, people are touching into states of realization and becoming doorways through which new levels of energy are continuously initiated into life.

To me, radical change occurs only at the moment we realize our perfect identity as Consciousness. Then we are At-One with that which is changeless, without any characteristic, beyond time/space and causation. Such experiences are relatively rare; yet mystical experiences are common to all people. It is time that we begin to honor this dimension and stop apologizing because we can't prove its value or adequately find a way to express it.

We are challenged to bring these dimensions forward, but not as "specialness" to adorn our egoic personality. It is time to recognize the spiritual heart of our lives. It is time to own the naturalness and the universality of this without dogma and the creation of new ways to separate ourselves.

Most important, we must reflect on what these experiences show us about the nature of reality. Have we ever attained deepest meaning and value through our own efforts? Do we make love happen? Can we through our own efforts fill the emptiness we all feel at times—an emptiness we may not even perceive until, through Grace, it is filled and we overflow with aliveness? We can, at best, set the stage, but the actual fulfillment happens in another way. We all know this. For example, when skiing becomes effortless and is in a sense doing us, time stops and there is an opening in consciousness which can be ecstatic. The result is a freeing of energy, a kind of self-transcendence. We have gained greater possibility within the domain of that particular activity. This is why any activity that tends to carry us toward such moments becomes so attractive, even addictive. Such peak experiences give us a taste of mystical unfoldment, but the change is localized, involving only a compartment of our nature. Whether such moments contribute to a broad expansion of consciousness depends on who we are, our depth of awareness, and the consecration that is pulling us into life.

Undeniably, transformation is having new experiences, learning new ways of thinking, so that life works better. But this is only part of it. Transformation is also a process of radical inquiry and undoing. It begins, for example, when those of us who want peace in our world can also accept that we really do not know what peace is, or how to find it for ourselves. It is much easier, too easy, to substantiate our basic identity over and over again in service to valid and noble causes that purport to change the world for the better. Certainly such efforts are part of the transformational impulse, but we must also face the fact that real change is far more radical and demanding. It goes beyond any concept or hope that we may have for a better life. If our efforts bring sufficient self-esteem and satisfaction so that we unwittingly turn from the deeper inquiry, these efforts may in the end decrease our aliveness and the possibility for a fundamental change in consciousness.

Transformation is about desire and intention, but it is also about intuition and surrender. Most importantly it is about awareness. We stand on the threshold of radical change at every moment. Certain societies, the West in particular, have saturated the energetic potential of their existing structures. We are, like Laura, bursting at the seams with energy that is often expressed morbidly because it is held in too small a container. Like her, we are doing everything we can to grow and heal, but our very efforts inadvertently strengthen the container, creating as much destruction as good. Opening to a larger space where the energy naturally finds harmonious expression is a process of radical change.

❋

The experience called Realization or Enlightenment is the archetypal experience of openness—of relaxing the container of our outer consciousness. It is stepping beyond the walls that define reality as we know it. It can be likened to contacting the heart of life. It is the sacred heart from which all conscious experience arises, especially the sense of our personal self. From this heart pumps the blood of infinitely renewed possibility. Laura's case is a partial representation of this category of experience. Hers emphasizes more the bodily transformative potential than the mystical wisdom that we usually equate with our notion of realization. Clearly, there are different levels of realization, levels of greater or lesser inclusiveness. Thus it would be a mistake to think that there is only one kind of experience. While there is certainly an underlying similarity in essence, the effect of it and the manner of embodiment depends upon factors unique to each person. It is the totality of all such experiences diversely expressed by individuals of all societies in the various arenas of human endeavor that form the basis of human culture.

Realization manifests everywhere; it underlies all that we are. The inclusivity of the way of life this understanding bestows is the soul of my work. Like Laura, I saw the relativity of myself. For a little while that self dropped away, becoming a minimal locus of self-consciousness from which to observe a whole other dimension. "I" became identical with Consciousness Itself.

Realization immediately shifts the ground of understanding.[2] Our humanness becomes far more than a physical or even psychological reality. From this larger point of view, we are also energy systems in dynamic interaction with everyone and everything. Individuality, as the expression of a separate self, enlarges its meaning and becomes *The I That Is We*, the title of my first book. Our responsibility to life changes as we see all reflected in ourselves. Every moment of life becomes a sacred relationship. The workplace becomes a new community in which the very energy of our shared service is an environment for individual growth and transformation. But, simultaneously, our sense of how to act and for what ends becomes less clear, for we have seen the profound unity of Consciousness and we know that we are already whole.

To our ordinary awareness the world is full of disease and wrongness, but in the state of Realization we see that every individual, no matter in what circumstances, is already perfectly whole. Laura was always whole. Before her opening, that wholeness required cancer and diabetes to express her full aliveness. After her opening, she was whole once again, but the new expression of wholeness no longer required cancer and diabetes. Laura was like a firecracker exploding in a closed hand. Her cancer, her diabetes, her whole self-perception and relationship to life were the automatic expression of that dense, confined, unconductive aliveness. All at once the hand opened, the container of consciousness itself went from a closed fist to the vast, conductive, mystical inspiration of an entire ocean. In this context, the energy of the firecracker was transformed. In Laura, what had been disease became radiance.

The term *wholeness* does not imply that we are perfect when measured from our ordinary perspective. On the contrary, it is

---

[2] It can be argued that to generalize from such a subjective experience as Realization, which cannot ever be replicated in a laboratory and thus become the basis for scientific pursuit, is an error. To this I acknowledge with deepest respect the work of Franklin Merrell-Wolff. In his book *The Philosophy of Consciousness Without an Object* (Julian Press, 1973), he brilliantly discusses why it is a mistake to exclude (from the arena of factual and relevant knowledge) understanding gained through the process of Realization. This represents a true weakness in Western science and psychology.

our self-perceived flaws that usually guide the direction and pattern of our Becoming. But if we are not simultaneously whole, then where does wholeness come from? Is it something that we can bring about while we perceive ourselves as unwhole?

When I was in fifth grade, I had my first real experience of education in the true sense of the Latin word *educare*, which means "to lead out." The teacher drew a line on the blackboard and a grasshopper at one end of the line. He asked how many jumps it would take for the grasshopper to reach the other end if he jumped halfway each time. I threw up my hand and called out "two." His silence told me I was wrong and in an instant I had my first conscious experience of infinity. For a few moments I stared into an abyss and something deep inside of me shifted. The world was never again the same.

Is our jump to the other side a moment of identity or an endless effort to reach something that we ever approach and never attain? Do we work to reach some goal or do we see the goal as realized here and now? This is the fundamental paradox, the gift and wound, of wholeness. It is not merely a metaphysical question. How each of us answers this question, moment by moment, in our very relationship to life is the key to our aliveness, our health, our intelligence and our humanity. We may no longer be at a time in history where we can retreat into a monastery and thereby limit the variables that assault our personal lives in order to pursue the awakening of higher consciousness. The awakening must be engaged in our day-to-day living and become a part of the fabric of our culture.

It is the essence of the egoic nature to struggle, to strive, to aspire—yet the awakening is not attained by any effort based in the egoic consciousness. Again and again, as we give ourselves to the transformational process, the very attitudes, values, and relationships that have all along been motivating and sustaining us become obstacles or become empty and meaningless. Even our desire to grow spiritually or to be healed becomes too safe, too easy, too "good." We have crystallized ourselves once again in another secure but too limited niche for our aliveness.

We must utterly surrender if we are finally to know wholeness. But how does one surrender? We cannot, at least not on our terms.

Thus, we fall into periods of unknowing and uncertainty—dark nights—only to rediscover our old values and relationships, but at a new level of meaning and consecration. This is a process of dissolution, of death and rebirth. It seems wrong, needlessly painful; it is not what we intended. Yet it is this very process that is empowering us.

✻

Radical Aliveness: It is in each of us, in our very being moment by moment, that the Infinite and the Finite continuously marry and incarnate as new possibility. The most mundane moments, or the greatest joys and fears, each lead to greater aliveness when we begin to see the face of God lurking within them. The fruit of this marriage may not be obvious at first, for it is happening primarily in a dimension of consciousness. Thus, from the egoic point of view, it is difficult to see what we are achieving, if anything. And this poses a problem in terms of personal fulfillment and ongoing motivation.

Our egoic natures are enlivened and motivated by the energy we receive through our worldly achievements. It is the hope of reward—whether material, psychological or spiritual—that drives most people to pursue transformation. When the growth turns out to be in timeless consciousness and in ways connected to all of life but not necessarily immediately personal, the journey can lose its appeal. We can even feel that we will die if we persist. We are complex beings: Part of us is personal, time-bound, becoming, while another part is referent to infinity, thus completely impersonal, whole. This latter part requires no feedback or reward. But the finite and personal, ego-driven aspect requires continuous feedback and nourishment. The issue of personal fulfillment, of meaningfully meeting our human needs, becomes more and more challenging as our openness to the infinite grows larger in the process of awakening. And this is another paradox, for surely nothing is more fulfilling than the inspiration and vision of expanded awareness. But, while this is undoubtedly the case, our personal natures rely on very mundane bread for nourishment.

To marry these two dimensions as a way of life is the challenge of our time.

It is not a matter of belief, but of awareness. Inspired by our most profound moments of insight and wholeness, we must truly seek to encompass the ordinary and the transcendent. Perhaps we will see that this is also the greatest service we can offer our fellow man. We cannot deny our ego-driven motives, but we must finally come to understand their limits. There is a deeper impulse toward life. From this deeper impulse, we can access sufficient authority to Be, especially at the times of exceptional challenge.

❉

At the edge of the unknown, every moment carries the possibility of fundamental transformation, every moment has a tremendous range of aliveness, far beyond that which we ordinarily allow. Laura's experience demonstrates the powerful possibility of such a moment. We must learn to confirm our own experiences and not accept simplistic and unchallenged beliefs and explanations. More often than not, our unknowing and uncertainty lies closer to the Higher Possibility. The greatest aliveness that we can experience will rarely come to us on our terms. Humanity has crossed the oceans, bridged the continents, walked on the moon, and approaches a global society. But the modern individual is no closer to approaching the "fierce enigmas" of his or her own nature than our counterparts of millennia past. And unless we make this approach, I fear we will not have the spiritual strength to govern the forces already unleashed by our rational faculties.

Yet already there is paradox. To acknowledge the possibility, just to describe such a remarkable experience as Laura's, invites the ego-driven self to hold this as a goal. But to have such a goal is to no longer approach each moment freshly, and thus we limit the intrinsic possibility for aliveness. Emphatically, to be radically alive has to do with energy and consciousness, not phenomena and attainment. We must acknowledge possibility, yet simultaneously understand that no phenomenal change may occur—or even needs to occur. Laura's experience is merely a moment in a far larger process that has its greatest meaning and substance as a way of life.

We do not change so easily, nor should we. The perspective of even the wisest of us is not large enough to fully grasp where we are going or how we should get there. The forces that retard change are equally as wise and holy as those that demand we grow into new possibility. Facing the intrinsic mystery and grace of fundamental change, we are moved to shed our naivete and arrogance about getting there on our terms.

Realization (or Enlightenment), the traditional goal of spiritual development, is at most a beginning. The realities, pleasant and harsh, of life remain, albeit with a whole new understanding. Yes, we are already whole. Yes, we grow only from wholeness to wholeness. But also, we are ever-unfinished, ever-evolving, ever-changing. As we move forward, seeking to create a way of life that honors our highest possibility, the personal man cannot be debased before the Spiritual Man nor the latter betrayed for the former. And it is this effort consciously to grow amidst these tensions, to stand reverently poised at this exquisite edge, that is to me authentic spirituality. The door of realization and healing may only open a crack, or not at all. In any case, it is ultimately a mystery. It is no more a personal achievement than puberty!

1 ✳ THE BLACK BUTTERFLY

Swiftly arose and spread around me the peace and
*   joy and knowledge that pass all the art and ar-*
*   gument of the earth;*
And I know that the hand of God is the elder hand
*   of my own,*
And I know that the spirit of God is the eldest brother
*   of my own,*
And that all the men ever born are also my bro-
*   thers. . . and the women my sisters and lovers,*
And that a kelson of the creation is love;
And limitless are leaves stiff or drooping in the fields,
And brown ants in the little wells beneath them,
And mossy scabs of the wormfence, and heaped stones,
*   and elder and mullen and pokeweed.*

WALT WHITMAN
Leaves of Grass
(Song of Myself, 78–89)

YEARS AGO I BEGAN *The I That Is We* by say-
ing that, like an earthquake, I had all at once been changed forever. I discussed the effect of that experience, the insight and work
it had led me to, the giving over of my life to fulfill a new possibility, but I did not describe the experience itself. At the time
I did not want the attention (whether positive or negative) such

a discussion might bring. Perhaps more wisely, I needed additional time to place that experience in fuller perspective.

Change comes with many faces that conventional thinking simply is not large enough to embrace. We toss aside what we do not understand, or create definitions that convey a sense of pathology. Often this becomes more an unconscious defense of the status quo than a fair or meaningful appraisal. Sadly, many people go through life considering themselves either defective or special. In either case, we miss a larger vision of life.

To be sure, deep change involves risk. The energy of the opening process will be more than one can integrate if it is approached as other things in life have been approached. The result can be intensification of neurotic patterns, psychosis, or even formation or acceleration of actual physical disease. Ego inflation is perhaps the most common danger of any rapid expansion of consciousness. And as Jung has pointed out, ego inflation is often followed by severe collapse. Afterwards, integration may only be achieved by regression to an earlier level of development. Yet, even these interpretations are not dead ends. What can look like the worst nightmare of collapse can become something quite other, depending upon our capacity to engage creatively with courage and perseverance.

Awakening is going on in varying degrees in every person. It is not something from which we can turn away. On the contrary, it is something that all humanity must engage more consciously. Yet its manifestations are so varied that, in the end, it is not the label we give or that others may place upon us, but the depth of integration that is of real significance. Many people are having opening experiences of various kinds. Many are terrified and attempt to deny the experience if they can. Many simply have no idea of the possibilities that are dawning in consciousness during these episodes of multidimensional transformation. New models are needed, contemporary examples of the awakening process, its trials and wonders, what it brings to life, and how it may be integrated. The greatest gift of any such model is not that he or she can tell you what to do, but rather that they expand the panorama of what is possible. Their very lives grant permission to trust more deeply, to invite a creative relationship to oneself. It does not matter how bizarre, difficult, or wondrously transcendent your experience may be. What matters is what you do with it. It is for this reason that I wish to share my own experience.

❋

I don't believe there is any point where one can say realization begins. It is something interwoven into the whole of one's life. In the months before my opening, I was already working extensively with energy and had begun to teach groups. Nearly every day brought some new level of phenomena, some new experience, as I explored at the edge of my psychical boundaries. For most of my life, driven by a deep restlessness and pain, I had been seeking. I had explored all kinds of therapy, and then began the exploration into consciousness along more esoteric paths. All these things played a part in the opening. Yet none can be really measured as the cause.

The actual period of greatest opening began on my thirtieth birthday. It is hard to recall this time objectively because of the multidimensional nature of the experience. As my understanding deepens, I regard it differently. But as one does not have access to hindsight at such times, I want to relate this experience as closely as I can to the way it seemed at the time.

On my thirtieth birthday I worked with a client, even though I had set that day aside for personal retreat. He said he had advanced cancer and was desperate. Reluctantly I agreed to see him. He did indeed have the disease, but his deeper problem was suicidal depression. We talked for many hours and then I shared energy with him. Afterwards he said that he felt as if the depression had been lifted off. However, I felt a nagging uneasiness and a sense of foreboding. For the first time in my life after seeing a client I washed all the sheets, aired the room, and attempted to do a ritual of purification for myself. But the foreboding persisted.

Two days later I traveled to Lone Pine to meet Franklin Merrell-Wolff. I was sipping coffee in a restaurant while rapidly scanning Dr. Wolff's book *Pathways Through to Space*, trying to complete it before the visit that evening. All at once the words began to dance on the page. As I looked around, everything seemed alive with energy. The very air itself was on fire with radiant light and my body felt like an atomic reactor gone wild.

I left the restaurant and headed up a country road toward the mountains. I felt nauseated, as though my body would explode. A shimmering brilliance pervaded everything, and I began to dissolve into the world around me. After a few hundred yards, I sat down in some brush. A cow was grazing in the field. As I looked, I felt myself enter the plants. I coursed through the intricate tangle of stems, into the sap and cells. With a blink, my attention turned to the cow and at once I began to dissolve into it. "I" and the world "out there" were almost but not quite indistinguishable.

The part of me that was observing all this was trying to regain control and thus resisting the process. The foreboding of previous days had set a dark tone and I became afraid. Thoughts raced through my mind so fast I couldn't rationally evaluate them. But that didn't matter to my medical mind. It offered a chain of distressing diagnoses: seizure, stroke, psychosis, adrenaline-secreting tumor. Although I had walked slowly and was just sitting, I could feel my heart pounding; my pulse was around a hundred and twenty. I was in excellent condition, yet my body felt as if it were falling apart. I tried to breathe deeply in order to center myself. I found nothing I had learned gave me any authority over this experience. I told myself to let go, but then I began to dissolve even more and the fear became overwhelming.

I don't know how long I sat at the side of the road, perhaps an hour. I felt ill and returned to the restaurant to use the bathroom. Everything was significant: the position of stones on the ground, the banging of the water pipes in the bathroom, all seemed to be communicating to me. It was not that I could decipher the communication, or that voices had some message for me. It was more that everything was connected; everything made sense, not rationally, but because it was all part of one living thing.

I returned to the table where I had been reading to discover a very dear, wise friend of mine, Edith Sullwold, sitting in the seat I had vacated. We had discussed the possibility of meeting there but I had completely forgotten about it. That morning she had awakened in a state of joy and peace unlike any she had ever known. All during the drive to Lone Pine she'd felt that she was being prepared for something, although she had no idea what it was. When I saw her waiting for me I was grateful, but also reluctant to admit how disturbed I felt. However, this was not a time for false pride. I walked to her and said quite simply, "Something is happening. I need help."

Together we made the visit to Dr. Wolff. He was a wonderful man, nearly ninety years old. I found that in his presence the sense of intense agitation calmed. He did not have much to say when I told him what was happening, but he did speak of a difficult episode in his own life. He had faced an energy that he referred to as "Mephisto." He had found that sitting up at night allowed him to maintain the focus of will necessary to pass through this period. These words lingered and helped me face the long nights ahead.

After the visit I knew that I couldn't return home. Edith invited me to her home, where her husband also welcomed me. For the next week she set aside her therapy practice and with love and wisdom provided the best possible support I could have received at that time. She was a Jungian analyst and dismissed the idea of psychosis. She obtained "holy" water and lit candles that burned day and night, and thus we surrounded the process with the sense of a spiritual ritual. When I became obsessed with thoughts that I was being destroyed, she just kept reminding me to let go of such thoughts, stating that I didn't really have any way of knowing what this experience was and where it would lead.

The state of intense energy continued uninterrupted for four or five days although the sense of blurring boundaries was never as intense as in those first hours. I was standing at the edge of an abyss, afraid and unable to let go, yet too anguished to remain where I was. The level of excitation, often mixed with intense anxiety made it almost impossible to sleep. On the second day, I called a mentor, Brugh Joy, whose opinion I valued, and described the experience with the depressed man and what I was going through. He told me he really didn't know what was happening and used the word *takeover*. That ominous word intensified my fear, recalling Dr. Wolff's discussion of Mephisto. I did not know what to do with such ideas. But he also said something else that proved to be more directly valuable. He said that he was not gifted enough to help me. I knew then that, while I was loved and supported, I was also on my own. This proved to be a crucial turning point.

He also recommended an experienced psychic. The psychic's interpretation was that I was being severly tested, but it was not a takeover. By that time, I gathered that takeover was another name for possession. In her loving presence, I again felt the cessation of my turmoil. In addition, she told me not to sedate the experience with any kind of drug or alcohol. I knew immediately that this was very important advice. Yet, I was so exhausted that I finally felt I had to get some sleep. I phoned in a prescription for a single ten-milligram Valium tablet, which I carried around like a talisman. Some months later I threw it away.

For years I have hesitated to discuss this aspect of my experience because I felt that people might become frightened or cynical at the idea of evil forces and unduly reject the transformational journey. However, I now realize that others are bound to encounter similar experiences, and thus my experience can be helpful. While there is no need to exaggerate the danger, it is unwise to go forward without a broad perspective on some of the possibilities. In those first days of radical opening, one part of me felt that I was involved with such powerful forces that I was literally fighting for my life. Yet at another level I could not fully accept this; to my deeper intuition, it did not resonate as truth. The psychic scolded me that I was in danger precisely because I didn't believe. She did not understand that it was not that I didn't *believe*, but rather that I had a sense such explanations were incomplete. Nevertheless, I was in distress and was profoundly grateful for the love I was receiving from my friends. I utilized her advice. I visualized protective light, and entered into invocations of the Christ. Although unaware of it at the time, I was soon to touch an experience that showed me we were both correct; it was an experience of Realization.

Today I never deny the existence of malevolent forces, but I also know that such forces only exist at certain levels of consciousness. They are configurations of energy that one encounters as the usual egoic boundaries break down. As long as one's realization does not penetrate to a more universal consciousness, these forces have a formidable reality. However, once the deeper consciousness is reached, they are in a sense conquered, or in the scriptual sense, "the devil has been placed behind." We can scoff at such ideas as evil spirits only if our ego-structure is of sufficient density to render us relatively impervious to these dimensions. Then it is easy to hide behind the mask of scientific rationality wherein the unknown is merely an unexplained phenomenon that will someday yield its secrets.

This is not the case in the process of reaching real wisdom. There is a point where such forces may be met directly, and here they cannot be easily dismissed. Yet, it is scarcely any greater wisdom to acknowledge them and live as mankind has for millenia, immersed in occult rituals of invocation and defense, than it is to deny their reality. One must penetrate to a deeper level, and in retrospect I can clearly see that part of me understood this. Yet it is paradoxical. We are multidimensional; one can have realization and know the relativity of the domain of evil-as-a-thing-in-itself and yet, at another level, have the greatest respect for the potency of such forces in their own right. One may never again ascribe malevolence per se to such forces, but they are nonetheless unpleasant and the first tendency is to want to shield and protect yourself. In the end, this is no protection. In fact, it is just a more subtle version of the same kind of process that goes on all the time in the form of warfare where, from our relative point of view, some people are the good guys and others the bad. Deeper wisdom is called for and this implies turning to a higher dimension.

To resist such forces gives them reality and power. The task is to know that even this is the very Divine. We must learn to center, to maintain attention to the deeper space of consciousness, so that we are no longer reacting. Of course, when the dragon is at the door and its energy is larger than what you can meet, it is a good idea to flee out the back. At this level there is wisdom in employing ritual to protect and center onself; it is equivalent to going out the back door. But eventually we have to open the door and incorporate this energy into ourselves. To do so implies that we have already reached a fairly high degree of centeredness and trust. It is easy to understand why egoic man has thought of God as a champion against evil. But this, of course, is ascribing a quality to God based on our personal preference, and this concept of God is meaningless. In fact, it is wiser to realize that as we are drawn toward a higher consciousness, evil is a level of ourselves that we meet on the way. *There is no war of good or evil being fought in the universe save at that level of human consciousness in which the wholeness of God is polarized into the forces of order and chaos.*

*

How does one describe an event of such multidimensionality? From the moment the energy awakened in the restaurant, I was no longer in one reality, one time frame, one perspective. The state-bound levels of consciousness broke down so that the subject/object consciousness and the non-time, non-space, acausal dimensions were superimposed. One can liken it to a dream that, when measured as a burst of REM/brainwave activity, lasts only a few moments. But when we think about the dream and narrate it, it appears to have taken place in an extended and linear progression of time.

Looking back I realize that in those first days the center of gravity of my awareness still remained within the subject/object personal dimension. This is a level of consciousness in which the knower and the known are irrevocably split. This is a basic consciousness of all human beings, the consciousness that makes language possible. I often refer to it as outer or egoic consciousness. It is outer (i.e. oriented to the objects of consciousness) as opposed to the inner or subjective principle of Consciousness itself. It is egoic because individual identity is presumed as the "I" that views the ever-arising content of consciousness. At this level we are always saying, "I am happy, sad, tired, confused. . . " as if this were the truth of who we are. From this level of consciousness, our certainty about things is always at the expense of the knowledge of self.

Perhaps it was my youth, perhaps it was my own inordinate egoism, perhaps there is no easy way through this process, but for whatever reason I could not surrender. The timeless energy represented an overwhelming force of utter dissolution. To the degree that it could be represented to the egoic consciousness, it appeared primarily as some terrible and negative process. God, the perfect Undifferentiated, Uncreated Consciousness, literally appears as evil from this point of view. It was not until the point of view shifted, and identity was then in the timeless space, that all at once the experience became one of supernal peace and wholeness.

Looking back, it was natural that Dr. Wolff, Brugh, and the psychic drew the conclusions they did. And I was all the richer for their thoughts. Yet I knew deep in my heart that it was not evil I was facing, but the fruit of my own arrogance, my own belief that I could heal the man with cancer. . . and others. In the fervor—literally, *inflation*—that came of having already awakened to new dimensions, I was imposing truth on only one limited aspect of experience—the realm of order and goodness—and building my identity from the new powers and seemingly magical possibilities of the awakening consciousness.

From another point of view, it could be said that I had been spiritually ambitious. I had begun teaching about energy by emulating my mentor, without realizing I was exploring forces that cannot be safely held by the basic ego. It was only a matter of time before the scales would have to be balanced. In retrospect, I would say that there are no mistakes. I had moved with integrity, but I did not know my own limits. I had entered into metaphysical realms, accessing higher energies and becoming more open without a deeper mystical base of wisdom. Now, ready or not, I was getting that base.

For all the fear in those first days, there was something else going on, something deeper. The first night alone in a Lone Pine motel, I had a crucial insight. Just a month before, a priest friend had given me a copy of the Gospels. I had read it through in a single sitting, finding myself profoundly moved but not quite knowing why. That night as I sat alone trembling in the energy, I realized that this space of profound disorientation was not unique to me; it had been lived through and thus redeemed by Jesus and others. Through them a Way had been forged. I realized that the Gospels and all scriptures are maps of the psyche, maps of the hinterlands of human possibility that few ever know directly. I understood that no experience is ever lost, that it lives forever in the realm of consciousness. Jesus' realization, Buddha's, and so many others', wait forever for all humanity to rediscover at the moment when we each come upon the boundary of our being and reach out into the unknown of ourselves. In this space there is no time, and it is here the real struggle that evolves consciousness has been waged and will always be waged. It is here the fruits of those who have gone before forever await us, forever parting the walls of ignorance and allowing us to step one little bit closer to the Uncreated. Our egoic interpretation and deification of these great souls does them a terrible injustice and relegates our own exploration to little more than a childish emulation of an already misinterpreted appreciation of the meaning and message of these lives.

At that time I had very little background in mysticism. And even if I had, I doubt that I would have been able to act much differently than I did. Attention is controlled by that which carries the greatest intensity, and in those first days it was the fear. But, on the basis of this intuition, I knew that there was a way forward. The resolution lay in another level of consciousness called Christ Consciousness, Realization, or Enlightenment. I had no idea how I might reach this state, but in retrospect I understand that this intuition reflected the nearness of that possibility.

Passing through to the higher consciousness was a remarkable synergy of events, a kind of cosmic theatre. I had reached a state of resignation. It was clear to me that resolution could not come through thought. Thoughts either absorbed my attention and distracted me for awhile, or they produced greater anxiety. I had done everything I could think to do. All that was left was acceptance. I vowed to myself that I would live one moment at a time and, even if I knew nothing but this misery, I would learn to be grateful.

Looking back on this phase of the process, I realize that positive thinking has its place in realms of ordinary egoic consciousness as a counterpoise to the tendency to become mired in negative states. But this is only a counterbalancing within a limited dimension. To transcend to a higher dimension, the negative or positive nature of any thoughts arising within the old consciousness are irrelevant. To affirm a positive state by repetition of a mantra or inspirational words has the power to soothe, but not to produce a new possibility. I found that as soon as I relaxed efforts to hold my mind in a positive mode in which I felt better, my thoughts spontaneously returned to negative associations and feelings. Thus I simply began to release all thoughts. As soon as they arose, I would simply notice and let them go. This is a common form of meditational practice, but I was discovering it in a new way, with a new significance. I saw clearly that any effort to change my condition was really just a form of rejection. I reached a point of utter emptiness in which there was neither hope nor hopelessness.

It was in this state that I was sitting quietly in the morning sunshine. I observed two butterflies dancing in the air. One was predominately black and the other white. They alighted on a branch and, to my amazement and delight, I saw them mate. I watched their wings opening and closing in unison. After some minutes, they once again resumed their dance in the air. Suddenly, the black one flew to me and landed right between my eyebrows.

At that moment life changed forever. The descriptive words that came in the following days all involve the imagery of Marriage and Union. I am at once the Lover and the Beloved. All of Existence confirms me and is none other than Myself. The personal, physical, existential me is nothing except the Grace of God. It is only through this Grace that "I" (the individual me) exist at all. Every thought, sensation, perception unites me with the Divine and is the Divine.

In that moment, all of creation became a single consciousness, a state of indescribable glory and unspeakable peace. The fear that existed when I stood rooted in egoic consciousness was now the most exquisite nectar. I was suffused with a current of aliveness so transcendently blissful that there is no analogy within ordinary experience that even approximates it. It was a living bliss, but it was also the most profound intelligence. There was a flood of knowing, of understanding as though all of existence stood before me in its totality with its secrets uncovered and revealed.

In the months that followed, I contemplated things that I had never known before. It began with an immediate understanding of mystical statements such as those in Handel's *Messiah*, but it soon penetrated into the domain of medicine and psychology. I saw the whole process of human unfoldment in terms of the unfoldment of consciousness and began to consider how this could be expressed. I wrote the treatise "The Individual and Collective Levels of Consciousness in Health and Disease," which later expanded into *The I That Is We.*

Even more important than the sense of having a vast storehouse of understanding to call upon was the sense of fullness of meaning. Life had always had a kind of emptiness. I had always been angrily questioning, always skeptical and pessimistic to the point of despair. I had wondered if there could be any meaning in all the suffering, the genocide, the pollution, and the mindless way in which most people plod through their days. All of that vanished forever at the moment the black butterfly landed on my forehead. Life now appeared to me as having a fundamental and immutable meaning and value. This value did not have to be attained; it already and always is. I perceived and knew with the force of complete identity, and not mere ideological conviction, that we are already whole. That wholeness reconciled for me all the questions as to life's meaning.

There is immutable Law that governs the unfolding of consciousness, that has been guiding everything that humanity has done or will do. While I do not belittle the problems that face us as we look from ordinary consciousness, I know that nothing we have done has ever been outside the Law. Everything has and is contributing to build the energy of our individual and collective transformation. It is easy to think that we know better, that someone or something else is wrong or to blame. But I saw that we each make our choices, draw our conclusions out of our level of consciousness. For all my complaining and better ideas, I had done very little of substance. All that noise had been to substantiate me, not life's wholeness. All at once I was freed from the darkness of pessimism and blaming, which I realized had been nothing more than a way to create boundary, a way to exist as "me." I experienced compassion for myself and for all of humanity's struggles and achievements. How radically different to offer ourselves to life from a sense of wholeness than from fear or hope.

We may well make ourselves extinct, but I knew then and continue to know that it is not because we are malevolent, not because there is original sin, because of ignorance, perverse will, or our inability to love. If it happens, it will be because there is no guarantee in the process of transformation. It is the gravest mistake to believe that because there is a teleological order—inherent Law—in the universe, such order has any personal intent for our well-being. We will and must keep trying to improve our world. Yet to the degree that such actions unconsciously create a bulwark against the kind of fundamental death/rebirth that occurs in the transformational process, all our efforts will only carry us to even graver circumstances. The Apocalypse is not outside ourselves, it is the process of discontinuity of consciousness in which identity shifts from the ego base of subject/object consciousness to a higher level. There is absolutely no reason that we must destroy ourselves, save that the very possibility is precisely what is carrying us toward the capacity to internalize more deeply the process of creation/destruction.

✱

As the state of Union or Oneness subsided, I went for a walk. I was barefooted, yet the coarse ground felt like it was caressing me. Every house I passed radiated aliveness. I could sense the occupants, their joy and suffering, their aspirations and fears, as though they were telling me directly. I had no preference; there was no high or low in the perfect naturalness of it all. I was in a state of devotion, but not to any abstract deity. God was immanent, inseparable from all that entered and was "my" awareness. I celebrated God in the pavement, the litter, the grass and the trees.

Within a short distance I reached the cliffs overlooking the Pacific Ocean. And there, seemingly just below me, a whale was circling in the cool blue water. I had the distinct impression that the whale had been drawn by the Realization, in a kind of cosmic acknowledgement. A sightseeing boat stayed several hundred yards beyond the whale and, judging by its wake, the whale had turned toward the coast from several miles out, perhaps an hour before I began my short walk. For a long while I sat watching the whale, distinctly feeling that we were communing in the same consciousness. As the whale turned back to deeper waters, I reflected on the kind of consciousness whales may have evolved. Perhaps, lacking prehensile hands, they have explored deeply into the domain of Being while man has evolved as a doer. If so, they carry a very important balance for the consciousness of man. The extermination of the whale may be locking humankind all the more into the relative prison of subject/object consciousness. Whatever the case, I look back upon that encounter as a gentle celebration of life's mystery.

After the unspeakable freedom of the opening, the whole initial period of profound undoing came into deeper perspective. I saw that all that had comprised my former identity, that made "me," was a relative defense against dissolution into a more universal and transcendent dimension. In particular, fear functioned in this way. Standing at the threshold of the new, it was expeditious, perhaps inevitable, to be filled with fear and thus create myself as the one afraid. I understood the whole of personal identity as a kind of reactive structure, a ceaseless creating of boundaries, an endless seeking for the security of identity, whether pleasant or awful. One by one the illusions of my life paraded before me and I saw how even the most noble of these, my career in medicine and my work as a healer and teacher, were fundamentally selfish, self-creating. It was me creating myself (the ego creating an identity) and never, not even for a moment, a true or genuine selfless service to another. I needed to be needed. Unconsciously, I needed others to be ill to substantiate my identity as doctor and healer. In short everything "I" experienced was self-creating; my moods, my fantasies, my hopes and fears, all of my works, and most especially my search for higher consciousness; these were all forms of self-love, all ways of denying the Divine.

Most difficult of all was the understanding that I had never loved anyone for their own sake. The love that I thought I had known was the most powerful self-defining force, the most addictive way to substantiate myself. It was never my lovers who mattered, only the way in which I knew myself through them. For the first time

I understood that narcissism isn't mere vanity, it is the very essence of subject/object consciousness. We look out into the mirror of life and see only ourselves.

Those first months after the opening were absolutely without precedent in my life. Even turning on a faucet and watching the water flow seemed miraculous. How could the Divine take such an amazing and functional expression? How was it that "I" still knew how to do such things? I read Walt Whitman and understood every nuance of his changing voices. I devoured esoteric and scriptural literature and read of the saints with a sense of complete understanding and brotherhood. People around me sometimes spontaneously broke into tears. Some found their skin reddening as though they were being sunburned. I would simply speak without any prior consideration and people began to ask me if I were reading their minds. I could see the pain we all share, but far more real was the beauty and wholeness. But when I moved into consideration of myself, of the days to come, of what I would do, I was as a blind man and simply trembled.

I had been profoundly humbled. Even today there is a part of me that remains in awe. I can trick myself into thinking that "I" had achieved something, but I know that it was only by Grace that it became the doorway into new life. The ineffable opening had given me everything, but simultaneously it had taken everything away. There was no more hiding in the illusion of myself, no more believing in any self-image. As it says in *The Gospel According to Thomas*, "The son of man has no place to rest his head."

The first and primary challenge was simply surviving with the new energy. One can picture this as a machine ordinarily operating on one hundred volts suddenly being wired to a thousand-volt source. I had touched a new consciousness of extraordinary value but the old, while subsumed, still tended to take over my state of being. In ordinary consciousness I became less transparent to the energy, and when it waved through in a new pulse of intensity I would feel myself being undone once again. While it was never as intense as the first five-day episode, I relived dozens of mini-versions of the same process in the first years. I would be afraid and reactive, then gradually bring myself fully into what was happening and suddenly enter a state of peace and radiance.

The power of the energetic current was literally teaching me to remain open and conductive.

I was more than a little frightened about returning to my work as a teacher of consciousness. In those first months, the energy of an evening group would propel me to tremendous expansion, but I would hardly be able to handle the current for the next day or two. I learned to go for long walks, eat small amounts of meat every few hours, take frequent baths and showers in order to harmonize the energy in my body. It was during this period that I discovered the value of spontaneous singing and dancing to keep the energy moving. But despite the fact that group energy would carry me nearly to the edge of dissolution, I never missed a session or cancelled an appointment with a client. My deepest intuition told me that, while I must not push for more work, I must meet everything that life naturally brought to me. In this way, I learned about the balance of will and surrender.

As the years passed, that first realization proved to be only a beginning. Life became far more meaningful, though not easy. That first time, I had seen the Law that unites existence in fundamental wholeness and had almost paid for the understanding with my sanity. But seven years later without disruption or intensity a new realization occurred and I knew myself as that Law. I thought I should celebrate and mark the day, but instead laughed and made the bed. Rather than declare myself enlightened and complete, I declare myself just as assholy as holy! Awakening is not just one experience, it is a process that unfolds in its own timing and has many levels and is never complete.

❋

Today I marvel at how the universe seemed to conspire to create the moment of awakening. No conscious intent could ever have choreographed or even conceived of such an orchestration: the exquisite love and friendship I received, the symbolic mating of light and dark butterflies, the alighting of the black butterfly upon my forehead, and the meeting of a man who forty years before had passed through the discontinuity of consciousness and awakened. As I look back to contemplate the role Franklin Merrell-Wolff played in my opening, I am filled with gratitude. Nearly a year after that initial visit he remembered our brief time together and, turning to me, said, "Now you can do great work, but you can't afford to daydream."

On October 3, 1985 Dr. Wolff died. I was one of the last people to speak with him and it fell to me to voice the permission for him to let go. I told him that his life was finished and his body was ready, that he was completely free to go as soon as he chose to do so. Then, standing quietly for a while, I said that we all thanked him. He emerged from delirium to reply that we were all entirely welcome.

For me, Franklin Merrell-Wolff represents a kind of lineage that says there is a life to be pursued dedicated to the Most High. It is not a life that is conventionally religious, rather it is the life born of realization that is the very basis of religion. It is a life born of spirit, born of Consciousness, upon which all else rests. At the time of great trial, Franklin Merrell-Wolff offered me little advice and, if I had taken his words literally, I would have held my experience in too small a context. But through his presence he did offer something of immeasurable value. It is the knowledge that I am not alone and have never been alone. Others have stood at the door of the Unknown and sung the song of possibility.

Every generation will have its few awakened souls who by their very existence say unto all Life: Here come unto me, that you may know the ground upon which you stand, that you may not fear to continue the journey of radical discovery and meaning upon which the future of all life rests.

❋

The process of mystical awakening reflects life's intrinsic mystery. That which carries us beyond ourselves and into wholeness, making us whole, even for a moment, is beyond our control. Real growth and healing, while intrinsic to life, are ultimately beyond rational understanding. Man as he knows and believes himself to be, can never be the full authority for his own unfoldment.

For many people this truth is unacceptable because it seems contrary to our rational and intelligent efforts for serious self-improvement and social transformation. They hear it as inviting the consolation of blind religiosity or, worse, regression to primitive superstition and a sense of helplessness before God. But what I am articulating is a paradox and we haven't learned to hold both sides. As great and important as our own efforts to grow and change are, we dare not turn away from that understanding wherein we are finally humbled. It is in this humility that we are made worthy stewards of ourselves and our world.

Reason has validly triumphed over blind passion, ignorance, and emotion, but it can never triumph over life's fundamental mystery. To honor the deeper mystery is to understand the relativity of our consciousness and the inherent illusions of any perspective. Finally, it is to understand and accept that there is no guarantee, neither that we will awaken nor that, in doing so, we will arrive where we would like to be. Walt Whitman understood this dilemma when he said that his work could do as much harm as good.

> . . . for I confront peace, security and all the settled laws
> to unsettle them;
> . . . and the threat of what is called hell is little or
> nothing to me;
> and the lure of what is called heaven is little or nothing to me;
> . . . Dear friend! I confess I urged you onward with me,
> and still urge you, without the least idea of what is our
> destination, or whether we shall be victorious, or utterly quell'd and defeated.[1]

All humankind is being carried toward the darkness of self in the very process of coming to realize the great blessing of wholeness. We are opening even now. Will we be overwhelmed? Will there be a panicked scramble for familiar territory? Will years pass while we deny the glimpse of eternity that has been eroding the old basis for our lives and readying us for a new potential? As-

[1] Whitman, Walt, *Leaves of Grass*, Signet Classic Edition, 1955 p. 261. "As I Sit with My Head in Your Lap, Camarado."

suming we have opened deeply, will we have the patience and strength to let the new consciousness guide us? Will we reject our own lives? Will we be patient until the new consciousness becomes more accustomed, more ordinary and our life is sublimed gradually and naturally? Can we be sure that along the way we won't empower the basic egoic structures and become inflated or even messianic? Will we take this new energy and empower old, destructive or disease patterns and thus take ourselves out of life even faster?

When all this is considered, we can understand why the path of radical aliveness, of true healing or enwholing requires tremendous courage, wisdom, and a good dose of humor. Awakening has its own timing for each person. Even if we enter religious life and prepare for the release of the self-involved ego by the routines and ego-reducing habits of such a life, how easily will we release our concepts about God?

Even with preparation and understanding, the moment of opening is still ineffable and unfathomable and the process of embodiment as original as every man and woman.

2 ✳ THE WISDOM OF IGNORANCE

The heart is like a grain,
  we resemble the mill,
Does the latter know why it turns?
Many stranger things will happen:
Silence!
Ask God to inform thee.

RUMI

SOON AFTER THE AWAKENING, when I was just beginning my teaching work, I had a dream. A man was in a hospital bed. Light poured from his head, silhouetting his skull; it radiated from his whole body and poured from his hands and feet. He was clearly suffering and seemed a little crazy. The doctors were anxiously conducting their tests and proposing diagnoses without any real understanding. All they could see were his symptoms, not his radiant energy, his extraordinary aliveness and sensitivity. I walked into the room and immediately felt a wondrous spiritual presence and knew that the light was the higher energy of consciousness and that the psychical and bodily phenomena were consequences of this illumination. I began to explain this to the physicians. The radiant man beckoned to me. He was no longer so distressed and seemed even playful. Leaning close, he instructed me to isolate myself from conventional thinking and study the wisdom of ignorance. After this dream, my medical mind relaxed somewhat, and I could watch the phenomena of the awakening process in myself with a growing detachment and occasionally even playfulness.

The radiant man was an aspect of my own being. In the early phase of the opening, I experienced much physical discomfort and a psychical sense of affliction and confusion. I knew this tremendous restructuring of my being was a result of the awakening. In a real sense this harrowing process was Grace, and a part of me knew it. But I had also been trying to interpret the symptoms medically, thereby limiting a more creative relationship to what was happening and causing myself a great deal of anxiety. While I do not deny the validity of scrutinizing human experience from the medical standpoint, I know now that it is an incomplete orientation. This incompleteness is not simply in the domain of knowledge, which can never be complete. It is intrinsic to the level of consciousness which a priori defines what we call knowledge and which interprets our experience. Since that time an aspect of my work has been to make the translation from the clinical/pathological model of humanness grounded in Becoming (how to get well and why we aren't), to an energetic model based on our ongoing wholeness.

The wisdom of ignorance: For me it is a sacrament. The acknowledgement of ignorance—that I lack full comprehension of anything—is a sacred act that takes ordinary experience and makes it a door to infinite possibility. It is not a mere intellectual assumption; this would be futile. It is an orientation towards infinity, towards God.[1] It is a profound turning of one's awareness away from the things or objects that form the immediate content of consciousness to the space in consciousness from which this content arises.

---

[1] The word God is problematic for many people. It reminds them of their religious upbringing and closes them down. They do not want to have the old image of God-the-Father imposed on them as it was when they were younger. I heartily sympathize, although I personally find it hard not to speak of God. On the other hand, there are those who speak of God as though He were their closest friend. I understand the mystical value in this, for it invites a relationship to the unknowable and infinite. But rarely do those who speak so comfortably of God ever mean it in this sense. They have literally created God as an object of consciousness and they confuse this self-created object with its Transcendent Root. Belief in God, in this sense, has become perhaps the greatest block to true mystical realization, and I have found deep rapport nearly impossible with people who believe in this way. *(continued)*

It is easy to name things: the sun, the sky, the car, my husband, my job, this is wrong, that's good, and so on. But if you try to answer the question "Who am I?" you find there is no simple label—no statement that fits completely. We look, and there are sensations, thoughts, feelings, ideas, beliefs, arising endlessly in our awareness, but never do we see the cognizing self that underlies all this. We can give a label to anything we perceive or think, and in this limited sense we know it, but we cannot know the one who knows in the same way. It is like the uncertainty principle in quantum mechanics, where, within the conventions of geometrical position and motion, it is impossible to determine the position and velocity of a particle simultaneously. If we know where it is, we don't know how fast it is moving, or if we know its velocity, we can't determine its position. As long as we remain at the subject/object level of consciousness we can have relative knowledge of things, but we can never know wholeness. This is the challenge of transformation, to make subject and object a unity.

Direct knowing comes through identity, Being At-One with ourselves, so we experience the transcendence of subject/object consciousness. It is what Jesus referred to as the Kingdom of Heaven when he is quoted in the *The Gospel According to Thomas*, "When you make the inner as the outer and when you make the above as the below . . .then shall you enter the Kingdom of Heaven." It is here, for the first time, that we have become truly reconciled and connected to our world in a living reciprocity of aliveness.

Our ordinary consciousness is rooted in appearance instead of the underlying Reality. The sacrament of ignorance is a way of talking about a new kind of attention that begins to bridge this separation. Now as we move into life, we acknowledge the relative

---

Nothing in my experience suggests the existence of God as an entity outside of Consciousness. At the moment of my realization, I had the distinct impression that God was in me and I was in God. Therefore, I assert that God is knowable in the mystical sense by becoming At-One. Also, there is no sense, at least as I speak of God, of implying a teleological significance, some divine purpose that could be regarded as personal for man. God is neither wrathful nor beneficient. God is not a champion of humanity, but rather a Higher Principle that when Realized lifts the ordinary person to a new level of being. However, while this is so, I nonetheless acknowledge the part of my consciousness that requires a more personal or feeling sense and which is constantly intuiting and even speaking with "God." It is a strong temptation to have a Daddy or Mommy and I do not deny the part of myself that relates to God in this way. Let each individual use the word with the utmost honesty about what level of consciousness is speaking.

reality of our experience. The compelling pull of the outer mind begins to turn back to its source in undifferentiated consciousness. It is as though we are intuiting: "Who am I that this is my experience?" The effect is a subtle undermining of our usual stance. The moment our experience and the "me" that makes it possible fuse, we move to a new level of energy and understanding. Objectively the world is the same. Yet it is shot through with a sense of new meaning and presence.

Practically speaking there is a lot we know and can be certain of. But the appearance of knowing and of certainty in the ordinary sense always means we are operating in a restricted context. We have placed a relative boundary around our experience. For example, in the mathematics of quantum electrodynamics, equations only become useful for practical technology after all the infinity symbols have been removed. This process of sacrificing truth for practicality is called *normalizing*. Similarly, whatever level of consciousness we are operating from is always normalized relative to the larger mystery of life. This unconscious normalizing, inherent in the fact that we only operate out of a few of the probably infinite levels of consciousness, makes it possible for us to act and to think we know what we believe and who we are. Meanwhile we are sinking deeper into illusion. The sacrament of ignorance is an acknowledgement of this. It is a turning to that which is in our hearts. It softens the brittleness of our subject/object reality.

To confess ignorance, which is not the same as acting ignorantly, is a key to aliveness. It is a law which we can confirm for ourselves: The seemingly hard facts of life, the absolutes that cannot change, will always soften and become ambiguous or irrelevant as the egoic forces are relaxed. You can fall in love with one person, but the moment you acknowledge that larger space of unknowing, where the you who is in love is recognized as relative, then you are in love with everyone. You may feel utterly indifferent, even cold, toward your former spouse and abhor any kind of association but, letting go of this, you could be in love once again. Every time we recognize the ignorance inherent in any interpretation of reality based in the content of our consciousness, we access a higher dimension of aliveness that unites us to life and other people. This is why I refer to it as a sacrament. This movement is extraordinary; we take the known and make it mystery and sacred; we take the unknown and make it love.

3 ❋ INTENTION, CONSECRATION AND UNCONDITIONAL LOVE

Let him who seeks, not cease seeking until he finds, and when he finds, he will be troubled, and when he has been troubled, he will marvel and he will reign over the All.

SAYING OF JESUS
The Gospel According to Thomas

IN EVERYTHING I TEACH AND LIVE, there is a dimension for which words are somehow inadequate. It is the sense of a space or context that unites our being to the fullness of life in every moment. It is not something static, but something dynamically alive, expanding and contracting as our being reflects a larger or smaller sense of the Divine in which we are continuously held. I call this dimension *consecration.* The intuition of this space becomes even more important as we ask questions about our lives, the directions we take, the things we act on or avoid, our values, and so on. When someone approaches me for spiritual advice, I often answer with the question, "But what is your consecration?" If we see ourselves in a smaller light, then we will behave accordingly, perhaps selfishly and defensively and with certain goals and concerns. If we see ourselves in a larger light, our goals and concerns are immediately transformed, as are our actions. The light in which we see ourselves is our consecration.

There is an active and passive aspect to consecration. In the active sense, consecration encompasses intention and aspiration. Yet in the passive sense, it goes far deeper, calling us to a kind of attention, a ceaseless intuition into our underlying relationship to existence. Upon this underlying relationship all our intentions and aspirations are predicated.

Intention in its highest sense approaches active consecration. Higher intention is a conscious relationship to life that involves self-purification and a desire to realize our highest potential: to be good, to be loving, to serve humanity. This level represents the basic esoteric expression of religion. But intention, no matter how noble or inspired, is always ego-directed, always reflecting some desire. It creates, as the word implies, a kind of tension. This tension mobilizes energy and provides a focus for will that is a valuable counterpole to inertia and crystallizing tendencies. Positive intention, in particular, produces a sense of direction, purpose, and self-worth that helps us to gather energy for incarnating new possibility or actualizing a higher value. But the fostering of intention is developmental in the maturation of consciousness. There comes a point where even our very intent to grow and purify is a defense against undoing, against realizing a more fundamental level of being. Inevitably, intentions born from our ego-based considerations must divide reality into a positive and negative pole. In this sense we are denying God as Wholeness.

It is the Catch-22 of maturing spiritually that intentionality, no matter how noble, empowers the personal egoic structure, and it is this structure that resists the moment of realization. In this sense, our intention inevitably leads to despair, and this is good; it is Grace. At a certain point we must surrender, and we cannot even intend it. We face a profound paradox where we may feel utterly useless and without hope or motivation, yet closer than ever to a new potential in consciousness. It is a difficult and dangerous time, a dark night. It is at this point that intention gives way to consecration.

Consecration comes from the Latin *consecrare*, which means "to make or declare sacred; especially, to devote irrevocably to the worship of God." In religious usage, the act of ritual consecration is restoring something to its true relationship in God, not intending it to become that. The difference is the essence of spiritual mystery. Thus, the question "What is your life consecrated to?" challenges one to move from the dynamic of becoming and intending, to a radical yielding into life, a radical gesture of faith. It is a probing into our underlying relationship to life. Does my stance presume that God is whole, that life is whole? Am I turning away from a higher possibility because I am afraid of my own uncertainty and helplessness? Do I really need to be more powerful? Is my pain the result of ignorance or wrong living, or is it because I am already embracing more of life than I can possibly integrate and control on my terms? Intention is often the end of questioning, the beginning of action. But consecration implies that we seek to see how our underlying assumptions about the nature of existence predicate the stance we take toward life.

Consecration in its deepest sense as intuitive attention recalls us toward the divinity of ourselves in every moment. It opens us to an undefended relationship to life where we may finally understand the subtle self-control that limits our aliveness. There is an unbinding of the heart, a relaxing in the very core of one's being. Suddenly, all of living is worship—our struggles, our doubts, our incessant need to keep doing, aspiring, purifying, becoming—all is worship. We no longer need a formula; there is no real distance between who we are and our highest potential.

As we reflect upon ourselves in this way, we are consecrating ourselves. We begin to see the subtle games we play, the self-enobling that hides in our aspirations and good deeds. It can at first make it harder to function in the world in terms of achievement and performance, for our old motives and intentions may no longer feel consistent with our deeper sense of consecration. But even if consecration is at first nothing more than a new concept, the very word conveys a spiritual feeling that invites timelessness, that invites letting go, trust, and Being. It suggests a coherence and an effective quality to the Unknown, something approachable, rather than a space of personal annihilation. Just as intention empowers within the plane of egoic consciousness, consecration empowers spiritually by reconciling us to larger dimensions of awareness. As the awakening process reaches more and more into our lives, the emphasis on consecration allows us to hold the new energies far more gently and safely.

*

We are consecrated whether we know it or not, but we have to look closely at the quality, motivation and content of our lives and begin to sense our energy before we can intuit the nature of our consecration. For example, when we want to leave a marriage because there is no longer real sharing and the passion has gone, where is the consecration? Is the underlying consideration loneliness or unhappiness? Do we feel that it is self-destructive to continue in this lifeless relationship. Perhaps (we think) the thing to do is to find another partner, fall in love again and try to regain that old feeling of aliveness. But how much aliveness is there in this? What if we are becoming aware that we repeatedly attempt to recreate a familiar condition and thus preserve a comfortable sense of self? At this point we may wonder if there is another possibility. Staying or leaving may not be the issue. Rather, we may choose to let go of (more truly transcend) the "me" that is unhappy and feels unloved. Releasing this self-perception could lead to a new level of aliveness and new space for the marriage.

In the first response, the consecration is to the known and the familiar. Underlying this is a sense of incompletion, and perhaps the fear of living life wrongly or of entering deeply into oneself. It is an unconscious consecration to life and oneself as less than whole, as needing to be completed from without. In the second response, the consecration implicitly acknowledges a deeper wholeness that moves beyond the "me" that I know. In this instance, marriage has become a sacrament precisely because it represents a level of commitment to oneself and another that is large enough to expand the basic consciousness and invite a new, albeit unknown, potential.

I am not implying better/worse, right/wrong in this comparison. Individuals must live what they feel is the truth for them. And from a developmental point of view, it is ridiculous to pretend that one can acknowledge the deeper consecration if, in fact, it is an ideal that results in repression rather than self-transcendence. Thus it is quite possible that releasing the dead relationship would be to move into the greater aliveness. The point, however, is that the deeper questions in life cannot be approached without a sense of one's consecration. No matter what question we ask, the answer is always relative to our consecration to life. And this is not something we decide as much as it is an attitude of ceaseless self-inquiry. Just seeing the light in which we are framing our lives automatically invites a larger possibility. It is a process of sublimation that changes our energy, our note. We become a little more conductive, a little more available, and this is reflected in the choices available to us. Life sculpts us even as we sculpt it.

Our consecration is like the iris of an eye that sees into infinity, regulating the light of the transcendent that permeates us moment by moment. As it enlarges, becomes more inclusive, the energy of reaction and defense is gradually transmuted and is replaced by a condition of expansiveness and radiance. More and more the ordinary is the sublime and we are enveloped in life's mystery. More and more our choices reflect life's wholeness and naturally call for the highest good of ourselves and all creatures. Simultaneously, there is a growing capacity to ratify our own experience, to derive our own sense of who and what we are. We are no longer veiled from our own native aliveness, a condition of ordinariness and divinity. Consecration—not any kind of desire, intention, or aspiration, but rather a profound intuition of that which is prior to any quality of experience—is one's personal relationship to God.

A SHIFT IN CONSECRATION

In 1975 I was physician and climber on a mountaineering expedition in Peru. This trip was a turning point for me, as it was then I first made a conscious choice that could lead to my death. Before leaving, I made a will and gave a farewell party for all my friends and colleagues. It was a ritual of separation and new beginnings. On the climb I became hypothermic at 20,000 feet and nearly died. Even though I never reached that summit, and in one sense the expedition could have been called a failure for me, something had shifted. I had reached a state of resolution of an identity crisis. It took the form of a simple statement, "I am substantial as I am." Deep within myself I understood that fear could not be conquered and that I no longer needed to prove myself by overcoming fear. I knew that there had to be another, more universal, principle that guided life. Simultaneous to this, I had the sense that I could now look any person in the eye and not feel the least diminished by her or his achievements. My consecration to life had been profoundly changed. I was no longer consciously controlled by fear and inadequacy. Thus it was not surprising that less than a month after my return, William Brugh Joy invited me to his first transformational conference, in which he proposed to explore unconditional love.

For the first time I experienced body energy fields, and the sense of my heart opening. The encounter with Brugh, also a doctor, was perfect for me, a young physician who had recently reached a turning point. Energetic awareness was presented as a subtle form of diagnosis and therapy; the healing relationship was still a therapist/patient dynamic for me, but at an immensely refined sense of rapport and meaning. This new dimension became, as it had been for Brugh, a stepping stone out of traditional medicine without requiring a complete break with the past persona. I recall that some people could not sense the energy which for me was completely obvious once I was inducted into that sensitivity. For me, it seemed like magic, a new power that I had been given. But it was not long, as I reflected on what I was experiencing, before the encounter with human body energies became revelation.

I was enthralled with sharing energy and took advantage of every opportunity to explore it when I returned to work. I taught it to some of the nurses in the clinic, and we would share energy with patients before and after any procedure that was physically or psychically traumatic. The results seemed impressive in terms of the patient's decreased pain, increased trust, and appreciation for our caring. For me it revitalized medicine. Now I had a reason to deepen my relationships to patients and I found this tremendously stimulating. I shared with every person who would let me. The result was that I continued to open into deeper dimensions of consciousness. Rather than closing down and losing the "high" of this first initiation, I let it continue to grow. However, spending more time with each person, I was seeing fewer patients and it became clear that the constraints of a traditional medical practice would not work.

A whole new evolution had begun. I wanted to gain as much experience as I could of the body energy fields, and I wanted to discipline my life in accordance with whatever practices would allow me to live at the highest possible energy. Again my consecration to life had been deeply changed, although at that time I would not have thought of it in such terms. The obsession with the personal, or finite, "me" was no longer central. Now, I was also oriented toward the infinite, toward the unlimited possibilities. I had experienced myself as more real than ever before. I was more than physical, more than psychological. Energy was a new dimension and it became the bridge to a new way of life, a new path. Within nine months I had stopped practicing medicine. Five months later I began to teach because I felt that there was nothing more important than to help others touch an experience that could change the base of reference in consciousness. Also, I realized that if I wanted to explore energy, the most accelerated way was to be in group energies. So I built my life around this. At the heart of this path and the work that I began was a new concept: unconditional love.

Unconditional love: It was something I knew in my heart, but couldn't explain. It became the ultimate goal, the most true condition. What Christ is to a Christian, unconditional love was to me. I would ask myself, "What is unconditional love?" What does it mean in terms of my relationships, in terms of my work? Unconditional love became my active consecration.

The consecration to unconditional love probed the underlying motive in everything that I did. As I sat listening to people, the notion of unconditional love began to part me from my ideas of therapeutic goals. Was I really loving another if I had to change them? Didn't this imply that they were unacceptable as they were? I became skeptical of how unconditional I was being when I saw how much self-importance I felt after helping someone to a new insight or understanding. I would let go of trying, of having any goal, and the relationships would go even deeper. I would watch myself as I shared energy. Here I was wanting to offer the finest quality of energy and at the same time my mind was filled with thoughts such as, "Does she feel it, is it powerful, am I a good healer, is it working, should I charge for this . . .?" Becoming aware of the sheer self-interest underlying everything I did began to show me my egotism and to erode it. I had set a standard for myself that I could never meet.

I believed, at first, that unconditional love was something that I could do—something we should all do. This, of course, is the greatest egotism. It is a common error in the New Age movement, and it represents a problem in translating between dimensions of consciousness. Unconditional love is a principle on which the universe is organized; it is an understanding at the moment of realization. But as soon as we enter into the dimension of time/space and causality, there is no such thing as unconditional love. Thus to hold it as an ideal for one's behavior only leads to paradox.

But paradox itself is a door to a higher level, and this was precisely my experience. I was committed to keep exploring relationships consecrated in unconditional love. Recognizing my selfishness and self-interest referent to this standard, I found that I began to release more and more of my self-involvement. I would watch the intent for the highest good, the need for recognition, the distrust of any assumption I made about my motive or involvement. Such self-awareness was painful, but I did not let any of this stop me. It became an exercise in awareness. I began to see that I didn't know anything; the good or the bad thoughts I had about myself were nothing more than thoughts. Thus all I could do was to remain aware. I would remain aware and simultaneously trust that something beyond me, something far purer, was actually taking place. In this way I began the deep intuition into the Divine.

This intuition eventually carried me to a new level of consecration. Why, I asked myself, is unconditional love any more real than any of the other thoughts that I have witnessed and gradually let go of? There came a moment when I consciously realized that even unconditional love as I had embraced it was a condition. No moment ever was what it was; it was constantly being compared and judged, albeit against a sublime standard. Suddenly I became aware of the underlying control in all this. If I really believed that there was such a thing as unconditional love, then I no longer needed to hold on to even that as a belief. This realization left me with a sense of emptiness and darkness. I became tremendously introverted, at the edge of what felt like the deepest grief. A few weeks later the awakening occurred and for the first time I knew unconditional love directly.

*

Clearly, in my teaching, the principle of consecration carries paramount importance. In fact, it is the beginning, the middle and the end of my work. As the beginning, it means initiation into a new level of energy and thus finding one's relationship to life suddenly brought to a new depth. One woman put it this way: "Ever since I was a child I knew there was a secret chamber and in it there was a dead rose bush. This chamber was like a knot in my solar plexus and, despite all that I have done in my life and the tremendous amount of growth I have made, I always knew in my heart that this chamber was still closed. Now I know, although I don't understand it, that finally the door to that chamber has opened. Light has entered and the rose has begun to thrive." This imagery is the imagery of a new level of consecration to life. As the middle, it is the new vision of life, the new commitment and discipline that such moments of deeper aliveness call us to. It is this which guides the purification of our natures and the manner and form of our living. But finally, consecration is neither an experience we have nor a new vision we pursue. Its essence is radical intuition that recognizes the transcendent in every moment. At this level consecration can be regarded as the highest form of meditation. And it is not an awareness outside ordinary life, reserved only for the religious aspect of our consciousness—something that we do on holy days. It is an ongoing awareness in the midst of ordinary life. And it is this very awareness that binds the higher energy into life.

4 ✳ THE TRANSFORMATIONAL MOMENT

Peace me together, Oh soul
Assemblage human and holy,
Peace together the life and the prayer,
That the Current flows strong in stillness,
And a twinkle in the silence catches the breath,
Oh wonder!

RICHARD MOSS

RARELY DO WE REALIZE how little we actually know, how our usual experience of life reveals only a narrow sliver of Existence. When opportunities for growth occur, they are doorways into the unknown, invitations to new life. They cause us to marvel at the unfathomed mystery and possibility that we are ordinarily unable to see, perhaps afraid to see. But before this sense of marveling is a genuine reflection of deepening freedom within our own being, we must allow such an experience to profoundly penetrate us. We must be willing to let ourselves be shaken in our own familiar and secure beliefs, to be troubled so that we renew our inquiry into ourselves, into how we live and what we live for. It is precisely this that the event of Laura's transformation offered to me, and in varying degree to those who witnessed it or who have come in contact with her since.

In the next few chapters I want to address this experience in depth, first describing the exercises that evoked her opening and then the general principles of transformation inherent in these particular exercises. Finally, I will address how her change has affected her and others in the years since.

I am aware of the potential dangers in placing so much emphasis on such a radical and relatively rare event. It can seem too desirable for those who are suffering, too much the goal they should work for and at the same time too far away, too impossible to hope for. Some may feel discouraged. Also, there is the danger of seeming to place too much emphasis upon dramatic phenomena, which is the very last thing I intend. From an epistemological sense, I question the validity of generalizing from one experience. But it is not just one experience. There are important similarities in what happened to Laura and my own awakening, as well as the experience of others with whom I have shared over the years. Taken as a whole, and in conjunction with the mystical literature concerning the process of awakening, they point toward universal principles, principles that I feel make the process of transformation relevant to every arena of human life.

For years I have been developing a teaching based upon my own awakening. I consciously worked to make the mystical unfoldment intelligible and immediate to seekers by developing what I feel is a contemporary language and, most importantly, experiential dynamics that actually evoke this unfoldment. Laura's opening was for me a confirmation of this effort. But, more importantly, she provided an opportunity that was like looking at aspects of my own experience from the outside. Thus it is not because I feel this kind of experience can or should happen to everyone, but because the ideas that I wish to discuss are best understood when they can be held in the framework of an actual experience. It is my hope that the wonderment and basic humanity of this story will inspire and trouble you, that you will feel yourself invited into the Unknown, encouraged to explore, unlearn, rethink— and to hold life with renewed reverence and compassion.

THE ENERGETIC DIMENSION

Laura's opening occurred during a three-day conference. The exercises and meditations used in that conference or in the longer conferences are for the most part spontaneously conceived as I attempt to make some area of exploration experientially real. The effective ones are usually continuously evolving and rarely are presented in exactly the same way twice. They all involve energy, or in some way point to a dimension underlying our usual level of awareness.

The concept and experience of energy is central to the understanding of transformation. It is also one of the most difficult concepts to describe because of its esoteric nature. To appreciate energy one must have direct experience, and this level of experience frequently transcends the dimensions expressible with words.

Energy is fundamental to existence; everything is energy. In its pure and unobstructed form, it is Consciousness. Franklin Merrell-Wolff writes of it as pure consciousness without an object and without a subject. Relative to this level of pure unobstructed consciousness, as we enter further into more mundane awareness and our experience becomes more particularized, energy gradually decreases. In other words, our ordinary levels of consciousness, in which things appear concrete and real, are lower levels of energy. As such, they are also lower levels of aliveness. It is not that manifest reality is less than or inferior to the higher levels. On the contrary, the energy of manifest reality is identical to the energy of pure unobstructed consciousness. However, at any given moment our ordinary consciousness only accesses an infinitesimally small part of the totality. This progressive narrowing of consciousness as it (and we) becomes more tangible, more "real," represents a contraction away from the dimension of realization.

Discussing energy with its infinite relative manifestations becomes quite complex because the meaning of the word *energy* differs according to the level one is referring to. At one level, it is *life force* and *vitality*. But sexual energy, emotional energy, and so on, are specific forms of that vitality. At another level of usage, energy means our relative state of *consciousness* at any given moment. In this sense, as we shift from one level of energy to another, our experience of ourself changes. Energy as Consciousness is crystallized or trapped in any subjective level of experience. Just as atomic energy is released when the atom is split, so too, when a particular thought structure or belief system is seen as relative truth and we recognize an underlying and more fundamental dimension, psychical energy is released from that thought structure. This freed energy becomes *aliveness* or *presence* that radiates throughout our being. In this usage, one could also call the energy that occupies and substantiates a thought structure, *attention*. Thus I might say that energy is released as we free attention from a particular pattern or belief.

Becoming aware of energy as the dimension underlying our psychophysical reality is crucial to taking the transformational process beyond a dynamic of continuous rearrangement of psychological and psychical structures. When we observe ourselves and our world from ordinary consciousness, we are continuously reacting or attempting to rearrange our experience so that we can evolve toward some idealized self-image, gain greater control and personal power, or simply eliminate some discomfort. But transformation implies freeing our attention from these considerations through awareness, thereby liberating our energy, so we are carried to a more expanded consciousness. Developing energetic awareness frees attention from relative levels of experience, thereby bridging the gap between ordinary subject/object consciousness and the consciousness of Oneness or Identity. Energetic awareness extends the sense of I-Am-ness from the subjective "me" that perceives everything as either interior and psychical or external and objective into a domain where the inner and outer merge. This is experienced as presence emanating from oneself and yet simultaneously including everything in the field of one's awareness. Thus, other people, the room or space one is in, the visual perceptions and sounds—as well as the thoughts flowing through one's mind—can all be experienced as facets of the encompassing energetic presence. Often there is a sense of stillness or emptiness as we are centered within this energy. Attention to this presence tends to deepen it and increase the stillness.

The exercises I work with in conferences are specifically intended to evoke this kind of awareness in ways that are immediately relevant to our contemporary concerns. They incorporate methods that can be readily grounded as a spiritual discipline that heightens body energies, creativity and one's sensitivity to others. The short-term consequences are an acceleration of the process of dissolution, the release of crystallized and defensive psychophysical patterns. Through dancing, singing and other physically dynamic activities (which also tend to evoke energy) our physical and psychical armoring breaks down (dissolves). In this way, rather than trying to locate our patterns on the basis of ordinary self-perception and concerns, we find them within the body itself. Energizing the bodymind in this way increases its energetic conductivity and begins to empower physical rejuvenation and transformation.

There are many ways to do this, but the key aspect is group energy. To me, group energy is only a metaphor for the human family; however in a conference it is possible to bring a group into far greater coherence than society in its vastness and diversity has the vision to appreciate. To accomplish coherence, each person must become an unreserved participant, not merely an observer. Personal needs, goals or issues must to some degree be set aside. In short, at some point in the conference each person must surrender fully into the process and become completely present. As more participants become available in this way, a tremendous collective energy is generated. This increasingly coherent field of energy acts directly upon each individual in ways that demand a new and ever-deepening relationship to themselves and each other.

Just to be within this energetic milieu is transformative in itself. People spontaneously move into expanded awareness and the personal issues and problems resolve naturally; often they become irrelevant when experienced from a new level of energy. This is important, because our usual approach to a problem is to attempt to resolve it at its own level. But from the transformational perspective, our problems are consequences of our relationship (availability and conductivity) to energy. When we become open to a deep, profoundly silent energy, many of our chronic concerns seem to melt away. For example, we may no longer fear the loss of love from our partner because we experience a profound relationship that exists regardless of external circumstances. Thus the focus is on activating the deeper energy while simultaneously learning to let go of one's resistance to it. To focus on the problem, no matter how real or tangible or poignant it may seem, immediately narrows the energetic potential. It is this that poses one of the greatest challenges to those who would pursue the transformational process.

I have discussed some of this in *The I That Is We* and *How Shall I Live*. As I plan to discuss energy later on, I will stop at this point. Suffice it to say that energetic awareness when held in a particular context of understanding carries one toward the threshold of mystical awakening to whatever degree this is possible in each individual. Obviously, kindling of the mystical element implies mental and emotional maturity, as well as thorough psychological insight into one's personal nature. Thus I address all of these areas in my work. However they are never the primary focus, just as healing is not the focus. Experience has shown me that the mental, emotional and psychological contents of consciousness are always secondary to a deeper dimension. If we are to approach the new, we must know how to release our usual preoccupations with ourselves and open to a more universal consciousness that tends to unify these other elements.

AN EXERCISE IN SELF-TRANSCENDENCE

The exercise which began Laura's transformational shift was a process of dancing in which the participants are in groups of four. One at a time, each person dances while the other three remain closely attuned to the dancer. Each of the three who are not dancing represents a fundamental force or vector of the transformational impulse. These forces are intrinsic to all awareness but are rarely consciously perceived. The three assistants specifically attempt to evoke and synergize these forces in the dancer, thus enabling him to move toward the transformational moment. In the course of the exercise, every person has an opportunity to dance and to explore each of the three vectors of transformation.

The first helper is called *Creative Involvement*. He or she verbally calls out images, word pictures, or feelings intended to help the dancer join more fully with the music and become freer with his movement. As a fundamental vector of the transformational impulse, Creative Involvement is far more than a conscious or willed intent. It is an *a priori* quality of spontaneity and originality with which we meet any experience. It represents the capacity to break the habitual stimulus/response equation so that a new and unanticipated response emerges. In the dancing exercise, the person who represents this capacity must become so attuned to the dancer that a simple remark may enable the dancer to become more connected to his or her dancing. Imagine, for example, that you are dancing in a somewhat practiced and controlled manner (you yourself are not aware of this because it is a habit) and all of a sudden you hear and sense the word *sunshine*. It immediately shifts your relationship to the dance. Just sensing the radiance and vitality of sunshine, your movements become more fluid and open. Now there is more energy available in your dancing. This is the gift of Creative Involvement. It allows us to enter the immediacy of our experience (the dance) with freshness, and thereby free energy that would otherwise remain bound.

The second helper represents *Will* or *Intensity*. This is another fundamental vector of consciousness that determines the inner authority or wholeheartedness with which we give ourselves to whatever we are doing. The intensity of our participation diminishes the psychical inertia that self-consciousness and laziness automatically create. It is this inertia that determines the limits of our aliveness, divides us from the immediacy of our experience. This division is the great abyss that separates subject from object in ordinary awareness. But movement toward either pole, i.e. greater identification with the subject or Self (the intent of most Eastern meditations), or with the object (experience), results in a tremendous increase in energy. An analogy of moving toward the object pole is the forced attention of a mountain climber during a difficult section of the climb. He or she is totally involved; self and experience are virtually united. Afterwards, despite being physically exhausted, the energy derived from such activity can keep one awake for hours. The important difference between this analogy and the sense of Will or Intensity as I am using them here is that Intensity is no longer the product of crisis or a particular desire. It is a continuous element of one's consciousness, a kind of tension that itself produces attention. The inner authority we possess in life is proportional to the natural intensity of the attention we bring to every moment.

Usually we do not know how to access the needed authority

directly; our inertia is such that only during crisis will we exceed our energetic boundaries. But there is a close correlation between Intensity, inner authority and willed effort. Perhaps this is why industriousness is a virtue in more than one religion. Thus the second helper can act as a throttle, urging the dancer to greater effort, more vigor, more involvement in the dance. For the dancer, the effort necessary to meet this physical demand has a tendency to cross over into a state of deeper involvement. He or she cannot remain peripheral to the experience of dancing. The distance between the dancer and the act of dancing begins to narrow. If it narrows sufficiently, the dancer will shift to a new level of energy. At this point the quality of the dancing will change, become more easeful, yet energy will radiate from the dancer. It is like the phenomenon of second wind. The second helper must be sensitive to modulate the dancer, either increasing or (occasionally, if the person is trying too hard) decreasing the force and vitality of the dancing in the hope of helping the dancer to be carried to a new energy level.

Finally, the third person represents the principle of *Unconditional Love*. This helper is asked to merge his or her awareness with the dancer unconditionally, to be At-One and at peace with the dancer, to accept the dancer no matter what. This dimension of love is truly unconditional. It is never something that we do, nor is it a feeling or emotion that we can direct. Rather it arises spontaneously when the barriers to communion with the moment have somehow fallen away. Love is intrinsic to the depth of Being, a natural force of integration that brings wholeness to what was formerly separate or even antagonistic. It is a direct indication of the breakdown of subject/object consciousness. It expands out to infinity, dissolving all relative forms until Love itself disappears into pure Consciousness.

The third helper doesn't say a word but stays fully present, breathing with the dancer, open to him and consciously holding him in an energetic embrace, an embrace formed by the helper's complete attention. It is a very particular quality of attention, fully cognizant of the dancer and the other helpers, yet simultaneously referent to the infinite, the already-present, perfect wholeness immanent in the outward appearance of things. This quality of attention provides space. It tends to act as a universal solvent for any state of consciousness in which the dancer may be stuck. Thus it inducts the dancer to a larger space, a higher energy. If the dancer reaches that moment of let-go, the energy field of the third helper will fuse with the dancer's and together they will become far larger than either one alone. The importance of this kind of support cannot be underestimated.

The third helper is the mystical Lover, the higher vision or aspiration buried deep within all of us that in rare moments carries us beyond ourselves. The moment this aspect becomes conscious for the first time, the principle of wisdom and the whole potential for transformation awakens. In this sense the third helper is exploring the function of the Guru, which in Sanskrit literally means "the uplifter." Clearly this function is the most subtle for people to grasp. Yet it is central to the whole exploration of consciousness. The latent higher potential within each person is most frequently kindled by recognition of it within another. To recognize the perfect wholeness that is Consciousness—to know that I am That—the Guru stands as a door, one aspect of attention united to the Infinite, the other in relationship to this world. The great contribution of the Guru is that he or she sees each person as they are, while simultaneously recognizing their wholeness. This is love.

In the act of representing this function, the helper is learning, albeit intuitively, that every person carries the awakening principle for everyone else. While this function is always proportional to one's depth of realization, it is universal, not a special attribute of rare individuals. I have seen participants reach such a state of availability that they carried the capacity to initiate awakening in some of their co-participants.

The intent of the exercise is to teach attention. The exercise is a metaphor for the process of self-transcendence that occurs as we have an intense, spontaneously creative and loving relationship with ourselves in any moment. By learning to help another enter a state where he is no longer dancing self-consciously and with very little energy, but instead finds that wonderful moment of *being danced*, each person learns how to access fuller and finer energy. When he stops dancing, his consciousness will be altered and simultaneously his perspective will have shifted. He may feel more open and available to others and pervaded with a warm glow of well-being. When the dancer touches those moments of being At-One with the dance, the effect reverberates into the three supporters and they too are carried into the dancer's energy. It is an experience of moving to a higher level of energy which demonstrates that this potential is available all the time.

THE SACRAMENT OF THE MOMENT

During Laura's conference, I was wandering around the room watching the small groups as they worked together. The dancers were discovering a deeper relationship to the music. The three helpers were trying to find that balance between empowering and interfering. At times, as one person or another lost himself in the dance, the groups drew together into a subtle bonding of energies. It was at this point I noticed a group that appeared lifeless and self-conscious. The dancer, who turned out to be Laura, was barely moving, and the others were standing around unsure of what to do. I walked up and asked her to put more life in the dance. She replied that she had cancer. Before I could even begin to consider this, I heard myself saying, "Dance! You aren't dead yet!"

Laura said later that at that moment she became furious, first with me and then with her own apathy. She realized that it was true, she wasn't dead yet, and she tried to dance, although it was not easy and caused her pain. While the shock of the remark did not open Laura to a new energy, it shifted her awareness of herself. She decided to try to participate more fully. This was a turning point.

Later that afternoon I asked the participants to repeat the same process in the same small groups, but this time with singing. Unlike the dancing, which can be exhausting if the space of "being danced" isn't reached, and which may be entirely too strenuous for an elderly individual or someone who is ill, the singing exercise has virtually no time limit and can go on for half a day or more. When engaged within the framework of this exercise, singing has the potential to amplify energy enormously and open the individual to profound states of consciousness.

The singing exercise is defined in this way: The singer must sing until there is a break in the continuity of ordinary awareness and he has entered an altered state of consciousness that inducts the small group into a heightened awareness. The nature of this heightened state will be unmistakable: The person may seem to disappear into the singing; time may seem to have stopped; fatigue and bodily discomfort may fall away; and the group may be lifted into a space of effortless presence. Once this occurs, and not before, the singer may stop. The others are there in their specific roles as in the dancing. They provide support, inspiration, provocation if necessary, to insure that the singer does not stop until the opening has occurred. Each one must be willing to give himself completely for each singer. It is the time involved, as well as the unusual nature of the task, that provides the intensity. On rare occasions individuals have sung for as much as six hours before shifting, but usually one to two hours is the average.

The quality of attention and support by the non-singers is crucial to whether the singer will reach a fuller aliveness. The group is small, but even four people united in their attention can become an immense transformative force. Some people refuse to stay with the exercise. They reach the threshold of their basic energetic inertia and feel blocked or afraid. If they have been singing for a long while without anything apparently happening, their sense of commitment falters. Usually this means they are getting close to the shift. However, this presents the singer with the important task of learning how to transmute resistance rather than being defined by it. It does not matter if we feel negative; *it is one of the paradoxes of transformation that the closer we get to new possibility the worse things tend to seem.* The key is to stay with it, to bring our attention fully into what is happening. Fear, anger, frustration, helplessness, are perfectly fine spaces from which to initiate the movement to a higher energy. In fact, every moment, no matter what it seems, can be a doorway to greater aliveness. It all depends on our *attention.*

To shift to a higher energy, we must find a creative relationship to where we are and not judge, react, or close down. One can argue that an exercise such as the singing invites resistance by the very effort it calls forth. This is true, but it is also true that life will continuously take us to the point where our energetic inertia will be challenged to stretch, and we will feel uncomfortable and want to turn away. We must learn to understand the reactive mechanism and, rather than being caught in it and defined by it, gradually appreciate how to find a new relationship to this kind of experience. This is what the exercise teaches.

I have explored the singing exercise with hundreds of individuals and observed the results. Most people reach a minor energetic heightening by singing loudly for a while, but then they quickly stop. It is as if they sense that going further requires a far deeper trust and self-abandonment, and they protect themselves from entering vulnerably into their experience. They sing songs that they know, over and over again, rather than trusting a new song to emerge. Most of us do the same thing with our lives, with our repeated attitudes, our repeated routines. Such unconscious routine and conformity is itself an aspect of the reactive mechanism whereby we perpetuate our identity by unconsciously barricading ourselves in behaviors that limit our aliveness. When we feel blocked in the singing, we blame it on the "stupid" exercise, just as in life, we blame it on an infinity of "its, theys and thems." Our thoughts of how we should be, which have no immediate reality and, in fact, arise as a reaction to how we feel about ourselves, become more real than our immediate experience. But the unreal can never be the doorway to ourselves. In this way, we are split from our own greatest aliveness and the potential of the new. Our energy becomes bound within a circumscribed range of behaviors, feelings, and thoughts and "we" become the expression of the states of consciousness possible within that range. It is what we unconsciously do all the time.

In the singing exercise, it becomes very clear that reaction creates intensity, and this intensity is itself a more alive state. It is almost as though the threshold for moving to another level of consciousness first presents us with resistance so that we gather energy for another possibility. Thus we must never let the form of that resistance become a reality in itself or we remain within the bounds of our basic energetic structure. We must become completely attuned to our reactive mood and allow the "song" and our sense of being to become unified.

The singing and dancing exercises demand that we find balance between will and surrender, between trying for more and accepting exactly where we are. We recognize intuitively that it is not within our power to self-transcend, that we can (and must) give ourselves over completely to the process, that we can never know with certainty if an opening will occur. However, rather than risk failure, we often accept mediocrity. Human beings, in general, are addicted to premature resolution. We are unable to sustain much tension in our lives unless the ends are very clear to us or the alternatives to not going on are even worse. Even an intuition of the importance of learning how to open to a larger consciousness is not sufficient for most people to persevere when asked to sing to the point of entering an altered and expanded awareness.

To experience the sacrament of the moment, that space where the song sings us, where life lives us, we must be willing to let go, and keep letting go. But it is never a passive thing; we let go into an active, dynamic participation with the moment. In a sense, we are having a love affair with life. In that act of letting go, we are saying it is not so much what I can do, but what is happening to me now, that is the truth and significance of this moment. *The only thing we can give to God is ourselves,* our immediate state, whatever we are experiencing. We give it by becoming At-One with ourselves, whole in the immediacy of ourselves, and it is irrelevant whether we feel good or bad, whether we are content or not. When we begin to live this understanding, we live a life of faith.

Whatever is happening is energy. If energy is crystallized in a particular dynamic, we can label it (and ourselves). This happens the moment we say, "I feel good. . .I feel bad," and the like. Immediately we are cut off from the larger energy. To return to that larger energy, to approach God, we must free the crystallized energy. In this sense we give ourselves away; we give away our identifiable condition and it becomes energy, aliveness. We keep singing. The song reflects and expresses the energy of whatever we are experiencing. But we don't stop, we don't analyze it, we don't rationalize why we can't go on; we just keep singing. Then all at once we are not singing, we are being sung. The voice comes from some new place within us, but it is also outside us. We are ourselves and yet we are also space. For many it is one of the most extraordinary states of aliveness they have ever known.

We continually undermine our aliveness when we think that we can only offer ourselves to life when we feel good. Instead of giving ourselves over in the wholeness of our "negative" states, we withdraw or attempt to distract ourselves. We make plans, read the paper, watch television. If we are really in pain, we may even pray. Suddenly God becomes important and we make promises, set good intentions, read inspirational literature or repeat affirmations. But even prayers are only concepts about how we *should* or *would* like to be. Unless the very act of praying becomes an intense, spontaneous and creative involvement with the moment—comes from our hearts—such prayers do not arise from the immediacy of ourselves. They are the frightened supplications of a child. They are born of reaction to the suffering one is experiencing, rather than a dynamic relationship to one's suffering that transmutes the very self that suffers. This dynamic is negotiation with the content of consciousness rather than penetration into Consciousness itself. This is how we remain separated from the immediacy of our being. In this way, ordinary consciousness is split, not unified, and thus always at a lower energetic potential. Such a lowered state can never approach the Unknown, the deeper aliveness that awaits us in each moment.

The singing exercise is a way of teaching prayer. It is consecrated to the aliveness that always awaits us. It is the music of one's own being that becomes the inspiration for the song.

A NEW NOTE OF BEING

Laura began her song as inhibited as she had been in the dance. But the anger she felt gave her strength. She began singing a hymn from her childhood, while one member of the group ruthlessly demanded that she keep letting go, keep staying with it. Hours passed and then the great breakthrough that I described at the beginning of the book occurred. I do not want to repeat the details, but certain features bear further comment.

Laura did not simply access a higher energy by the release of a relative level of identity such as "I can't sing, I'm afraid, I am too ordinary to experience a heightened state, I have to do it, I need to try harder," or some such. These structures are powerful limiters of one's aliveness, and overcoming them forms the first hurdle in the singing. Most people pass through this and then begin to access a depth of creativity that is frequently astonishing. But here the fundamental energetic structure has been stretched to hold new aliveness, it has not been transcended. With Laura, it was precisely this self-transcendence that occurred. Her whole conscious identity released. She realized that everything she had known and lived and believed up to that moment was not real. Her personal identity was not real; her cancer was not real. There was a sense of witnessing; at no point did she become lost in the experience. But none of the structures of egoic mind carried the weight of reality while she was in this expanded state. She was Reality, Perfect Wholeness and Peace, but her old structures, which she could recall like phantoms, were not. At best they were veils, curtains of relative unconsciousness. It was the relative unconsciousness of her life that she had mistaken for the real. Immediately, she understood that nothing mattered as it had before. She was free in a way that she could never have dreamt possible.

Her group sensed that something astonishing was happening; the four of them had been there for hours, and now it was as though time stood still. The whole space had taken on a feeling of holiness. They found themselves being profoundly nourished by the energy that poured from her. Wisdom guided them and no one interrupted Laura until the process subsided of itself.

Laura had awakened; she became and remains a person vibrating at a new note. Afterwards, she attempted to describe what had happened for the rest of the conference participants. She realized that she was an entirely new person, but didn't understand how or in what ways. It was as though she knew herself for the first time. She realized that she had ceased to be fully alive as early as age two when she started developing her sense of identity, the sense of being "Laura." She could look back and actually see how the development of the egoic self began to imprison her aliveness. It was then she began to die. Her report is on tape and as one listens to her voice, there is a powerful induction as though one were listening to a mystic. In fact, Laura was describing aspects of realization fundamental to all mystical development, although in her outer life she had no such background. Her insight was awesome because it was spontaneous, out of the immediacy of her transformation. She did not speak from ideas or memory; her sharing was not intellectual, not some personalized transcription of what she had learned from others. As she spoke, her words were like an open door to her soul, to dimensions beyond her personal consciousness. This depth became available to her simultaneously with the realization of oneness with existence. The fact that this same energetic shift also triggered a major healing makes it all the more important that Laura's experience be given the deepest scrutiny.

5 · LAURA'S STORY CONTINUED

When you make the two one, and when you make
the inner as the outer and the above as the below,
and when you make the male and the female into
a single one, so that the male will not be male and
the female will not be female . . . then shall you en-
ter the Kingdom.

THE GOSPEL ACCORDING TO THOMAS

THE DAY AFTER THE SINGING EXPERIENCE, the whole group of forty-five people entered into an energy sharing ritual with Laura and another woman.[1] It was after this that the actual physical healing became apparent. Laura says, in retrospect, that while the essential experience occurred during the singing, in her mind she needed the energy sharing, which she perceived as a healing ritual, to acknowledge that she was now whole. As she felt the energy pouring into her, her heart stopped. She

---

[1] Energy sharing is a ritual relationship that is a central teaching form in my work. The energy of any relationship depends on the level at which our attention abides. Energy sharing is a way of learning to maintain conscious attunement with another person while simultaneously freeing one's attention into more subtle or universal dimensions. The result is that we can charge ourselves with energy. So that the reader may have a visual image, when the energy sharing is done in a group, one person lies on a table while the rest gather around the table. Energy can be shared by light touch with the hands or simply by being present without actual physical touch. When performed in a group, the energy field can become quite intense. It is a phenomenon well known in all shamanic, mystical, and religious traditions and it is perenially rediscovered and reinterpreted. For a fuller discussion of energy sharing see Chapter 14.

thought, "Well, this is a perfect way to go. I'm ready." Then, when her heartbeat resumed and the tremendous force of the energy flooded her every cell, she understood, "This is mine to do with what I like." At that moment, quite spontaneously, she chose to be completely well. She had always been somewhat ill with diabetes and its related problems and had practically learned to take it for granted. Now she found herself stating, "I want to be totally well. Not just healed of cancer. I want to be completely well."

It is important to differentiate Laura's spontaneous choice to be well from the reactive orientation to health that nearly every sick individual makes. Once we discover that we are sick, something naturally rallies and wants to get well. As a result we go to doctors, begin to read and learn, and maybe alter our habits. Most of the time this is sufficient to result in some improvement; sometimes it results in moving in a new direction, but it never results in fundamental change. All such choices are being made within a closed system of consciousness; they are merely reflexes. In terms of touching the threshold for radical change, this level of response, while inevitable, actually can be a defense that diffuses the creative intensity which might lead to a really transformative involvement. The desire to live, the new-found appreciation for life, the resurrection of relationships that now seem precious, so that we become caring and more receptive and giving, all of these are common gifts of illness. This *does* represent a kind of energetic conversion. But to the degree that it is a reflex out of our pain, it is often superficial and does not represent a potent force for healing. I am not saying that such feelings aren't genuine, but they should not be considered a signal that we are fundamentally changing. Thus, when I hear individuals speak of "learning so much from their illness," or "getting the message" of the disease, I recognize that, while this is true from one point of view, it is usually the voice of the ego subtly congratulating itself and not a higher energy that has been accessed. We must learn to go deeper.

The difference between choosing life as a survival reflex and choosing life the way Laura did is that she made her choice after she had already "died." She had transcended. She had experienced the relative reality of her egoic state. At that point, the choice to be completely well was not merely a wish; it was an expression of her whole being. It did not arise out of fear. Neither the person who was sick nor the one who wanted to be well were real to her. The decision to choose complete wellness was, in fact, not a choice. It arose spontaneously from within her at the moment when what she *thought* was inseparable from what she *was*. It has been said that a man is as he thinks in his heart. But to think in one's heart is not the same as rational or logical thought. It is not thought in the usual sense that arises as an object of consciousness, that is mentally evoked or called forth as affirmation. To think or know in one's heart is knowledge-through-identity. It is conception coincident with Being.

Laura's experience confirms what I have heard from people who had remarkable deathbed transformations with accompanying healing. In these cases, the individuals were on the brink of death and had given up. Suddenly they realized a new relationship to life and "miraculously" recovered. Typically, as they realized that they were going to live, a deep conviction arose that they were called to serve others. In short, these individuals no longer saw their lives as their own but as a part of a larger life. Here again, we are dealing with an understanding that arises spontaneously from deep within the being, an understanding that completely possesses these individuals at the moment of its realization. It is not a reflex or a desire arising out of the situation.

Does this mean that we have to die or nearly die before fundamental transformation is possible? I believe the answer is yes. If we don't want to surrender completely, if we want to keep growing in ways that we think are the best for us, very little that is new will eventuate. If this seems shocking, look more closely at our world. We teeter on the brink of destruction, and we responsibly try to avoid this. Yet with each new effort to control or mitigate this threat, it becomes even worse. We are now faced with the consequences of aeons of this same kind of maneuvering in the form of imminent nuclear holocaust and environmental ruin. Perhaps we unconsciously invite our own undoing again and again in order to touch a transformational moment. And when it approaches, we cry and scream that it is not right and try to avoid, manipulate, modify ourselves and life in the unending dream of how it should be. It is time that we stop trying to make it right, stop searching for the thing we imagine we should be, and just fall into life. This is precisely what happened to Laura. She fell into aliveness; she was tricked—lovingly tricked—to enter a new moment not of her fabrication. She forgot about trying to be healed, for how could she have possibly conceived of the wholeness she awakened to? That wholeness is already ever-present. Laura's experience suggests that what we need to do is learn how to get out of the way. We really don't know what will happen when we let go.

After the energy sharing ritual, Laura said she felt absolutely naked and vulnerable. It was as though everything around her were part of her; she had no boundaries, no walls, no defenses. It was not pleasant being so unformed, so open. It was as though her whole being had been put through a cosmic grinder. This was something she had never experienced before. She protected herself in the only way she knew. She took a nap. Upon awakening, she walked across her bedroom and realized she felt different. Unconsciously, she reached down to support the tumor as she had done so many times before. It was gone. So were some of the other metastases that she had been able to feel. To her amazement, and it brought a laugh, her slacks were too big for her!

As I looked at Laura, she appeared at least twenty years younger. She was fifty but looked almost teenage. Her skin had a translucent appearance. I've compared a photograph taken three days before the conference and another taken directly after the "experience." It is almost impossible to recognize the woman in the photos as the same person.

It took Laura several days before she realized that she had not taken any insulin and felt fine. It was several months before her routine visit to the ophthalmologist showed that her detached retina was fully restored. Furthermore, Laura had been on regular doses of morphine and percodan for pain. She never took any more of these medications after that day, and didn't realize until later that there had been no withdrawal problems. Eighteen months later she was hospitalized after a fall and was thoroughly examined. No sign of cancer or diabetes was discovered.

Laura had severely impaired kidneys as a result of her diabetes.

After chemotherapy, her kidneys failed and she had required dialysis. In the weeks following the realization, she made one little "miraculous" discovery after another. Her kidneys returned to normal. Almost humorously, she was surprised to discover herself recoiling in pain when she did the dishes. The loss of peripheral sensitivity common to diabetes had numbed the sensation in her hands. For most of her life she had done dishes without ever knowing how hot the water was!

The transformation continued to unfold in dimensions beyond physical concerns. She would find herself crying for hours for no apparent reason. She could feel the "wind," the spiritual current, blowing through her. For months, it was difficult to do anything that required planning or focus. Fortunately, her husband made sure that all her needs were met and that she could have periods of undisturbed solitude. For the first few weeks, as the body purged itself, she had diarrhea of the foulest kind and mild intestinal cramps. Eventually the foulness passed, but the rapid bowel movements and mild cramps continued. I too have experienced this phenomenon in varying degrees since my first opening. At times, the body seems to require huge amounts of food to cool the energetic fire that moves through it. Yet most of the food passes undigested. At such times, it is not advisable to be vegetarian and particularly dangerous to fast.

Throughout the early months and periodically thereafter, she had periods of moderate mid-sternal chest pain. Medical tests were normal. The pain was greatest when she felt the most transparent, as though the world were passing through her. In my experience, this has to do with activation of the energy center in the chest. Laura's "heart" had begun to open.

During the following months, she says she seriously questioned her sanity, but as with anyone who has had such an experience, she seemed to draw to her the needed support. *The I That Is We*, which discusses some of the phenomena of opening to a higher energy, proved helpful. In addition, a wise friend she had met at the conference, an associate of mine, kept in contact and helped her to trust the process. Specifically, she needed to be reminded that this was a totally new dimension unlike anything she had ever thought or dreamed of. There were no fixed rules now, no experience from her past she could draw upon for guidance. She simply had to learn to trust the depth of the experience and stay in touch with the new sense of aliveness and energy within her.

One of the problems she encountered was that many people were willing to believe that she could be healed, but they couldn't accept that this had occurred in a nontraditional spiritual setting. Some even felt that, since Jesus hadn't been invoked, perhaps her healing was the work of the devil. This is a sad confusion, for it reflects how little the life of Jesus or any of the great teachers is understood, and how little the Christ-like consciousness, which Laura had briefly entered, is recognized. Laura had briefly fulfilled the very words, "When you make the two one. . . ."[2]

In the moment of her singing, the inner and outer became unified, her self-consciousness and the consciousness of existence became a single living reality. At that moment, one could say that she was suffused with a transcendental energy and was made whole. But making the statement in this way implies some agency outside of Laura, and this is how such experiences are commonly understood in conventional religious settings. Certainly the higher energy is outside of her (or anyone's) ordinary level of consciousness, but it is not outside of Consciousness proper. Thus I feel we need to discuss this kind of experience differently. For one who knows the Transcendent from direct contact, it becomes far more appropriate to say that she realized the Archetype of Wholeness. In that Identity we are ever and always whole. While to my knowledge no one remains completely in this state, once it has been realized the individual continues as a kind of doorway through which the transcendent radiates forth in varying degrees of purity. When I met Laura again a year-and-a-half later, I felt this the moment she entered the room. To be near her was like bathing in a gentle nectar.

The relationship with her physician, who had suggested she attend the conference, and had himself attended, was interesting. He maintained professional skepticism, but after a while it be-

[2] I heartily recommend the contemplation of *The Gospel According to Thomas*. In my own search, I have found few documents that more clearly discuss the awakened state of consciousness in ways that parallel my own unfoldment as directly as this does. While the reader may find the parables similar to those in the synoptic gospels, it actually enhances the understanding of the latter. It places the emphasis on the mystical character of Jesus' life and emphasizes the fact that this is a journey for all of us.

came in her eyes a subtle hostility. He had her come back several times to test for diabetes and to look for the cancer. She grew tired of this and asked him to pay for whatever further tests he might want to do; he refused and she stopped going. Such clinical and laboratory confirmation is, at first, the responsible act of any good physician, and I suspect that the hostility Laura perceived was her own fear that doubting would bring the disease back. This is not uncommon. When something beyond the expected has transpired, many people simply want to close off whatever preceded it, as if even thinking of their old self will curse them to return there. The point, however, is that the physician continued to regard her from his basic viewpoint rather than asking the crucial questions, "What am I? What is real?" and thus beginning his own transformational exploration. He waited and continues to wait for her to return to the disease state, so that his own reality (and it is not just his; it is "reality" at the current collective level of consciousness) can remain unthreatened and unchanged.

It was not only her doctor who maintained his basic stance; it was also many of the people at the conference, including some of Laura's friends. They kept urging her to attend the next conference presented by the next visiting teacher. They couldn't accept that, at least for the time being, Laura had no need to look for new understanding. She had transcended to a new dimension where only the deepest teachings have meaning. Just integrating what had awakened within her was sufficient challenge.

In point of fact, there is much about herself that Laura might have learned from such experiences. Her opening did not make her a saint, and at the level of her ego she had many patterns that made it difficult to be with her. But she was far too vulnerable in that first year to even consider this. The problems between herself and her friends were of dimensional incongruence. They were at a lower energy level and had no equivalent experience from which to comprehend Laura. Her sense of transparency and openness to existence, what she describes as "God is the only truth," was so powerful in those early months that she couldn't imagine adding one more thing to her experience. In this state, she had no need to modify or explore what she already knew to be unreal. But, she could feel that her friends had these needs, that they didn't know this sense of fullness.

✱

One unquestioned assumption is that which equates information and experience with fundamental knowledge. There is a tacit belief that real knowing is the result of some special experience: "If only I had that experience, then. . . ." Thus, in human potential jargon, we are forever "working on ourselves." But the underlying assumption that this will bring us to a state of knowing or sureness about ourselves is unfounded. The state of consciousness in which we are striving to understand, or in which we believe that something is missing that will give us the ultimate key to ourselves, never is continuous with or an avenue to the state of Knowing. The two conditions—striving/desiring/searching, and Knowing—represent entirely different states. The former is in time, defining a self out of memory, comparing to some ideal seen as distinct from this memory and projecting how "I" will be in the future when. . . . The latter—Knowing—is not in time, not a process, not an evolution. It is realized all at once and is complete in itself, independent of any cause. It is always by its very nature unimaginable and cannot be derived or extrapolated by any process of the basic egoic consciousness in which desire/striving resides. Literally, this consciousness must cease to be operative or dominant, and in this sense must die for the Knowing to be present.

This is precisely what Laura demonstrated and it was specifically to invite this possibility that the exercises were designed for the conferences. But there can be no attempt to define in advance what will be experienced at such a moment. This is not possible and has never been possible. One can only assume that the deep underlying themes of one's life and the quality of the immediate context may have something to do with the nature of what is realized. The classic example is Newton being struck on the head with the apple which, whether factual or not, simply represents that the moment of Knowing is Grace and never born directly out of the desire to know. There is a discontinuity, a surrender if you will; the search is unconditionally set aside (whether for moments or forever is irrelevant). There can be no guarantee that what is realized, if anything, will be that which is sought. This is analogous to the experience of a mental block. All efforts to unblock simply disguise the forgotten information all the more. Later, having entirely forgotten about it, the datum is recalled quite spontaneously. Still we foster the delusion that if we keep striving we will someday arrive at the place we imagine we should be. This paradox between effort and surrender is one of the great challenges on the path.

To the degree that we associate effort with attainment, Laura is a contradiction, at least at first glance. She had no conscious intention toward transformation. She had never heard of my work and had only attended the conference because her doctor invited her. She was not involved in any other kind of consciousness exploration and only occasionally attended church. When she came to the conference, she hoped to find a little energy so that she could die. Also, she wanted to show her friends that she hadn't given up, that she was still trying, like a good girl. But when we look at Laura from another perspective, the possible reasons for her radical transformation become more plausible. She had been a dynamo in her life. She was involved in a service-oriented career and had reached the very top. For several years she was the head of one of the largest unions in the country and had twice been voted most outstanding woman of the year in her field. It was to this powerhouse that the cancer appeared.

Laura is to me the classic example of an individual whose intent may not have been transformational, but her consecration to life embraced the world in a way that few do. She was given over to the good of the many, a true lover, although she would never have thought of this as a spiritual impulse. Furthermore, she did everything at full throttle; her aliveness engaged many levels of life and she did not compromise. She worked in an area where negotiation was both mentally demanding and emotionally tumultuous and she gave fully of herself. Perhaps we could call her a workaholic, but the point I am trying to make is that she was energetically saturated, that she was living at her full potential, at least at the level available to her. Her life was challenging and she lived with intensity. One can imagine that, given the opportunity provided by the transformational focus of the conference, she was ready to jump to a new energy level. I suspect that the cancer contributed to weaken her substantial egoic control. It forced her to surrender. She had retired and returned to her childhood locale reconciled to die. In a sense, she had given up the search after a full and intense life. She was emotionally vulnerable, but more important she was energetically open and available. At these times the discontinuity of consciousness becomes most possible.

*

Laura is alive and well but, like her doctor and her friends, she too finds it difficult to know just how much significance to give to her transformation. With the return of her health, the outward openness and vulnerability that cancer had brought her closed. She is a paradox, energetically radiant and available, yet outwardly, at the personality level, cautious, domineering and conservative. In fact, as is the case with many people after an opening, there was a tendency toward ego inflation once the initial vulnerability passed. I suspect that this is a natural attempt to encompass the new energy in the old egoic framework. It is so common that perhaps it even provides a kind of shield, holding people away and giving one the illusion of being in control. However it certainly invites a lot of pain that can lead to a serious fall. Some of this is unnecessary where there is greater self-knowledge, but no one can be fully prepared for the demands of a radically awakened aliveness. And this leads to an important understanding: Realization is whole and complete within itself, but does not necessarily extend the same integrity into other levels of reality. The work of self-purification, of bringing the balance of our lives into a new richness and openness, is a slow and often tortuous process. Realization, to whatever degree, brings new aliveness, and new vision and understanding, depending on our own natural capacities, but it doesn't tell us how to live.

I regard Laura's idiosyncrasies as natural in the human drama. While a part of me is disappointed that we have not been carried more deeply into mystical association, I nevertheless have a deep appreciation for her. Her life has undergone what, for most people, would be a very radical, perhaps insufferable, change. Some of her family members distrust her, are even afraid of her. Most simply want her to be the woman they remember and trust, without realizing that this would mean that she once again would be terminally ill and in terrible suffering. It may be easier to lose someone to death than to a transformational shift.

Laura and her husband sold their home and gave away most of their possessions. They bought a motor home so they could travel, day by day. Living simply, their combined retirement money was sufficient. She says, "When life is so rich with aliveness, who needs all these things?" Life became a pattern of moving from place to place, staying months or longer and offering service wherever possible. At times it has been difficult, but much of it has been a joy because she can feel the current of aliveness flowing within her. Sometimes it is stronger, and everything is right and effortless. When the current is imperceptible the whole experience seems like a dream, and at such times she admits wondering if letting go as they did wasn't madness. Before they started roaming she considered returning to her old career. At first she was cautious, fearing that she would get caught up in it. But gradually, she wisely came to see that this old self had much in it of basic value. She even returned to her work for awhile, to discover that she could do it with joy and freedom. Then she stopped because it was no longer important to her. Thus she has reverence for the past without being recrystallized within her old image. The new energy continues to radiate from her and she is very much her own person.

Perhaps most important, she has learned something more of the nature of love. While this understanding is still, for the most part, intuitive and not fully represented in her behavior, she knows now that love does not come from "outside." She is much less afraid to risk being herself. She knows that her self-image, the new one that arises in the moment, like the "old" one before the transformation, is not real. This is not where she looks for the sense of realness. The realness arises in the core of her being. It is a living presence, a current, a nectar that makes the whole of life, the immediacy of the moment, her true lover.

To me, this is the sure sign of a complete healing, of a life emerging from a new energy and not just a transient alteration of consciousness. Many people are briefly lifted to a new sense of well-being and purpose, but often (as will be discussed later) the shift has not been deep enough to really require a new life style. Some alterations are made and there are new values, new beliefs, but the change has not occurred in the basic note of consciousness. After a while the individuals once again identify themselves in the old self-image. At this point, if some healing has occurred as a result of the energetic shift, the disease often returns.

I expected that Laura's experience would give a tremendous sense of freedom and new possibility to all who witnessed it. However, many of the participants, like her doctor, were unable to generalize that Laura's experience, and the basic exploration that was the context for it, could represent a way of life for them. To glimpse the Mystery doesn't necessarily mean that one will be invited into it. Most of the witnesses of Laura's transformation continue the search for new experience and new understanding, believing, I suppose, that if they can learn enough about subtle energies or maneuver their psychological realities appropriately, they will ultimately arrive at some ideal attainment. Clearly, few are able to embrace the transformative abyss of surrender, energetic communion, unknowing and ordinariness. The message of archetypal wholeness and of Grace suggested by Laura's experience is to them, at best, an intriguing riddle. In everyone, there exists a tremendous search for growth, but only in a few does the search lead to such a fundamental transformation.

✱

Why is it so difficult to take in a happening like Laura's? Why aren't those who witness such an event immediately and profoundly intrigued? I remember how it was, sitting in the conference room when she announced her discovery. The room was filled with an awkward silence. I could sense the disbelief and skepticism. I myself wondered if she were not exaggerating in the exhilaration that comes with expanded awareness. Quietly I hoped that she was not inviting great disappointment. Most people remained open, but simply didn't know how to respond. It is as though our outer consciousness is unable to grasp such an event. We hear, but somehow we cannot feel it, join it, enter it. In part, we don't want to. It is beyond our rational understanding, and it is disconcerting, if not frightening. Perhaps it is akin to our inability to conceive of our own death.

An experience like Laura's stops the mind, stops our world, as Castaneda would say. It invites us into a space where all of a sudden we are not in control. But we don't really want our world to stop. We search and call out for a better life, but we really do not know how to finally trust our wholeness; we continually look for it, continually try to fill ourselves with something more that we have to get, some understanding, some experience.

Our defenses against the Unknown, the unexplainable, vary from outright denial to much more subtle psychic maneuverings. Egoic consciousness has difficulty understanding anything that lies outside the egoic realm. A few people actually accused Laura of lying about ever having had cancer and diabetes in the first place. Some rationalized that the medications had finally cured the cancer. Curiously, a variety of subpersonalities emerged that pretended to grasp the event. The "scientist" in consciousness evokes the catch-all explanation "spontaneous remission" and thus never has to leap into a new adventure. The "believer" invokes God and once again the event is explained. What we gain from such a perspective is security, the continuity of our basic position. We never have to ask, "What is my relationship to this experience? What do I believe? Why? How do I know?" Thus our world keeps turning and, like a soap opera, we live vicariously out of unchallenged assumptions and inherited beliefs.

In reality, the invocation of God is stopping the world. But this is only true for one who lives so close to the sense of mystery that in the very act of saying or thinking "My God . . .," he or she has undressed the security of personal beliefs and stands naked before Existence. And this is not an easy or necessarily a comforting state. It is said in scripture that the fear of God is the beginning of wisdom. We might think of it as the-fear-of-God, a singular condition of one who is peering into the infinite unknown of himself with no answers, no point of reference. No!

God is never an explanation. It is the most profound and utter declaration of "I don't know," and yet even in this unknowing lies the I Am. Fear-of-God is that existential anxiety that arises as our seeking carries us beyond our familiar self. But, many of us are still egoistically involved in the search, still standing outside and maintaining a distance. Love-of-God must become worship; the infinite unknown is not a source of loss but of wonderment. But many people have lost touch with this fact. For them, God is no longer an awesome doorway requiring nothing less than the complete hallowing of their lives. If it has any meaning at all, God has become a safehouse, protecting us from the depths of ourselves. It is a great Parent, a being who stands above, outside, rather than within. As long as we continue in this belief system, we remain immature, unable to truly stand in our own light.

This level of belief invariably accompanies a low-energy life dynamic. When I am with people and they begin to speak of their parental God in a this-explains-it-all manner, I can literally feel the energy level drop. And there is nothing that can be said, because built into such belief is a structure that cannot be challenged. All I can do at such times is experience the pain as the door closes. As Simone Weil has said, those with greater sensitivity are always afflicted by the unconsciousness of others. This suffering can be redemptive. If we can allow this suffering without rejecting the other or ourselves, it becomes energy in which we expand. Then, in some degree, that unconsciousness may be lifted.

Laura's story suggests that, while one part of us is fascinated by miracles and even believes that this kind of "evidence" will open us to the new, for many people such experiences mean very little. Unless we are at the very edge of ourselves, immensely available and fully committed to realize truth, these experiences remain peripheral; they do not cut to the heart. It is much healthier to say "I don't know" and to enter the resulting discomfort than to disguise that unknowing with mental speculation or simplistic beliefs. It is of immense value to be profoundly disturbed, profoundly challenged in our souls, for our familiar living is at best limited and relative. There is a greater Life and we will never know it if we insist on turning from whatever upsets the security of our cherished beliefs.

But the discomfort arises from more than admitting that we don't know; it also means coming to terms with the fact that radical change demands that we must die in order to be reborn. And this is something that we cannot do in any usual sense of doing. We have been shown the "Pearl of Great Price" but its price is not in our conscious power to pay. And this is the real disturbance. It can lead to self-surrender and wonderment or it can just as easily lead to pessimism and despair. There is a great risk here. Now we are no longer safe. Now for the first time, we begin to realize how unprepared we are, how little we know in our hearts what we really want. In our fear of facing this fundamental disturbance, we continue to reach out into life in the familiar ways that give us the sense of power and accomplishment. We unconsciously turn aside again and again before the door of undoing and thus very little transformation is actually possible. It is time to be honest with ourselves about whether our commitment to change is really transformative, really bringing us to the edge of the unknown in ourselves, or whether our very goal of transformation is yet another way to defend the status quo of our being.

6 ∗
TOWARD A PSYCHOLOGY OF ENERGY

IT IS A PROFOUND BREAKTHROUGH for most people to realize that to know themselves more completely, and incidentally to heal themselves, is not so much a process of trying to solve their problems, but of entering fully into life as it is. This is a radical understanding. We can begin to work with the quality of our relationship to life, rather than our reaction to life's ever-changing appearance. In modern business jargon this is proactive rather than reactive. The basis for the enhanced transformational potential in a proactive orientation is that it creates a higher level of energy because it is a natural tendency to move into the present moment.

In comparison, trying to understand or analyze our moods or behavior frequently generates little transformative energy because we are not really meeting our experience, but rather reacting to it. It can become self-indulgence that potentiates the reality of the very mood. On the other hand, responsible self-inquiry that creates a new relationship with ourselves is utilizing the vector of Creative Involvement. When this inquiry is carried out with a wise listener, and consecrated to the highest potential, the energy of the group of two creates a significantly transformative environment.

To me, this is the great breakthrough of psychoanalysis. First, Freud made the incredible jump of creative relationship by seeing that his own dreams were a doorway into the unconscious. He simultaneously looked into the dreams of his patients and began to see the forces underlying their symptoms. He discovered and described universal unconscious dynamics and pioneered the process of free association as a means of making these forces conscious. He found that at times this process resulted in a cure. But it was the form of therapeutic relationship (what Erikson has termed a kind of psychic nonviolence) that was perhaps his greatest breakthrough. He pioneered a whole new quality of attention to his patients, a way of listening that neither judged nor reacted. Instead, Freud (and later all trained analysts) learned to remain present, and in so doing created a heightened energetic milieu. With his attention to dreams and the process of free association, he brought the vector of Creative Relationship to a field that virtually assaulted patients with pathological diagnosis. And in the very process of the analytic listening, he began to approach the vector of Unconditional Love. In this way, our Western psychological understanding made a move toward wholeness.

In a relationship where even one person holds an open, nonreactive attention, a finer level of energy is automatically invoked. This heightened energy is naturally more inclusive; what was unconscious (and perhaps limiting aliveness) automatically begins to surface into consciousness. Once conscious, the dynamic begins to lose its potency. This is the basis of cure. The unconscious is not a thing in itself; rather it is consciousness that is not directly accessible to us because we have not achieved a sufficiently high energy. Thus all therapy is transformative to the degree that it heightens and refines the basic note of consciousness. Since fundamental change is Grace, most therapy can only work as a perturbing force. (We shall discuss this in greater depth later.)

It is the level of energy reached in the therapeutic relationship that produces the therapeutic possibility. The theoretic understandings about the workings of the psyche are secondary, born in the heightened energy. But if we work from these ideas without understanding the process, the ideas eventually create distance and diminish the healing relationship. This is my objection to Freudian psychoanalysis and to most one-to-one verbally based therapies. In fact, there is a tendency to personalize psychic content to such a high degree that it becomes trapped in a verbal process at the level of subject/object consciousness. Studies have shown that long periods of analysis do not seem to lead to discernable change. But here I feel we are attempting to measure effectiveness by the wrong criteria. Psychotherapy is not necessarily a cure for suffering. It is a relationship that inquires into the nature of mind, a process of revelation, for we are learning to see ourselves anew.

Yet it is the very strength and weakness of all therapeutic relationships that they begin from the level of a problem that must be treated. This assumption binds the creative relationship by defining both therapist and client in a circumscribed set of roles. As long as these roles are maintained, the whole context of relationship is subtly bounded and the energetic potential is limited. Perhaps this is inevitable at this point in history, for we still limit our relationships to serving special needs, rather than engaging a free and open attention with everyone. If this were possible, we might see the therapist/client relationship as that of lover and beloved. The whole structure of therapy would enter into the presumption of wholeness, rather than into the defining of pathology and modes of treatment. In fact, it is in this direction that we can appreciate Carl Jung's great contribution. His concept of *archetypes*—universal forces that define the basic expression of all human beings—moves a long way towards defining a universal psychology. With him the therapeutic relationship became a context for allowing the psyche to creatively work out its natural potential for understanding and healing. The tendency to personalize psychical content was diminished.

Now, it is not my intention to critique psychoanalysis. I am not an expert and I recognize the profound contribution that has emerged from this exploration. It represents a major shift in our understanding of human beings. Yet from an energetic point of view it is limited. Ego-based therapies are firmly grounded in subject/object consciousness and this limits their energetic potential.

Jung's psychology certainly moves toward embracing the numinous and underlying principles of consciousness. In fact, Jung's understanding itself rests upon realization. I believe he awakened to the deeper dimensions and, given his cultural context and religious background, expressed them uniquely. But I don't know whether he ever saw himself (and the psychoanalytic process) as really being capable of generating realization, for the mode of exploration itself scarcely touches the levels of energy in which the archetypes of which he wrote are consciously realized. Verbal discussion, listening (even with a fully attentive listener), dream work involving play dynamics, or encouraging artistic representations are all valid, but only work with a fraction of the bodymind. The energy levels are thus intrinsically smaller than that which is possible with an approach that includes the whole bodymind. With the Jungian therapists or any of the ego-based therapies that I have observed, the capacity to work directly with the energies of consciousness does not seem to have been developed.

Finally, there is the hidden assumption in most schools of psychology that there is a normal psyche. I would claim that we really do not know what this is. Whatever we call normal or functional is always somewhat myopic, always relative to the cultural and historic context. It is not a normalcy relative to what *can be*. Normalcy must never really be the goal. It is already too small.

I feel we are now approaching the point in group dynamics where we can actually reach levels of energy in which we approach these archetypal forces. It is, principally, the jump from a dyadic form of inquiry into a group process that allows far higher energies to be achieved and thus a major expansion of consciousness. But the key is that such inquiry is not therapeutic (i.e. not oriented toward a problem), that it has no ultimate agenda beyond creative exploration, that it does not tend to personalize psychical content, but instead sees all content as relative to the level of energy.

It is working directly with the energies of consciousness that marks the breakthrough of transformational group dynamics. The quality of energy that occurs in moments of unified consciousness is universal and resonates with all the participants. This is why people work together best where there is a higher vision that creates a common cause and cuts through levels of relative individuality. Thus, to come to a state of greater coherence in a group process, we need to develop dynamics similar to the psychoanalytic listening approach where there is no constraint on what a person can share, but which also invites the whole bodymind actively into the energetic. In fact, the transformational group dynamic is one in which all the participants learn to hear, observe and physically (dance, sing) interact with each other from a space of open, detached attention. But this kind of relating must always be balanced with working directly with the energy so that the content that is shared begins to arise from deeper and deeper levels.

We are each unique in the expression of our personal psychical content. But since the content is secondary to the note of consciousness, to define one's uniqueness on the basis of this content is to claim an individuality that is in essence unreal. At lower levels of energy, individuality can have a tendency to be idiosyncratic and separating. At higher levels of energy, while our delivery will have the flavor of our unique nature, it will reflect common and unifying themes. Then the individual speaks and everyone hears their own story. Thus the art of orchestrating a heightened group energy resides in the ability to welcome and include each person unconditionally while simultaneously inviting them to set aside certain separating stances that will limit the energetic potential.

We fear immersing ourselves in a group energy, fear the stultification of our personal individuality in the homogeneous identity of the group. Yet when the process is consecrated in unconditional love, the result is a tremendously empowered sense of personal uniqueness as well as the capacity to honor the uniqueness of others. Clearly transformational group dynamics are only possible once we have reached a certain level of maturity. If we believe that self-determinism requires the exclusion of others, if we define ourselves by saying what we are not, by rejection, then the transformational potential inherent in our communion with people and our environment can seem like self-annihilation. We will turn away in fear or judgment and rationalize this by saying we are really taking care of ourselves.

Yet we all face this tension. The promise of a global society will be consciously and unconsciously resisted by the impulse toward personal uniqueness that grows from the sense of separation. Realization shows us that this separation is at best a relative perception, that we are always the whole as well as the part. To the ordinary consciousness this movement toward wholeness is intuited as a kind of dying. Often it is only the pain intrinsic in our separation that eventually pries open the door of our being, so that we are able to intuit something more than destruction and, in faith, enter the deeper adventure.

The wealth of any human being is his or her knowledge of self. To lack depth of self-knowledge is to be in poverty. Yet something like radical awakening, which immensely expands one's self-knowledge, is not itself the product of such knowledge. At the time of my own awakening I realized how true this was. I had years of therapeutic exploration and some work with nontraditional approaches such as that of Gurdjieff. I had grown immensely in self-understanding, yet at the time of my awakening I had the strong impression that none of this had directly contributed to the opening. In fact, rather than serving to assist Realization, I distinctly understood how much of what I had done had actually functioned to siphon off the energy of the awakening process. Thus from one perspective, therapy slows the transformational impulse. I believe this is likely when we use the process to run from ourselves. Also whenever therapy operates out of a presumption of health, it limits the inquiry to an understanding of pathology rather than allowing a relationship of real creativity and aliveness. Yet at the time of awakening I was grateful for every experience I had undergone. My therapy had worked like a pressure valve to release the tension of the building energy in ways that were far less self-destructive than they might have been. The awakening process was thus slowed down until in natural timing I was ready. Furthermore, because I had already thoroughly explored psychological structures that might have proved extremely confining and very destructive at a higher energy, they posed no great mystery to me; I simply wasn't drawn to reinterpret my experience at this level. I am certain this enabled me to explore more creatively after the opening, and it immensely helped the difficult process of integration.

INTENSITY AND CREATIVE INVOLVEMENT
IN THE TRANSMUTATION OF FEELINGS

In general, any transformative approach that primarily uses the mental faculties rather than the whole bodymind to reach into the depths of consciousness rarely creates the maximum potential for unification of consciousness. Thus such an approach transmutes very gradually. There is a wisdom in such gradualness, but there is also the limitation of never fully coming to realize the relativity of all of our personal experience. Thus we tend always to live in the content of life, the *known*, and never reach the states of aliveness in which we commence to explore the larger context, the *unknown*. But even if ego-based therapy is not a direct route to realization, it is part of the foundation that can allow realization to yield greater fruit and to emerge less destructively in our world. It is essential that we learn to observe ourselves and that we thoroughly examine every presumption that determines our way of meeting life. But a discipline of this sort must not be a rehashing of memories in an attempt to explain a feeling. Rather, it is a precise inquiry into the immediate content of consciousness in order to discriminate this from the space of Consciousness itself.

Because the releasing to a deeper level requires the capacity to recognize where we are (i.e. to name our state or condition), we see the tremendous contribution of the whole movement to help people sense and express their feelings. If we can name our state, gestalt it, so to speak, it becomes conscious content and automatically consciousness is more self-aware. While we were unable to recognize our feelings or describe our condition, it remained unconscious and dominated us. Inevitably we are then reacting to the content that is secondary to the unrecognized state. For example, if we do not realize that we are feeling disconnected from ourselves, then we act this out by being defensive, angry, remote, biting, or competitive.

However, merely to bring people to recognize their feelings often leads to another form of illusion. Now the feelings become real in themselves, concrete new objects of attention, new self-discoveries that once again entrap. Thus it is not uncommon to hear people speaking of "my" anger, "my" sadness, "my" holding back, and even worse, thinking they had these feelings stored within them, or that they had finished with them. Then, finding themselves feeling anger once again, the jargon goes on about having to "work on my anger." Such a statement implies that although the individual has moved to a larger space by discovery of the feelings, he or she still has not looked beyond the content of consciousness to the space. The fundamental illusion continues; only the content has changed.

The expression of feelings or the capacity to discuss one's condition represents a further step in the ceaseless principle of Creative Relationship. It is at the root of all inquiry into life that we are, in fact, having a creative relationship with ourselves. Finally to notice how one feels or thinks and then to give it some new form of expression is the natural process of transmutation that is slowly lifting mankind to the Divine. Now, if the expression is intensified—some of the common pop therapeutic ways are to pound pillows or to beat telephone books with pieces of hose— the individual is accessing more vitality and will. This is the transformational vector of Intensity. No wonder there is a sense of catharsis and release. Such practices carry the person to a higher level of energy and their former "negative" feeling has transmuted. They think they are healed, freed, or even enlightened.

Of course, to think this is to misunderstand the workings of consciousness, and unfortunately many well-intentioned teachers exploit this delusion when they employ cathartic techniques to transmute feelings such as grief or guilt that they themselves may have evoked in their students. There are some popular teachers who are considered heroic by a certain stratum of individuals for their power to invoke emotion and sentiment as they speak. Having done so, these teachers then counsel acceptance or encourage deep cathartic confession to release the "blocked emotion" or "negative state." The individual so released is grateful, and clearly the intention of these teachers is good. Yet from the perspective of a higher possibility, one form of ignorance has been substituted for another. That this has value in terms of a developmental sequence cannot be denied when we take the larger overview. But such intentional induction of emotion followed by cathartic release is a kind of masturbation that is far from a breakthrough toward new understanding or wholeness.

It must be said again and again that human beings *are* consciousness. Whenever the energy reconfigures in a particular way, the content—be it anger, sadness, joy, or whatever—will be there once again. It was not "stored" inside as if the psyche were some great bottle. Perhaps one can say that it is projected whenever the structure of consciousness once again grips too tightly on reality and turns the free energy of consciousness into a firecracker of intense psychical content. There is no shortcut to salvation. What is required is understanding, and such understanding must embrace the context as well as the content of consciousness.

WORKING WITH THE WHOLE BODYMIND

To work with the whole bodymind, energy must be invoked through dance, song, speech, bioenergetic exercise—any dynamic that invites participation of all modes of consciousness (i.e. cognition, sensation, feeling). Ritual has a potent place here, for in ritual these modes come together in an enactment of being that transcends the elements that comprise the ritual. But the true heart of any ritual is the creative spontaneity, intensity, and consecration with which it is engaged. A ritual can be repeated again and again, yet for it to be alive the performer must self-transcend, go beyond the formal elements of the ritual with his own consciousness. In this way spiritual ritual, in particular, becomes a source for continually renewed wonderment. But rarely are we so yielded to a repeated ritual that the inherent mystery endlessly emerges regardless of the frequency of repetition. It is said that when the great Catholic mystic Padre Pio performed High Mass, the power breathed through the congregation like a living flame. I have seen a photograph of him that remarkably recorded a nimbus of radiant energy surrounding the uplifted chalice.

One need not be a mystic to appreciate the power of ritual. Ritual is part of life everywhere. Anyone who has learned to concentrate and immerse into an activity, a jogger or skier, for instance, is involved in a ritual of aliveness. The key is our ability to go beyond memory. We must be able to free ourselves from time, to be immersed completely in what we are doing. Exercises like the singing and dancing are constructed to make the process of invoking energy conscious, to invite expanded awareness in which the whole bodymind, not just the intellect or the emotion or the physical self, participates. We learn to release the higher consciousness and free energy from smaller egoic patterns, while at the same time training the whole bodymind so it can become a channel for the spontaneous and natural expression of higher energies.

Ancient activities, such as whirling or the more complex ritual of a sweat lodge, carry us, like the singing, to the point where control and letting go become one and the same. This creates a doorway between the physical, egoic self and the infinite, unbounded being. In this doorway the psyche unifies, and we can receive and express a far larger dimension of aliveness. We learn to recognize that our multidimensional natures are capable of accessing more energy than we allow ourselves to express within the confines of our usual egoic patterns. Unless we learn to give this energy freedom to move and live within and through us, it can become morbid, physically or psychologically.

It is crucial for us to understand that *our problems cannot be resolved at the same level of consciousness from which they originate; we must move to a higher level of energy.* Most problems in life stem from the autonomous functioning of the various modes of consciousness. At our usual level of energy, thought and feeling tend to remain separate. We think about something and it engenders a feeling (or vice versa) which in turn generates new thoughts. Thought itself can only go so far before it turns back on itself and begins to circle round and round, a process that can become quite disturbing when our energy heightens and we are trapped in our heads. We must move to another mode of energetic activation and expression to free the energy from such a cycle. There is an intrinsic nonrationality in physical movement or singing that transcends conception or emotion alone. We can understand how our body moves only so far, and then we reach the place where movement is initiated out of another space in consciousness that we cannot measure or recognize. Thus to allow the body to express freely and uninhibitedly in dance or physical work provides space for understanding that cannot be reached directly through reasoned thinking. Feeling does a similar thing. For example, we cannot imagine death with our thoughts; yet grief brings us into a far more immediate and inexpressible relationship to death. Our whole body participates and there is great healing value in this.

The movement to a higher level of energy is a movement toward a unification of the psyche, so that feeling, ideation, sensation and the sense of the ALL, which is really behind and above our experience of reality, begin to merge. At a lower energy, the intellect tends to operate separately from our deeper feelings. We live in our ideas and emotions, and there is a brittleness to our lives. When the psychic energy heightens, as it does in the singing the moment the process becomes effortless and unselfconscious, there is sufficient energy to bring intellect and the deeper feeling states together. This experience is commonly called an opening of the heart and the love of life flows through us. For a little while we feel our understanding; emotion and conception are unified in a common awareness. If neurotic behavior has been created at the energy level in which these modes tended to remain separate, such behavior will now be understandable and a "healing" will have occurred.

As the energy level goes even higher, sensual perception, physicality, conception, and feeling begin to unify. The body becomes Light, flooded with a feeling that is both sensual and intelligent. The mind is quiet in the usual sense and the conception at this level is shared with the whole bodymind. This state marks the awakening of the deeper psychical energy, sometimes referred to as Kundalini. But rather than a dormant process that resides in the body, it is more an aliveness that is only possible at certain levels of energy. When this unity is attained, many physical ailments that evolved at a lower and more divided state of consciousness may begin to resolve. Yet even at this level there remains a sense of an experiencing self that is somehow separate or other than the experience. There are even higher levels of energy in which the whole subjective and objective reality becomes a single divine Consciousness. This is what we call Enlightenment.

We have an analogy for this process of unification of ordinarily separate modes of consciousness in theoretical physics. The four basic physical forces in the universe (electromagnetism, gravity, and the weak and strong nuclear forces) were thought to be unified at the moment of the Big Bang. But in order for scientists to test this theory, experimentation needed to be done at higher and higher energies. To attain these energies involves accelerating electrons or other particles to very high speeds and then colliding them. For brief moments sufficient energies have been reached that unification of some of these forces was observed. Work proceeds on even larger and more powerful particle accelerators in order to see what occurs at even higher energies.

There is something quite stirring to me in the image of modern physics moving toward higher energies in order to peer backward toward a time in which the energy of the universe was infinitely higher than it is now and unity dominated diversity. Simultaneously through yoga, meditation, depth psychology and religion, millions of people work to reach higher psychical energies in order to unify consciousness, to see life more clearly, and perhaps to attain enlightenment. To me these are different vectors of the same movement: mankind individually and collectively, materially and spiritually, moving to a higher energy. While physicists use linear accelerators, the great accelerator of the human spirit is communion and relationship. The energies of a group of people who merge into a more unified consciousness accelerates the movement of each individual into levels in which body, mind, feeling, inner, outer, higher, lower, all begin to blend into entirely new experiences of aliveness.

Physicists tell us that the universe is slowly running down, slowly losing its energy. Yet it is this very dissipation of energy that makes possible the diversity of life we see here on earth. It is the synergy of this life that in turn allows the embrace of new and higher levels of energy, evolving consciousness to new possibility. The laws of thermodynamics are correct in saying that there is a fundamental economy of energy. But this is only looking at one dimension of existence. Even as we dissipate and exhaust energy at one level, even as we die from diseases triggered by the residual pollutants of the very mechanisms that sustain our growing human biomass, another consciousness is taking shape out of the awareness with which we live.

LEARNING TO TRANSMUTE ENERGIES
AND AN EXPERIENCE OF EXORCISM

The exercises for transmuting energy that I teach in my work were spontaneous discoveries that kept renewing the sense of deeper balance and harmony during the early period following my awakening. At that time there was so much energy moving through me, that when I contracted due to old psychical habits, it was like having 1000 watts in a 50-watt system. My body would ache terribly, I'd feel weak, and my mind would race trying to understand it all. At such times I was particularly vulnerable to negative ideation. No rational analysis would bring either understanding or peace. In fact, I found it quite impossible to focus in my usual analytic way. Using meditation techniques helped me to become quiet; in fact I would fall effortlessly into deep meditation. But soon after leaving the passive meditative state, I would have even more energy than before; my discomfort would increase.

And so I began to learn *the basic law of awakening consciousness: Energy not creatively engaged and radiated becomes morbid.* It was during this early phase that I discovered that the easiest and most direct way to channel energy was through the body. Walking, especially in natural settings where I briskly forced myself up hills, would restore me to a sense of peace.

It was also at this time that I accidentally discovered the tremendous power in singing. I was parting from a client whom I had seen some weeks before. She had been experiencing recurrent hepatitis and depression. Her most recent relapses followed intensive Buddhist meditation practices, for she was in fact competing spiritually with her lover, while at the same time maintaining a professorship at a major university. She said that the more she meditated, the more her graduate students were attracted to her. They would come to her confiding their problems and leave feeling wonderful, while she would become progressively weaker. But then, with hesitation and embarrassment, she confided that she felt there were two evil spirits in her. As she spoke, an oppressive sense of darkness and heaviness pervaded the room. Immediately, a powerful voice within me silently commanded, "Be gone." At precisely that moment, a wave of heat passed through us and she burst into tears. Some weeks later, she wrote to thank me and called me for a second visit. She said that from the moment of her spontaneous tears, her hepatitis ceased, and she was feeling wonderful. She ended her relationship, modulated her meditation practice, and was already planning to leave academic life for a position in private industry. The experience had literally been an exorcism, something that my newly awakened consciousness seemed to understand and be capable of. (My ordinary awareness looked on in astonishment—and not without some fear.) As she was stepping into her car to leave, she asked me if I had any idea of the power of the forces I was dealing with. Instantly I was thrown into terror. I didn't really know, at least not with my outer awareness.

But, quite spontaneously, as she drove off I began to sing with all my soul of the fear that was holding me and of my need for help. I was oblivious to the fact that I was on the front lawn of my house in a rather sedate suburban neighborhood. I sank to the ground like a characer in a Wagnerian opera. (None of this was consciously directed or premeditated.) Suddenly I could hear my voice reverberating in the trees as if I were far above myself. At the same time, the energy moving through me was a fine hum and I fell into utter peace and stillness. Contemplating what had happened, a part of me smiled at such melodramatic antics.

In this way, I learned that fear or any mood is merely a momentary configuration of energy and has no reality in itself. The energy that is fear or hate is also peace, generosity and love. By spontaneously meeting the fear in a new way, singing (Creative Involvement) with real passion (Intensity), the energy was freed and "I" expanded into stillness. This had taken only a few moments.

The experience of transmuting fear gave me a new respect for the power of this emotion. It is perhaps the highest level of energy one can experience while passively bound within the basic egoic structure. I say *passive* because we usually experience fear acting upon us while we ourselves are not fully active. Fear takes over when we are no longer absorbed in what we are doing. In contrast, rage is the other pole; it is the highest energy available within the basic egoic dynamic when we are in an active mode. This is why it is not uncommon for an individual who is very afraid to overreact and swing like a pendulum into destructive rage. Rather than swinging to the opposite pole, I had transmuted the energy. I spontaneously moved into an active mode that had allowed merging with the energy of fear. At the moment of union, the I-who-am-afraid became At-One; the fear vanished and became space. The fear had acted as a door to Being—a rather high-energy one. At that moment of Being, inner and outer became a single one. This was very similar to the original awakening but on a much smaller scale. I realized that the awakening had opened a door between dimensions, thus giving me access to many extraordinary powers. But my ordinary awareness was not conscious of the door. I now set about learning to keep the door open continuously.

I began to sing out of the immediacy of myself whenever I was alone in the hills. In a few minutes, I would be lifted into silence and peace. The key was the authenticity of the song, i.e. that it emanated out of my present state and that I persisted until my singing became unpremeditated and unselfconscious. I suspect it is this power to break out of the local cocoon of one's basic energy state that makes singing or chanting a central part of religious and even military ritual. In fact, looking back I realize that on my front lawn I had experienced prayer for the first time.

Prayer is a complete self-abandonment, so that the very moment becomes the Living Divine. I soon learned that if this gesture of creative self-abandonment is not done immediately when a particular dynamic begins to arise in consciousness, the dynamic will precipitate fully into psychological space/time and will not release as quickly. If I had waited before singing and instead started analyzing what had happened and worrying about what to do, the fear would have had me, perhaps for hours. Any action I then took would have been a reaction to it.

That first episode of transmuting was Grace. But to master this practice required and continues to require tremendous self-awareness and immense attention. This kind of discipline, which is the heart of all meditation and prayer, has been central in my own unfoldment and work. I have only recently learned that in Tibetan Buddhism this is called the Path of Liberation.

Most people have no idea of the relative reality of their moods.

Instead they live at the effect of these moods. But this need not be the case. The exercises that Laura and the group were undertaking create the direct experience of another possibility; we can learn to transmute the energy of any state. I have given the example of fear but the same is true for sadness. Sadness can only exist within a specific range of energy. It can come from loss, but more often in the awakening process, sadness is what I call Yin sickness. It reflects that one has become too open, too transparent without simultaneously incarnating the energy into creative expression. Whatever the cause, shifting the energetic dynamic will change the sense of sadness. In the beginning this requires doing something spontaneous with the energy, such as singing (Creative Involvement). Of course, singing sadness may, at first, make it even more real, more overpowering. However, if you sing with greater and greater energy (Intensity), not just loudly, but with impeccable attention to every nuance of your tone, every note change, at a certain point, you may go through a door—you and the energy of sadness will not be separate. At that moment the sense of sadness will disappear. It may become laughter or just quietness. No matter what it becomes, the energy itself will be finer, and awareness will have changed.

If we continually analyze our moods, passions, fears—as we in the West are so wont to do—we are doomed to a life trapped within them until, having developed sufficient attention, we recognize them as energy. The energy that is released when we finally transmute them can be vast. The deeper we go in our inquiry into ourselves, the more subtle and all-encompassing are the processes we begin to observe, for there will always be dynamics that are larger than our awareness. Thus we are led into unknown territory within ourselves as we free the energy from the known. This process inevitably invites us to deeper consciousness, and to humility and compassion as well. But to spend an inordinate amount of time in the basic emotions once we are able to access higher states of consciousness is more a matter of indulgence that reflects the addiction to familiar kinds of intensity. We are allowing ourselves to live at a lower energy level where these painful states continually draw our attention. At a higher level of energy our attention is brought to a much more subtle dimension of consciousness. Thus we become able to witness psychical content as it arises and learn to free the energy into radiant aliveness.

This is very slow at first, because during this phase our experience still defines our identity, so that whatever we observe or give additional attention to is emphasized, making it seem even more substantial. Sometimes this can be uncomfortable, because bringing such attention to pleasant experiences tends to diminish them, while bringing the same attention to unpleasant states tends to intensify them. But this equalizing of experience means that we are actually moving toward a subtle and more universal dimension. As we grow more adept, we begin to witness at a point closer to the moment where the content is arising into awareness. This is when we begin to become aware of the collective and archetypal levels of consciousness, the very patterns that define humanity. Long before this, we have learned to free energy from our personal psychic dynamics directly and immediately into radiant presence.

Along the way, there are many dynamics where we will have to stop. There is no choice. Rather than simply watching, we will be compelled to say, "This is the real, this is what I am." But *it is a basic law of Consciousness that we are—in the totality of our nature—larger than anything that we can identify or witness.* Whatever it is that we call the truth, whatever pretense we require to undertake the journey, whatever vision we have of the goal (perhaps to know God, Jesus, Buddha), all along we are infinitely more than these archetypal entities. To the degree to which such ideas and goals exist as the content of our consciousness and we are identified with them, we have trapped our larger nature. At the moment we know these energies directly as ourselves, the energy is freed and we experience ourselves as Divine. But whatever this new sense of self, no matter how expanded and profound, it too is relative.

This is why I am always amazed at people who have profound experiences and use them to rationalize a new personal identity. They become "the teacher," or "the healer," but personalizing the energy immediately places the individual back into the straightjacket of self-involvement. Certainly, the experience of realization changed the base of reference of my consciousness, and my life changed radically in terms of function and capacity. But having new capacities and thus a new role to play did not cause the fostering of a new relative identity. The utter dissolution of the personal egoic reference in the process of awakening destroys the fiction that self can ever be defined in or through worldly involvement. There is a statement in *The Gospel According to Thomas* that says this very clearly: "The foxes have their holes and the birds have their nests, but the Son of Man has no place to lay his head and to rest." Therefore no experience, especially realization, can be the basis for renewing personal identity in the separatist sense. To the degree that our experiences help us to commune with each other and to understand our world, they have validity. But it is precisely because we have experienced ourselves anew that we can with certainty say that this is not who I am. Identity is wholeness when the natural expression of our uniqueness shines forth and we are At-One with life. But the private identity we work so hard to cultivate—no matter how elegant, wise, or spiritual it appears—is a dense energetic bastion separating us from the vastness of Being and the humility of ordinariness. It is equivalent to living in a hole in the ground like an animal.

Freeing our attention is the greatest achievement. Without it there can be no creative involvement with life; we are simply responding and reacting, always at the effect of our moods or the world around us. Thus, when a person comes to me for counseling, the first thing I ascertain is whether they can sustain a sense of self-awareness in the midst of their pain. If they can, then I encourage them not to turn away from themselves, not to be caught in some final interpretation of what is happening and some desperate need to be different. This self-acceptance is itself Creative Involvement and this begins the transmutational process. But self-acceptance does not mean that we must feel happy or content in conventional terms.

Happiness, itself, is not the best condition to invite deepening awareness; thus it certainly is not the goal of one pursuing transformation. Happiness, as it is popularly venerated, usually implies worldly security and a self-esteem that bequeathes relative impregnability, a diminished sensitivity and availability. People who are in pain are usually growing. Their deeper aliveness is awakening and bringing with it a greater sensitivity. Such sensitivity means an enhanced capacity for wonderment but also an equally enhanced capacity to suffer. But if we can observe ourselves, if we can witness our suffering, then gradually we will transmute the structure of suffering, and it will become wonderment. We all suffer at times, but suffering is not wrong in itself. It is only when we become identified within it that it becomes destructive. But this is true of any level of identification; it immediately binds our aliveness. And since it is easiest to become identified and forget attention when we feel good, in many ways suffering is superior to happiness. At least when we suffer we also tend to inquire into why, and this leads to attention.

Even negative or disruptive energy that seems to come from outside can be empowering to one on a transformational path. Instead of closing down or reacting when someone is threatening you, it is possible to transmute that energy. It can become a stillness that may even deflect the violence. In one instance a man I know was crossing a picket line. Each day the strikers cursed and threatened him. They even tried to burn his car. He told me that most days it was frightening, but one morning his heart spontaneously opened. To his astonishment their hatred filled him with love. It made him blissful, almost drunk. After this, the strikers stopped paying attention to him.

While such capacity is unusual, it is nonetheless a very real and continuous possibility. I often have this same kind of experience, although it has never involved violence per se. On one occasion, I was at a football game. When an overtime touchdown won the game and the crowd was on its feet in exultation, I fell into a Samadhi-like state from the sheer force of that collective energy. A similar thing happens when I am at airports or in any situation where there is a high degree of diffuse emotional energy. It isn't always pleasant at first, but it soon becomes a deep meditative state that is often calming for people in the vicinity. Along a similar vein, the attention, sometimes positive and sometimes very negative, that certain spiritual groups attract because of their unusual appearance (long hair, special clothes) is a valid source of aliveness for those sufficiently adept to tap into it. Perhaps these groups start out only intending to symbolize their faith and establish a group identity for their own sake. However, attention whether from within or without is energy, and it is foolish to think it should only be positive. For those who are truly religious, this energy can be freed to become a boon for the sake of all. Unfortunately very few religious people understand this possibility, and rather than use the energy to empower expanded awareness they use it to further empower their separatist group identity.

The transformational process requires a lot of energy. To access this energy means that we have gradually explored more and more of our potential and freed the energy from relative levels of identity. In the conferences, when people are first inducted into energetic attention, it is amazing how exhausted they become just sustaining the consciousness for an hour or so. They simply are not used to placing this kind of demand upon themselves except during rare moments of intense mental and physical concentration. We cannot get something for nothing. We cannot expect to be able to sustain the kind of attention that allows us to step beyond the ordinary content of consciousness unless our whole life is consecrated to that possibility. Even to indulge in casual socializing, which is effortless and seems so natural, means that we are habituating ourselves to a very limited level of aliveness. If we think we can turn from such an unconscious and comfort-oriented life and expect to be able to access higher levels of energy and aliveness, we are not only naive, we are arrogant.

THE IMPORTANCE OF GROUNDING
AND THE PROBLEM OF HYPERSENSITIVITY

Everything in life is of a piece. The energy it takes to develop attention, which seems exhausting at first, returns to us as radiance and reaches into every level of life. Nothing is lost; everything we do has greater aliveness, greater freedom. We can literally transmute the substance of our consciousness as it arises and radiate this as pure presence in any activity or situation. It is a space in which everyone is lifted into greater wholeness, and yet nothing outwardly has been done. This suggests a crucial new understanding of both aliveness and service. Most of humanity generates aliveness by doing, rarely by *being*. The popular call to aliveness is a "go for it" mentality that creates energy by continuously challenging oneself or the world; there must always be something to push against and change. Thus this level of aliveness and empowerment inevitably leaves a tremendous wake of building and destruction. Likewise service, as it has come to be respected in our world, is also a *doing* orientation. Whether all this doing is really helpful will be discussed later.

For myself, the greatest energy and fullest sense of being comes when I simply relax into stillness. It is as though a door opens in consciousness and a current circulates through me that is a nectar of peace and fulfillment. Life seems permeated by softness. Time stands still and every breath is a celebration, a gentle rapture. The body relaxes and the mind is quiet. The distinction between inner and outer, between breathing and being breathed, diminishes. This is a far richer feeling than I have ever known from the occasional tranquilizers and psychedelics I explored earlier in my life. If I am tired or some problem is troubling me, in a short time I am completely restored. While the problem may still be present, my commitment to face it is once again certain and strong. If anyone is with me at these times, they also feel the effect and are similarly restored.

Yet this nectar cannot be abused. I have found that if I remain in it for too long there is a taxing effect. It is as if I have run too much current through the physical circuits. Thus, as we learn to derive energy from higher dimensions, it becomes very important to feed the ordinary self the energies it is used to. Exercise and simple work like gardening and sculpting make it possible for me to dip into the current safely and to sustain it for prolonged periods during my conference work.

In general, modern living frees us to explore consciousness, but it has also decreased our tendency to be in our bodies. This poses a problem as we access more and more energy. In the past, the sheer arduousness of daily life naturally involved the body in the awakening energies. But nowadays such natural grounding is rare, and each person must develop a special discipline of manual work, exercise, dancing or singing that includes the body in the transformational process.

If we are well-grounded, the attention participates with our physicality, our ordinary humanity. When we cannot hold the attention at this level, but tend to move out into the subtle body and value psychic and energetic experience over physical ordinariness, there is a tendency to become ungrounded. Then the heightening of energy can result in a hypersensitivity or allergic condition. It is as though the body calls us to earth, to flesh, demanding our attention by creating suffering. I have had quite a lot of experience with hypersensitivity, both personally and in my work. For some people, hypersensitivity to the environment develops because they have outgrown their life structures, but they are so unconsciously bound to them that the naturally increasing level of energy takes on morbid dynamics. By releasing the structure (letting go of the marriage, the job) and simultaneously learning to free energy in ways that involve the whole bodymind, the allergic process is alleviated. For others, it is the spiritual pursuit itself that engenders the sensitivity. Higher states become activated and begin to consume the aspirant. When the consciousness moves up or out of the body, occupying the subtle levels, the physical form loses its capacity to integrate this developing transcendence and cellular sensitivity becomes a morbid pattern of resistance and rejection. Yet the same energy grounded more directly in the body provides the basis for developing sensitivity as a subliming of flesh, a transfiguration, rather than morbidity. The morbid energy becomes new aliveness and radiance.

A human being can be seen as a channel connecting heaven and earth. If we are not well-grounded, our first experiences of higher energies tend to be psychical. There are visions and ecstatic feeling states, and we equate this with enlightenment. In contrast, a well-grounded person may enter a heightened energy and feel virtually nothing, or merely pleasant clarity. A less grounded person experiencing the same energy may become ecstatic or terrified at a sense of annihilation or dissolution. But groundedness is not necessarily the same as density or unavailability. A person can be very transparent to the energies, but if they are well-grounded, this will not translate into powerful psychical experiences. Yet they will conduct these energies and help stabilize the overall energetic milieu. It should be noted that the best healers are often very earthy and not particularly sensitive

(in their own bodily space) to the subtle energies. This is the consequence of their groundedness. The movement into higher energies at the expense of being grounded in our bodies and in ordinary
... may mean that we will have powerful psychical experiences,
but little of this energy will radiate into life as a transformational
force. It is our task to become more open, conductive and radiant while simultaneously deepening our connection to our basic
human ... this grounded, ordinary, vital aliveness that can
sustain higher and higher energies without the breakdown of the
body.

The kind of hypersensitivity that is pulling so many seekers out
of the immediacy of life and into what is almost a narcissistic process of self-involvement represents a withdrawal from the stress of
incarnation. What is needed is to more fully ground the higher
energies in the bodymind. The awakening consciousness automatically becomes more sensitive. The air, the sky, the trees, the
whole psychosphere, including the by-products of man's technology are none other than self. At this level we are saying yes to
more and more that still remains foreign to our basic consciousness. The hypersensitivity reaction is a combination of this greater
yes at the universal level of consciousness and a simultaneous need
to say no at a more basic level. This schism can become a narcissistic self-involvement, a reductionistic process of continually trying
to eliminate the so-called stressors from the psychic and physical
environment and thereby protect the basic nature. This is the traditional medical approach, and even the thinking of many holistic
and psychic healers. It places the power outside the person (in
the stressor) and is a way of thinking that grows from sub-
ject/object separation. Clearly there are some severe environmental
toxins and we must eliminate these. But for the most part, we
are unaware of how much authority each of us has to transmute
these stressors.

My own approach (which has been quite successful in a small
number of severely hypersensitive individuals and a larger number of moderately sensitive people) has been to increase the conductivity of the bodymind to higher energies. This involves the
previously discussed group dynamics and exercises that allow us
to enter a higher energy and express ourselves within it. A large

part (if not all) of hypersensitivity represents a split or distance between the level of energy moving through a person and his or her ability to hold (ground) these energies in daily life. When this split unifies and the person is living and expressing at a level in harmony with his intrinsic energy, hypersensitivity simply ceases. I have known people allergic to nearly everything while the split continues and, an hour later, when unified in their being, they no longer demonstrate sensitivity.

The approach I use emphasizes the need to access levels of energy that have been severely repressed. They are usually related to the principle of fire (anger, directness, rage, potency). Once the individuals access this fire quality, they simultaneously have the capacity to ground the higher energies, and the hypersensitivity is automatically transmuted into aliveness and presence.

The challenge of this approach is that not every person is willing to look into the unknown of his being. We would rather have others take care of us or use their energy to eliminate outer stressors. While many people do improve through the reductionist approach, they use up an enormous amount of energy to push life away. It is a kind of individuation or self-empowerment through an adolescent process of rejection and control. There is so much fear in this that letting go to a higher aliveness is impossible. Thus, my own work has only been effective for those people whose love of life and desire to know wholeness was greater than their fear of illness. All of us at times need to watch our diets and avoid certain stressful agents, but this is as much a reminder to come back into a larger balance as it is any kind of limitation. Here we are seeing the importance of the underlying consecration in determining the way in which we approach this problem. Do we attempt to get larger to hold our growing sensitivity (God-is-love), or do we fight to eliminate that which threatens our basic identity (God-is-wrathful)?

BEYOND POSITIVE AND NEGATIVE

The transformational process can be regarded as learning how to heighten the energies of consciousness, while simultaneously softening the egoic grip on reality. Opening the fist is both ego-based (the process of releasing crystallized psychical structures) and energetic (the process of moving to a new note of consciousness). We work on ourselves to root out fear and prejudice, narrowness, or laziness, until we become more open, less controlling. We can speak of this as Becoming, or purification of the nature. There are infinite possibilities here, but the key is to realize that, while we have learned to differentiate when the egoic fist is contracted or open, we have not changed in any fundamental sense. A still deeper level of work is learning to put the firecracker down—to cease identifying with content. This is essentially the process of developing meditative attention that frees the energy. Again and again, we learn to release a particular dynamic until it no longer has the power to cause us to contract. Finally—and this aspect can neither be learned nor given—there is the mystery of realization, the discontinuous movement to Wholeness.

In the example of the dancing and singing exercise, the focus is on unification of consciousness. It is in this condition that we are at our highest level of energy, yet we are firmly grounded in the bodymind. It is possible that at this moment the basic psychoenergetic structure will simply release as it did with Laura. But even if this is not the case, as we heighten our energy, consciousness expands and becomes more inclusive; we come closer to that exquisite edge between form and formlessness, the known and the unknown. It is here that the sense of inspiration, beauty, and meaning are most strong. Even if this is only a transitory induction and we later return to our usual energy level, there is now a new reference point for aliveness, a new quality to our aspiration. Thus we turn back to the ongoing process of self-purification with renewed determination and an expanded sense of meaning.

It should be emphasized that the capacity to transmute states of consciousness is not just a new technique for manipulating unpleasant moods and enhancing desirable states, nor should it be regarded as a new approach to healing. Rather, it is a stage of development in which we are learning more about our true nature as Consciousness. By being able to shift from one energy to another, we learn that all reality is relative, that nothing we experience can be regarded as real in any final or absolute sense. It is a process that teaches us how to become more fluid, more transparent (i.e. we release identification with the various emotive and feeling states faster and faster—they pass through us rather than define us).

This understanding is quite different from that proposed by the positive-thinking and mind-science schools, where some states are decidedly positive and definitely to be preferred over those that are labeled (and collectively believed to be) negative—and the larger context of Consciousness is never considered. The labeling of reality into positive and negative conditions is both natural to our egoic selves and also a fundamental ignorance that itself propagates more suffering. This is not to say that we each don't experience some conditions as positive and preferable to others. Pain and suffering are definitely unpleasant and undesirable. But to go to a deeper level of consciousness, the positive or negative poles of experience provide equal access and potential and, in this sense, are identical. The value and placement of the whole positive-thinking, positive-affirmation thrust is a beginning stage in understanding the capacity to shift the energies of consciousness. These approaches provide the counterpoise to our identification with the negative. But shifting from a negative to a positive state is merely a reversal of the polarity, not a movement to a higher energy. We may transiently feel better in the positive pole, but it is a superficial well-being. Positive-pole spirituality feeds on people's fears, the universal inability to face death. It is seductive to learn to keep modifying one's state in order to feel on top and in control. Yet it is the deep self-surrender that comes from the contemplation of death that is perhaps the very root of religiosity. Thus such approaches are to me inherently nonspiritual. They would appear to be deflecting the transformational impulse except that, once people have learned they can shift from negative to positive, they have embarked on the first stage of learning to transmute energy.

A deeper level of understanding occurs when we realize that we can move to a finer or higher energy through either pole of experience. But very few people are willing to enter a creative relationship to their positive states. There is a tendency to be unconscious at such times. It is only the negative states that we want to do anything about. The failure to be attentive in the positive state (and thus, sacrifice that state into a larger and perhaps less immediately pleasurable awareness) invites the swing into the negative state. There is line from Isaiah in the Old Testament that speaks precisely to this: "The valleys shall be exalted, the mountains and hills made low . . . make straight in the desert a highway for our God." In order to move to a higher energy we must release the energy of our attachment to positive and negative alike.

At this point the whole process of transmutation moves from a voluntary act of attention to something far deeper and more mysterious. Since no state or condition has absolute reality, the need to transmute begins to fall away entirely and life is simply experienced as it is. This could look exactly like the passive acceptance of less aware individuals, but it is actually very different. There is a freedom from reaction. The content of consciousness arises, but the energy is liberated spontaneously. This does not mean that there is no pain, anger, or unhappiness. Anything can be experienced, but it is over as soon as it happens. Furthermore there is an unusual quality to consciousness at this level. The very forces that crush people can become profound radiance in an individual who no longer is resisting or attempting to modify life. Clearly this is difficult to describe, but the result is that we no longer hold or resist our experience as it arises. At this point, one can honestly say that everything is as it is. The discrimination of positive/negative, spiritual/nonspiritual, real/unreal, ceases. Even the need to transmute the energy of a particular state becomes irrelevant. In this sense one can allow sadness, for it is already perfect and not other than Reality.

For myself, I dip in and out of this state continually. At one point, I wanted to sustain the thinking that this is the ultimate condition. But I found that as I lived in this state more and more there was a subtle tendency toward disincarnating, toward leaving the body, and my health suffered. Thus I found that it is necessary to dip in and out, to allow my humanity to have equal expression, so that the transcendent point of view is contrasted and new depth of understanding arises.

It is all too easy to think that higher states of consciousness represent the transcendence of all previous conditions, but if one were to imagine the whole panorama of possibility as existing simultaneously, then every possibility, whether desirable or undesirable, evolved or unevolved to our relative valuation, is actually contributing to and an expression of the Whole. Thus transmutation must be seen as developmental, so that once a certain level has been mastered, there is a validity in surrendering that capacity and once again entering life without pretense or understanding. One appears thus to fall, but I suspect this is inevitable. Perhaps the Luciferian myth is not about doing it wrong, but more accurately one of the very appropriate, albeit disconcerting (literally) processes of psychic unfoldment.

7 * THE DIVINE BODYMIND AND VOICE CHANNELING

THERE IS THE BODY that we all know through subject/object consciousness. It is the body that we infer from our senses and we see when we look in the mirror. There is the body that we know through thought. It is a body that is conditioned by life experience, by our family and cultural contexts, that lives in our memory and associates new experiences through old impressions. It is a body known through inference and rational examination, the body that grows with education, that medicine dissects and treats. But there is also another body, one that few ever know directly. It is what I call the divine body. It is aliveness that is unconditioned, unobstructed, the reflection of the very principle of life. The accumulated beliefs and concepts of the bodymind no longer dominate. Subject/object consciousness is transcended, and with it all the patterns of energy that have been defined simultaneously with the development of that consciousness.

The ego structure is an energy pattern based in subject/object consciousness. This is why it was so revealing when Laura spoke of beginning to die by age two. From the perspective of her opening, the egoic development even by age two was sufficient to be-

gin the contraction away from full aliveness. But as this egoic development is subsumed in a larger consciousness, so too is physical reality animated in a new way. There is a literal
trans-substantiation, and the conditioned body of personal identity
gives way to one that is made in the image of God. It is this divine body that we may know in varying degrees in every moment
of being, and most fully in the moment of realization. To move
readily between the egoic body and the divine body is a valuable
way to envision the transformational process. It is also what I call
health.

The way we live in our bodies (how we move, the quality of
the voice) reflects in large measure our energetic conductivity and
aliveness. When we find a moment of free and unobstructed aliveness in dance or song, it is equivalent to freeing energy. The liberated energy is not merely psychic energy. A large part of the
bodymind participates. The integrative effect reverberates through
more of our being, freeing energy at many levels—including the
psychological, preverbal, and even cellular levels. Thus after touching that moment of At-Oneness in the dancing or singing, we
suddenly understand whole aspects of our behavior that had never
been conscious before. Simultaneously we discover that our back
has been healed or that some longtime physical disability has simply vanished. We move differently, with greater fluidity and grace.

In effect we are uniting flesh to Consciousness and Consciousness to flesh, with the result that the enlightenment process is
spiritualizing physically as well as psychologically and theoreti-
cally. So much of our spirituality seems to me wishful thinking.
There are many elegant hypotheses and visionary speculations
born of transcendental moments, but rarely does this penetrate
deeper than the mental or emotional level. Undoubtedly such
speculation is valuable as a process of Creative Involvement that
invites us to new perspectives about ourselves. But the art of incarnating such ideas is the heart of transformation. This implies
that the higher consciousness must descend further than intellectual understanding. It must become part of our cellular aliveness,
making us radiant human beings.

It is the movement from the mental level into full psychophysical aliveness that is the radical step. It is a far greater challenge

to live within the energy, so that it transmutes our bodies—and our sexual, emotional, physical and feeling natures—than it is to theorize about the transformative potential. Belief is simple, but actualizing any belief within the body as new aliveness is a long and difficult process. The more the energy descends into the body, the more paradoxical the whole process of awakening becomes. At the mental level things can be very clear and the path of action obvious, but as we penetrate more deeply into the heart of our being—what I refer to as the center of gravity of our consciousness—this clarity is no longer obvious. Mathematics provides a good analogy. Pure mathematics is elegantly self-consistent and its application technologically is relatively direct. It is the next step, the entrance of the pure idea into the culture that is quite complex.

If we imagine pure mathematics as a mental dimension that closely approximates the transcendent in its internal consistency and universality, then we can speak of such mathematics as one of the purest levels of incarnation of the Divine. Conversely, we could also speak of it as one of the highest penetrations of materiality into the realm of the transcendent. But look what happens as we watch pure mathematics descend further and further into materiality, into the body of humanity. It becomes technological power over the environment, with new machines, new instruments. We begin to interact with life in more and more complex ways, and soon a theoretical breakthrough of exquisite elegance that integrates and reconciles whole branches of thought becomes the instrument of profound consequences philosophically, psychologically, emotionally and physically for every human being. Now the value of the breakthrough becomes extremely debatable, because at the level of the body, the level of physical reality, any higher possibility is always expressed as a polarity, a fundamental duality. Relativity theory and nuclear energy are a case in point. The theory is elegant and simple, the incarnation equally as creative as destructive.

As we attempt to study life and to enter into a transformational process, we must engage as much of our being as we can. The awakening of man must involve the whole being; it must be bodily and cellular; it must engage the emotional and feeling nature as well as the mental and transcendent parts of us. A realization that descends into the physical and cellular level while extending out to the Infinite and Eternal is unlikely to be accurately expressed in any one level of consciousness. Perhaps it can be partially conveyed as a parable, and for those who are sensitive it can be partially conveyed through induction by a radiant individual. But it can never be conveyed fully, precisely because it is paradoxical, involving spirit and matter simultaneously. It incarnates into life everywhere all at once, but it is realized in time most slowly at the level of the body, at the level of human culture. Thus it represents a principle of growth or change that is holistic, not linear or quantum. For the same reason, there is no direct application for realization. It serves neither good nor ill. It is neither appropriate as a means of fixing oneself, let's say psychologically, nor is it an instrument of destruction. This is precisely why we make a grave mistake trying to interpret mystical scripture from only a mental or psychological level. Such scripture comes from a process that was centered at the heart, that engaged the whole body as well as the mental and subtle aspects of consciousness. The only possible way to know this is to experience it directly oneself. It is this and only this that scripture invites—and not the terrible positive and negative expression that always results when whole-body realization is heard from a more limited level of consciousness.

We must begin to include the whole bodymind in our exploration of consciousness and in our idea of spirituality. From the point of view that transformation involves the whole being, the task is to engage as much of consciousness as is possible in any activity. Exercises such as singing and dancing teach us how to move beyond the boundary of our ordinary energy level by becoming creatively At-One. But they do something else as well; they simultaneously incarnate that energy into active embodied expression.

✽

There is a further refinement of this. It is the capacity to give verbal expression to higher states. Now, I do not mean reporting about such states after we have returned to a more ordinary level of consciousness, nor do I mean creating various theories and cosmologies as a result of our experiences. To do so is part of integrating the transformational process, but it indicates the gap between higher states as we experience them directly and the level of energy we are actually able to carry into the world. Said in another way, reaching up into a higher state is one half of the process; the other half is bringing the higher energy back. Thus, an important mastery is to begin to learn to speak right out of the immediacy of these higher states. It is the voice that conveys the energy of the state and inducts this in the listener.

The voice is perhaps the most complex human activity, for it involves not only physical coordination, but also elaborate mental functioning. Language itself is intrinsic to subject/object consciousness; we cannot speak save that we have already evolved a functioning ego; we have identified ourselves as separate individuals. We can expand into states of unitive consciousness that exist at a much higher energy, but the moment we begin to speak, or even to think, we immediately return to the basic level of consciousness in which language evolved. At this point our words carry the barest adumbration of that original energy. But this need not be the case; language can also become the vehicle for the expression of a higher energy. It is possible to speak, just as in the singing exercise, without premeditation. In a sense it is using the voice with words, images and tonal quality to gain access to oneself, to narrow the gap between self-consciousness and immediacy.

Ordinary speech is timebound. We report from memory or we plan for the future. Thus it is always a copy, an imitation; it is never original. But to speak in such a way as to convey the higher consciousness requires complete originality. The voice becomes an extension of pure attention. It penetrates inward into our being. It is active inquiry that is, itself, the answer. It is probing toward infinity, toward that which we have never expressed, even as words are flowing out from us. This is an extremely difficult thing to learn. In effect it is simply being oneself, accessing the spontaneity that flows from us at any moment of unself-conscious play. However, it is being oneself at a far finer and more universal level of consciousness.

The gap between what we can realize or intuit in a passive mode of attention and that which we can actively communicate grows greater as we enter the deeper levels of consciousness. But it is precisely this gap that we must address if we are to confront the problem of bringing our highest knowing and aspiration into day-to-day living. Many people can touch higher states, but this state remains bound at one level of consciousness and does not generalize to the rest of their being. It is like teaching medicine to students when they are drunk. They can recall the material later when they are drunk again, but not when they are sober. This is precisely what happens with the transformational impulse. It is profoundly real to us at the level we experience it. But because this level is often a spontaneous moment of Grace, or the result of the heightened energy of a conference, it becomes almost impossible to access the same knowing and dedication when one returns to ordinary consciousness. This becomes far less the case when we learn to incarnate the higher state directly into words.

When one is speaking out of the immediacy of oneself, the effect can be immensely enlivening. In a sense, this is what is meant by speaking in tongues or the process of channeling. It requires letting go of the basic consciousness and inviting a deeper level of consciousness as one speaks. It is not so much a special gift as it is a discipline or meditation on the path to actualizing higher consciousness. Every actor or actress knows the power of reaching the point where even memorized words are being spoken with such inner authority that there is no distance between the words and the speaker. This is when the performance becomes compelling, when acting becomes art, and the performer is functioning as a door between dimensions and enlivening all who are present. But the energy of this level of channeling is not as great as when the source is utterly spontaneous, emanating out of the deepest level of our being.

The importance of the capacity to allow a higher consciousness to speak through us is exemplified in the interaction between Jesus and Peter. Jesus asks, "Who do you say that I am?" and Peter answers, "You are the Christ, Son of the living God!" Jesus then tells Peter how blessed he is, for "It was not your own nature, but my Father who revealed His truth to you." It is upon this "rock" that Jesus says he will build his church.

I assert that the rock is not the literal words, "You are the Son of the living God," but the space the words came from. Having brought people for years to higher energies, I am aware how difficult it is to teach them to give voice to these levels. We must be so full, and yet so completely yielded that the mystical voice comes forth spontaneously, and with simple clarity we express things we never imagined we knew. And when we do speak, there is a sense of authority that is neither pompous nor pedantic, but rather conveys a living force that moves everyone who hears. By the end of a conference, many people have moments of such communication that the room becomes a cauldron of ineffable presence. Their hearts are wide open, the throttle of aliveness has expanded to its fullest. It is upon this "rock" that the church of greater life can be built and not necessarily upon the words used in such moments. When we see deeply, our language is ecstatic and requires a language of ecstasy. At this level, all of us may look at one another and say, "You are the Son (or Daughter) of the living Father." And when this flow of voice has ceased, the person is suffused in stillness.

Today, more and more people are learning to access higher energy in words. This often takes the form of writing or verbal channeling of the kind where the source is identified as coming from someone other than oneself. A channel is a person who sets aside his or her consciousness and becomes the vehicle for another dimension of consciousness. In some instances the setting aside of basic consciousness is accomplished by entering a deep trance, and the individual who does the speaking recalls nothing at all of what has been said. Often this is cloaked in esoteric and occult ritual. The source is regarded as other-worldly, i.e. an entity that is extraterrestial or who has died and is "working" for humanity from the "other side." I do not put these words in quotes because of my own skepticism. However, these interpretations or beliefs are not natural to me. While I do not discredit the validity of such beliefs for others, I place the quotes to emphasize them as part of a special category of understanding.

The occult nature of communication from the beyond is an age-old phenomenon, and one that carries a great deal of influence for many people. Most people are not aware of what a universal process this is. They fail to regard the inspired poet, scientist, musician, or leader as a channel; instead the phenomenon has been co-opted by occult considerations. Channeling attributed to an other-worldly source seems somehow to have a greater veracity and importance than the same information presented under more ordinary circumstances.

In fact, there is a certain validity to this impression, because a good channel does demonstrate powers beyond the ordinary. Often there is a great feeling of energy as the channeling begins, and then a sense that the material is very relevant personally. One feels as though one is really being seen and understood by these "entities." This leads to a further tendency to attribute great power—and therefore wisdom—to them. The fact that every person is in degrees of telepathic rapport with everyone else and that this is naturally enhanced when one sets ordinary consciousness aside and enters a higher state is not considered. To beginning explorers, when they first come across a channel, it seems they have found a magical phenomenon and there is a compelling need to attribute higher truth to these experiences. We may have outgrown our biological parents, but we have not outgrown our need for a special "higher" authority to guide us and help us understand our place in the universe.

Nevertheless, the phenomenon of channeling is important. It reflects the growing level of energy in our collective psyche. Thus more and more people will find themselves spontaneously speaking out of higher levels of consciousness. This should not be suppressed. On the contrary, it should be encouraged. But wise discrimination is crucial, so that we do not needlessly set aside our personal responsibility for the energy that is generated by encouraging a loss of personal consciousness in order to engage the process. Precisely to the degree that we set aside the validity of our personal space, there will be a need to personalize the higher energy, to attribute it to a special source. From a developmental perspective, I can appreciate the value of this splitting of consciousness. It allows us to separate our basic humanity from the higher understanding. This protects in some degree from ego inflation, but it also limits the humanizing and the transformative element in whatever material is brought forward. The channeled material is a thought form without a body and, as such, for all its depth and wisdom, cannot carry compassion, for to do so requires that flesh and spirit are one. To the degree to which we incarnate the energy, we are no longer a channel, we are a source.

Sometimes the process of becoming a channel begins spontaneously, and the first occasions are often quite disturbing if one is not familiar with this phenomenon. The power of the higher energy can seem to be of such a magnitude that we might even feel that an alien or superior consciousness has invaded our own. (In my own experience, the energy did have a superior force. However, it never occurred to me to regard it as foreign. Instead I began the process of immediate and direct integration.) But it is understandable that this "invading" consciousness is characterized as being extraterrestial or from the spirit world. Individuals who are likely to find themselves opening in this way have probably not had much exploration of self-awareness in the deepest sense. There has probably been a sincere effort toward personal transformation that has been grounded more in belief about how one should be than in meditative awareness. Thus the tendency to personalize the energy grows from an inadequate understanding of the roots of personal identity. The characterizing of the energy in order to give it an identity occurs simultaneously with the protection of one's own relative egoic state. Again, this may be a natural process, but it is nevertheless a process that deeper meditative self-awareness automatically carries us beyond. Thus channeling tends to be regarded with caution (from the mystical point of view) because the unconscious protection of one's own identity is a kind of short-circuiting or side-stepping of the process of realization and incarnation. Rather than being carried deeper into the radical discontinuity and rebirth, we have gained a source that can often carry a higher vision and wisdom but have paid the price of fundamental transformation. Since the latter is probably not understood as a possibility, it may be wise to regard the phenomenon of channeling as a natural manifestation of the awakening process that represents an intermediary state of incarnation between egoic consciousness and full realization.

To me there is a higher form of channeling that can be developed through conscious discipline. First we must understand that the higher levels of consciousness are simply not bound within the limiting structures of personal consciousness; they extend far beyond our ordinary sense of identity. Thus we can begin to explore opening to expanded energies through the voice, as a yogic technique rather than as an occult power. It is an ancient and respected technique. The Sufis practice a form of prayer that is simply the opening of one's heart in the moment and allowing the voice to speak one's love of God. Once individuals have learned to open in this way, a tremendous energy can be accessed. The early Christian church not only recognized the phenomenon of glossalalia (speaking in tongues), it was actually encouraged as a way to allow access to the higher energies. However, I would concur with Paul when he scolded that the phenomenon is not important if the energy we are channeling is not universally understandable by others. I would go a step further. Not only must it be universally understandable, but we must begin to realize that we are training a natural attribute of consciousness and not mystify this with words like "holy spirit."

For me, personalizing the energy diminishes the real mystery of what it is to be human and alive. Since I have never had to relinquish my humanness to be a vehicle for such energies, I speak for the immense importance of not subjugating one's self-consciousness to the higher energy. Self-consciousness becomes dormant at the moment of transcendent realization, but it is not closed off or denied. For me, this is the greatest problem with channeled teachings. Besides its seeming magical aspect, which leads many to ascribe to it wisdom and infallibility, it is impossible to make an accurate cross translation from the higher states of consciousness to the more mundane levels. This error in cross translation becomes even greater when one has released the ordinary human level to access these teachings. The "entity" that is speaking doesn't have to deal with the paradoxical and contradictory aspects of any higher understanding relative to other levels of one's humanness. These levels in the channel have been put on hold in a way that is quite different from what occurs with realization. Thus all channeling, while it contains what can be called wisdom, is a wisdom without a body. Certainly the person who channels is gradually affected by the energy channeled and thus gradually becomes conductive of a higher level of energy. But the teaching itself is misleading. Without a body, it is easy to preach love, nonattachment and mastery. With a body, one has to be far more honest, far more compassionate, because no teaching in its literal form can ever speak to the whole of us.

In my work I place an emphasis on each individual's learning how to express higher energies verbally. But there is no sense that such communication is wisdom per se, or that now one will have the truth of his or her deeper nature. Rather it is a process of learning how to bring the higher energies more fully into embodiment. Communication at this level is no longer a process of trying to convey identical information from one individual to another, nor of trying to access higher energies to solve problems. Rather it is a process of learning to celebrate more of what it is to be human. Such expression becomes a process of evoking meaning or actually inducting the listener to the level of consciousness from which the words are emerging. There is no guarantee, nor really any need, that the meaning be interpreted literally—that the listener understand precisely what the speaker has said. Rather, the speaker is more a catalyst, a form of Creative Involvement that presents the listener with new possibilities without defining what these possibilities have to be. In a sense, this kind of communication is spherical rather than linear. It is not involved in truth as an absolute, but is rather involved with the Principle of Relationship in which we are constantly evoking new possibility in each other. The depth of this possibility depends on the depth of our realization and the degree to which our communication carries the energy of that realization. Thus I have had the experience of speaking spontaneously out of the energy and having a physicist approach me to say how a very subtle problem on which he had been working suddenly fell into place. It is also common that people report feeling heat or being healed while listening. Obviously it was not the words I used, but the energy that was radiated. Still we must learn to use language as precisely as possible to try to express the most difficult and subtle ideas. This is not because it is absolutely important that others understand as we do. Rather, such discipline means that, when we attempt to express the higher dimensions, we are that much more adept in bringing those energies forward. In this way, the higher energies have truly incarnated into the animate world.

8 ❋ SONG OF THEODORA

Is it love that wounds,
or the wound that creates loving?
Hope and aspiration,
Yes, even for wholeness
wound me.
How can I serve? cries the soul.
Yes, and how can you not.

RICHARD MOSS

THE NEWS OF THE DEATH from breast cancer
of Theodora, a woman with whom I had shared quite deeply during a conference, provides a stark and important contrast with
Laura. Theodora also had a shift of energy, although quite different from Laura's, and in the days that followed she noticed a pro-
nounced decrease of the inflammation in her breast and a
shrinkage of the lymph nodes in her armpit. However, the nature of the energetic shift was not as spontaneous nor as deep
as Laura's.[1] Thus I was not surprised to learn that some months
later her disease had resumed and, in fact, had spread. She died
about a year after our first meeting, despite the brief remission

---

[1] Here I am utilizing purely subjective criteria based upon my memory of the energetic presence that
radiated from the two of them at the time of their openings and in the subsequent months. I acknowledge that no real comparison of significance or depth can be made in any ultimate sense. From
the perspective of the higher consciousness, both were always whole whether before or after their
changes, and in this sense the criterion of depth is meaningless.

with its auspicious indications. Theodora was a remarkable person, and learning of her passing brought a sense of tenderness and loss.

In order to appreciate Theodora's energetic opening, which I believe precipitated her transient remission, I need to go more deeply into my experience of her. Clearly this is subjective data and, as such, limited. But, as we are dealing with a dimension that cannot yet be approached by traditional scientific methodologies, it is the only place we can start. Here I am not merely speaking of superficial impressions, but rather of a deeper intuitive gestalt of how Theodora's presence affected my consciousness.

First of all, I liked Theodora immediately. She radiated intelligence and beauty. She was a rising opera singer, immensely talented and rapidly gaining recognition. She had traveled from Europe for the conference. I was flattered, and felt responsible that her experience be as rich as possible. This should have been the first warning that I was losing my impartiality. Clearly I was being seduced and, in retrospect, it is easy to see that I wanted to be. Yet at the same time I was being pushed away. Theodora had powerful self-determination. She wanted to be her own guide, which is admirable, but she gave out a mixed message. On the one hand she was saying, "Help me, I am open," while at the same time she had already determined what she wanted to have happen and what she thought she needed to learn. It had the feel of brittleness. Her self-determinism had an element of more than the usual degree of control.

Theodora invoked in me a sense of spiritual richness, as if a part of her had known, or soon would know, transcendental wholeness. Perhaps this was a result of her impending death. I could feel the lure of this higher aspect. I could sense it bleeding through in her voice when she sang. This part reached out to me and to life itself for union, for something beyond this world. Yet as one got close, there was an equivalent force that created separation and distance. It took the form of self-control, of keeping things on her terms. This was reflected even in her medical approach to her cancer. She had refused traditional treatment and tried some rather exotic approaches. Perhaps she felt that a mastectomy would ruin her singing—as it very well might have. In this sense she valued her talent and career more than her life. But it was more than that; it was as though the cancer held some deeper significance—that she needed it and wouldn't release it until something else had happened. I could sense that Theodora didn't just want healing; she wanted breakthrough. This made her even more attractive to me, and thus I was less unconditional in my relationship to her.

I tried to understand and resolve the subtle push-pull that I felt in myself when I interacted with her. I knew that I was attracted and simultaneously intimidated by her beauty and talent. I knew that I longed for her as an energetic counterpart, as I have for many others who energetically represent continuations of my own body and being. There was a recognition of depth and of possibility that drew me into personal involvement. Thus I was in direct conflict with a deeper wisdom that knew I could not serve her fully in this way. Theodora was like a magnificent meal that I couldn't quite let myself taste. Yet, I also knew that when such a state is triggered in me, it is not only my process; I am resonating in the energetic dynamic of the other. I wondered what it was about Theodora that both invited and obscured, opening with promise and closing at the same time. Somehow she could not allow the vast energetic depth that I sensed in her to merge with her personal self. Looking back, I realize that her cancer was the battlefield in which that integration was undertaken. I sense that she knew this.

And then all of a sudden she opened. As the energy of the conference built to a finer and finer note, it began to dissolve her self-control. At first she was agitated and invoked all kinds of mental questioning to tie up her energy. But finally there was nothing she could do and she lost control. The sense of separation gave way and, for a little while, I could taste the promise that had always been there. But while Theodora became more energetically available, her subjective experience was that of great terror.

Unlike Laura, who opened to a sense of Oneness, a dimension beyond the domain of personal self and identity, Theodora opened to a place partway between. She was tapping a higher dimension while simultaneously crystallized in personal identity. From the point of view of her egoic self, such a condition is akin to being involuntarily dissolved or annihilated.

I did not know until months later that she had known this space before. I learned that she had been considered schizophrenic and institutionalized several times in the period from her late teens to her early thirties. These episodes were characterized by a state of existential terror that paralyzed her. With each episode her life would become scattered. But in her mid-thirties she managed a full commitment into her singing and her career blossomed very quickly. At the same time her terror faded. It was four or five years into her new life that the breast cancer appeared.

For Theodora the return of the existential terror during the conference represented failure, a horrible step backward. She was still trapped in the memory of her earlier life and this superimposed a negative and frightful interpretation on the essentially new experience triggered by the conference energies. It was this very possibility—to go beyond the crystallization of her basic psychoenergetic structure—that had drawn her in the first place. But as the energy heightened, with the resulting loss of control and loss of familiar boundaries, Theodora once again felt overwhelmed. She lacked the faith to release deeper, to trust such a frightening experience and thereby allow a fresh relationship to it, despite her otherwise potent self-determinism. In fact, it was the strength of her ego that made the space so terrifying. She couldn't let go.

As with doctors and therapists in her past, she desperately turned to me for help. Perhaps if I had known of her previous history, I would have emphasized to her how clear and full the energy felt and encouraged her to trust the process more deeply. But I had already lost impartiality. I was personally involved; thus I felt compelled to intervene and try to help her. Ignoring an inner discomfort, which should have told me to do nothing, I joined with her energetically to intensify and refine the quality of her space and perhaps help her to break through. Simultaneously I had her breathe deeply. In a few minutes she reached a state of release. I had only done this once before and at that time, it was a completely spontaneous intervention without any urgency. It proved to be profoundly appropriate. This time, however, I was acting from that memory and from a sense of urgency.

I understand why people believe in demons. Feeling the energy pouring through her and seeing her fear, one might think that something diabolical was occurring. Yet there was something more real about her, more available, beneath the outer intensity of her panic. Energetically, she was tremendously open, probably more open and energized than when she performed. It is during this kind of opening that a new integration of energies may occur if we are well-prepared and can allow the process to unfold naturally. However, Theodora could not release the egocentric perspective. This was not a conscious choice; it is just how the process occurs at times. It is like a sugar cube in hot water. The cube symbolizes identity at the egoic level. The cube can relax into its underlying essence as sugar and soon merge with the water and fill the whole space, or it can cling to its identity as a cube and feel that it is being destroyed. Some Sufis refer to this space as "the corridor of madness." Theodora was caught here. She never entered the transcendent sense of integration exemplified by Laura. In my experience, until the center of awareness releases out of the egoic dynamic, we can go no further. There is simply too much energy emanating from the undifferentiated or uncreated Consciousness for the vessel of the basic ego. Theodora's energies were heightened and she came to the boundary of her egoic structure. But her memory of her schizophrenic episodes was too strong for her to let go. She could not trust.

With my help Theodora reached a state of peace, and to her it was wonderful, liberating and new. But I knew, even then, that this peace was not as deep as it might be. She was at peace, but rather than transcending the dynamic to a higher level, she had dissipated or discharged the energy. She was in the calm that follows an orgasm, the calm that results after an intensely cathartic process. She was in control once again, albeit in a fine resonant aliveness, but the door that had been briefly open in the midst of her panic was already closing.

Processes that involve creating tension and then almost explosive release have always been popular for altering consciousness. They include methods involving hyperventilation, long periods of sitting still, chanting, or fasting. At one point or another I have employed all of these methods in my work. But despite the fact that I employed such a method with Theodora, which she herself would have regarded as successful, I am cautious of such routes. They do contribute to greater energetic conductivity much in the same way that rigorous exercise strengthens our muscles. They are techniques for developing will and focus, for learning to let go, and for learning to sustain higher energies. Thus all these approaches involve the transformative vector of Intensity and result in heightened energy, but they tend to become valued as ends in themselves. The transient expansion of consciousness is confused with spiritual progress and this deflects from a more encompassing aliveness.

Furthermore, our state of consciousness when we intentionally enter these processes is a context that subtly defines the depth and potential realization that is possible. The very desire to alter our consciousness is a kind of self-manipulation, and as such it is also a reaction against one's present condition. Change engendered in this way rests upon a shaky foundation indeed. While a "new" space may be temporarily reached, it is already premeditated and preprogrammed for some result. Thus, it is not a process that can produce real newness or freedom, because unwittingly the ego remains in control. It is another thing altogether to discover such a method spontaneously as one creatively moves into the transformational moment. It is quite possible that doing so is the very key that allows the energy to free into a fundamentally new note. The key here is the spontaneity of the Creative Involvement. Finally, the consciousness of the guide also subtly configures the possibilities. Thus, with Theodora it was my own conscious intent to do something that conditioned her experience.

✻

Theodora called me some days after the conference to say that her physician had confirmed that her lymph nodes were no longer palpable and the breast mass had significantly shrunk and was no longer inflamed. I once again urged her to keep letting go. I suggested that it may be wiser for her to go into a period of "free float" and let new possibilities emerge rather than to return immediately to her home and career. She agreed, but did not follow through. About nine months later, when she contacted me again, she had returned home and married her lover. She had confided her uneasiness about this relationship because his career was just opening up and it was his primary concern. He had no time, or real desire, to be with her in her cancer process. So why were they marrying? We'll never know, but I suspect she was avidly pursuing the relationship for its intensity and emotional aliveness as a substitute for her deeper openness and its existential pain. Within weeks of the marriage, the cancer aggressively reactivated and spread. She was in pain, and the original tumor was larger than ever. Again she wanted help to fight her disease. But by that time the energy was no longer available. She felt too weak to enter another conference and face another opportunity for undoing. She had retreated from that possibility and was back in control, now contemplating radiation and chemotherapeutic approaches. But these came too late.

I believe helping Theodora cathart the energy of her overwhelming fear was a disservice. In retrospect, it may have been better for her to remain in it, despite her terror, and to have found her own way through. Recalling the impressive though brief restoration this short episode produced, I am inclined to feel that her cathartic release actually short-circuited a healing crisis. However, just as it is Grace to go through the mystical door, so too it may be Grace when it opens partially or remains closed. There is really no way to know what is right. Thus, while I wish that it could have been otherwise with Theodora, I do not hold her or myself responsible. Yet, I am wistful. Radical doors are precious, and when the forces for deeper change finally converge and it appears that we are unable to meet them fully, it is hard not to feel regret.

Did Theodora really only take a partial leap? Did she fail to meet her full potential? Am I using the recurrence of her cancer and her death as evidence of this? It is so easy, even tempting, to think in this way. But I tremble at the assumption here. It equates health with rightness and fulfillment, and simultaneously equates disease with failure. It also equates radical transformation and healing with achievement, which it is certainly not. It is Grace! Yet this is something we are always unwittingly doing; it is implicit in our "wars" against disease. There has to be a winner and the winner is health, but I know this perspective is too small. Health includes disease; it is not the counterpole. Once again we have paradox. In approaching the wholeness of each moment we cannot compare one person to another. I compare Theodora's experience with Laura's only to make the point that there is a profound relationship between movement through a discontinuity of consciousness, and the restoration of the bodymind. I am even suggesting that there are degrees of discontinuity and that this may influence the psychophysical responses. But making such a discrimination does not mean that we can go further to judge the intrinsic value or success of another's life.

Theodora was one of the most inspirational people I have ever met. That she did not take a step I wished she could have taken says nothing of her intrinsic worth. After all, I cannot sing like her and I cannot account for my realization. It happened. Perhaps I had been preparing for it all my life in unknown ways; perhaps this had been the case for lifetimes. But so what. The significance of anyone's life cannot be measured in a relative sense. It must be appreciated in its own intrinsic wholeness. If we say she failed because she might have gone further (i.e. recovered), then we measure her life from a very narrow corner. In this sense, as ordinary consciousness tries to comprehend what is suggested by higher consciousness, it will do as much harm as good. The "good" lies in the act of pointing ahead to a way that is not the linear extension of where we are now. The "harm" resides in the fact that, in pointing to this way, we seem to be comparing and often devaluing where we are or have been. To observe life is one thing. To draw conclusions, the treacherous "therefore," is something else. That realization is often accompanied by healing is a reasonable statement. But to say that "therefore" we should work for realization in order to be healed is not reasonable. In fact it narrows our relationship to life, thereby undermining our capacity to live fully and to reach realization.

Pushing away one aspect of existence to reach another state of consciousness is not the kind of balance that allows one to make the transition to a higher understanding. In fact, I believe that when we try to approach the higher potential by devaluing where we are, we encounter resistance, anguish and pain.

The way of radical aliveness is paradoxical. Perhaps the greatest of the paradoxes is that, to go to a place where we are whole, we must take the route of wholeness. This is why deeper healing of the self or humanity cannot begin with the problem or the disease. It must begin with the fundamental realization that we are all ever and already whole.

✱

There are ways I might have helped Theodora out of my experience. Becoming emotionally involved was the last thing she needed. This shackled my capacity to act as a transformational door. In retrospect, I understand my deep love for her more clearly. I see that, while this love had its roots in a completely impersonal space, it became confused with a more personal involvement. This is an easy confusion and many of us make it. We are called to each other by a deep inner song of recognition. We sense the radiance of each other's aliveness, the door of the soul that has been opened into the timeless dimension, perhaps through the force of our living or the depth of our pain. We respond to this differently. We call it beauty or Grace; it produces empathy, which can become the desire to help or to comfort. We may not even have a good word for what they have kindled. We're attracted and, not understanding the source of this song, we try to respond to it personally.

Being a teacher is at times a very lonely work. Even with the friends who surround me, I am always struggling at the edge where personal involvement does not betray a deeper possibility. Again and again I try to wed these two, for it is my deepest yearning that they be wed. Yet at any point the relationship can become too attached and intertwined, and the objectivity and detachment necessary to allow a more co-creative level of embrace may be lost.

I met Theodora early in my work. I did not know then as fully as today that the deepest power does not come through my doing, but through my being. I knew that Theodora needed love. I knew that love without the passage to higher aliveness is too fragmenting. But the love she needed could not be given her by me; it had to arise spontaneously out of her. If there had been time to develop that relationship between us, perhaps the Grace of this would have been sufficient to carry her through the terror. In many of my relationships there is a deep mystical connection of love and trust that can be recognized intuitively and immediately, or it begins to arise in people after we have spent some time together. I do not do anything actively to invoke this— rather it is the spontaneous quality of their recognition and love that seems to empower their capacity to go more deeply into themselves. The realization of my Being somehow provides the possibility for this kind of relationship, but it is nothing that I consciously create.

I wonder if Theodora might have been able to find this space in relationship with me or someone else. But she had always been powerfully self-determining; she had never let herself be really vulnerable in an intimate way. Oh, I believe she knew love; it was the force that dedicated her to creativity and beauty. But this was too impersonal to ground the more mystical love that requires relationship in the devotional sense. I suppose that her devotion to her fiance, despite his seeming selfishness, was an attempt by her to honor the need to learn of this love—to give it space to bloom within her. But Theodora didn't have time. Her cancer was like a time bomb ticking away and she was pushing for a breakthrough (we both were) before all the pieces were in place.

I realized later, when her disease had resumed and I looked more closely at my actions towards her, that I had wanted to give her that kind of relationship. But I was confused. I wanted to be her friend, yet I was unwilling to acknowledge the personal love I was feeling for her. Instead I tried to express it in my work as an energetic catalyst. But I might have recalled my biochemistry; a catalyst is never consumed in the reaction. An effective catalyst is simply present, and a higher integrity mixes the ingredients and guides the outcome.

9 ✳ THOUGHTS ON CANCER AND SCHIZOPHRENIA

AT FIRST GLANCE, it seems so unfair that Theodora should finally outgrow her paralyzing anxiety, tap her immense creative potential, and reach a fulfilling and exciting life only to develop cancer. While there is some evidence that suggests that cancer tends to appear from one to five years after a major loss, here we have the seemingly opposite dynamic. Certainly, by conventional considerations, Theodora was moving toward greater aliveness and health. Was her cancer just another one of life's trials, or is there a relationship between the resolution of her "schizophrenia" and the development of cancer? If, as I have stated, greater aliveness is the direction of transformational unfolding, then why the cancer? Why did she enter into temporary remission and then resume her disease process? What was it in the nature of her terror and the near breakthrough that held such healing power for her?

First of all, I use the expression "greater aliveness" to mean a multidimensional expansion of consciousness, not necessarily the apparent aliveness of a professional singing career or the outer activity so often associated with the notion of aliveness. Aliveness is above all an attribute of awareness, a phenomenon of energy and boundary, of individuality and self-transcendence. I believe that the episode of intense fear reflected Theodora's opening boundaries. She was at the threshold of awakening where the individual ego merges into a larger dimension and personal identity is subsumed in its numinous source. Perhaps it was similar in kind to the dissolution of boundary that occurred again and again throughout her life—her so-called schizophrenia, which was both a nightmare and at the same time the deepest calling of her soul.

There is a Zen saying: "First there is a tree and the mountain, then there is no tree and no mountain, and finally there is the tree and the mountain once again." During my opening process, this saying came strongly to mind. While there are many levels of interpretation, it seemed succinctly to summarize the process I was going through. It gave my intellect a mystical ground of reference that proved to be a vital strength. I had been (we all are) living at a level of consciousness in which the objects of consciousness, the tree and the mountain, were unquestioned. Then, all at once, there was no "I" separate from these objects. While they continued to exist—I could see mountains and trees—they were also at once identical to myself. They no longer existed as things-in-themselves. Afterwards, subject/object consciousness resumed its dominance and the mountain and the tree were things once again. However, I had been changed and I knew the illusion of the separation implicit in ordinary consciousness. The realization gave me inspiration and the capacity to live anew. But it was also one of the most overwhelming and difficult experiences I can imagine any human being facing.

I believe this kind of experience happens all the time in varying degrees. When it does occur with great depth, it produces a profound existential shock few can integrate without help. Obviously traditional medical approaches and psychiatric assistance represent one attempt at such integration. Religion in its deepest, most esoteric, sense represents another approach to the same dimension.

I, for one, can testify to the profound assistance religious art and scripture provided as all of a sudden I plunged into the process of realization. I recall lying down and listening to *The Messiah* the evening after my opening. My friend had made a brilliant intuitive choice in playing it. All at once I heard my own experience being clearly described, albeit in highly symbolic language. But the meaning was apparent. Phrases like "all warfare is accomplished, all inequity pardoned" spoke of the inner peace that had befallen me for awhile some months before the opening, when everything was all right as it was and life seemed effortless. "The valley shall be exalted, the mountains and hills made low, the rough edges plain, the crooked straight. Make straight in the desert a highway for our God. . . ." spoke to me of the stepping back from identification with the emotional highs and lows of life. It conveyed the sense of my own experience, of giving my attention to the space of consciousness and not the content. It spoke of what could be a momentary doorway allowing the opening of realization, or an ongoing discipline and way of life.

Finally, statements like "Who shall stand when He appeareth, for He is like a refiner's fire . . ." and "In this flesh we shall see God . . ." conveyed the way in which "I" had simply been overwhelmed by the energy so that no level of personal identity could stand as a place of safety. Every aspect of self-identity, self-control and self-love was mercilessly held up before the light of an absolutely neutral and detached aliveness. To the degree I was attached or strongly identified in any relative structure of consciousness, it was like burning in a fire of refinement until there was only surrender. I could feel the whole body awakened in this force. Every cell was alive and the physical self was illuminated in a current at times too powerful and at other times unspeakably gentle and uplifting. Lying on the floor with a piece of music I had heard many times before but never understood, all at once there was a context for what was happening to me, and the very energy of the music carried me back into the state of union, peace and glory.

Many people do not appreciate the immense integrative legacy of religious art, thought and ritual as signposts for the integration and maturation of the awakening process. For people who do not find succor in mystical-religious understanding, an opening of this kind is very difficult. For some, the assistance provided by drugs and hospitalization is a life-saving benefit. Not every breakdown is a breakthrough.

Theodora's psychiatric care had obviously helped her to make significant integration from the functional and behavioral point of view. Witness her career. However, I question whether this level of integration represents a sufficient understanding of the human potential and the forces that drive us in life. I suggest that it was the transformational impulse that had been chasing Theodora throughout most of her life. She was, I believe, periodically approaching the middle or "no-mountain" space in the radical awakening process where the egoic self resolves back into undifferentiated consciousness. And, given her youth, with no model of wisdom to call upon, it was undoubtedly a terrible struggle. For me, the profound aesthetic depth of her being was closer to the mystical than to the artistic, although these qualities are very similar. Grounding her in the artistic was sufficient to marshal a functional and, in many respects, inspirational life, but her artistic expression was not enough for the full depth of her aliveness. I question whether any kind of functional identity achieved at the expense of the mystical impulse ever really represents integration. Only movement to a whole new note of consciousness, followed naturally by new life expression, represents integration. As we have seen, this is one of the most mysterious and difficult processes to understand or approach. It was the threshold of the new energy that Theodora once again began to enter during the conference. Even briefly approximating this space resulted in an immediate freeing of her deeper aliveness and, as we have seen, a partial healing of her cancer process.

CANCER AND SCHIZOPHRENIA: HIGH-ENERGY PROCESSES

The shift to a higher energy level always means a transient loss of boundary. During such a shift, the whole psychophysical nature reorganizes, reconstituting itself in varying degrees of harmony with an archetypal principle of wholeness. I suggest that such reconstitution *can* mitigate or cure any disease but, unequivocally, I am *not* suggesting a new treatment modality. Rather, I am pointing to a phenomenon that is going on continuously. We are constantly breathing between the basic structure of subject/object consciousness (the egoic body) and higher dimensions (the divine body). The way of life of any individual will be more or less transparent, more or less accessing this deeper aliveness. To be relatively dense or crystallized means to express aliveness in ways that are less immediately referent to a deeper wholeness. I suggest that this is one basis for cancer. Similarly, to be very transparent to larger dimensions but unable adequately to condense a sense of personal identity also presents difficulties. This may be a basis for schizophrenia.

I became interested in the relationship of cancer and schizophrenia after my own awakening. I recalled the interesting statistics that schizophrenics had only one-fourth to one-fifth the incidence of cancer of the general population. I began to wonder if the relative immunity to cancer demonstrated by schizophrenics had to do with their differing energetic openness. In the course of my work, I was slowly acquiring more and more direct experience with both categories of illness. In the first years after my opening a large number of the private "patients" I saw for counseling had cancer. I worked with them in a deep meditative and intuitive dialogue and with direct energy-sharing. At the same time, I became the "spiritual" consultant to St. George Homes, an organization that works with schizophrenic and autistic youths. While most of my interaction was with the staff, I had some contact with the young people. I was astonished at their energetic openness. I watched them align their bodies as if to use a part of their energy field as a shield when I would come close to them. It became clear that, while they were highly disorganized in their personal functioning, these children had exceptional sensitivity. Also it was clear to me that they lived at a higher level of energy than the "normal" individuals who were working to help them function. I realized that the higher energy always inducts the lower. Thus, if the staff were to have a greater effect on the children, they had to come to a higher energy level. We approached this problem by using the group energy of the staff in once-a-week sessions designed to generate higher awareness and by going on occasional weekend retreats. After the retreats the staff remained more centered around the children, and the children were more cooperative and self-controlled in the presence of a staff member who was operating at a higher level of energy. In contrast to these schizophrenic children, the people I saw with cancer had far less sensitivity. They were grounded in the world, highly functional, but all the higher energy seemed to reside in the cancer rather than in them.

What we call *cancer* is a tremendously diverse phenomenon. In fact there really is no simple definition for the disease because it does not follow any particular pattern except that of metastasis. It is *metastasis*, the capacity of the tumor to spread in varying ways to other parts of the body, that is the only agreed-upon phenomenon that defines the multiform entity, cancer. But even metastasis is a mystery. It is clear that sometimes cancer spreads by local extension or through the blood or lymph. But there is a whole aspect of spread that is unexplainable this way. This is implied in the very word itself. *Meta* means to move beyond, or to come following or in succession. This has a transcendent and transformative implication. The word *stasis* means stable state. Thus *metastasis* means to move beyond or transcend a stable state. And this is what sometimes happens. The disease appears in other parts of the body where there is no known form of connection. This reminds me of the way ideas crop up in different parts of the world at the same time without any outer connection.

Clearly, cancer is a transforming force manifesting at the physical level. There is a discontinuity of the normal dynamic into a new energetic process. In *The I That Is We*, I state that cancer is a high-energy disease. The cancer cells themselves display unusual powers. Besides the rapidity with which they multiply, they have the capacity to communicate with normal cells and have them do their bidding. Cancer cells call immune cells to them, so that the ensuing inflammatory reaction will insulate the tumor. They have the capacity to cause additional blood vessels to grow to the tumor to provide nourishment. The list of their capacities is truly astonishing. In certain cancers genes alter to trigger abnormal cell growth. These "genes," called *oncogenes* when they trigger cancer, normally function specifically to limit growth. With cancer, it is as though a signal has been given to transcend the age-old limitations on growth. Such limiting is so basic to life that the same genes found in men are also found in fruit flies. There is an intrinsic stultification of individual potential inherent in the process of specialization. This is as true of cells in the body as it is of people in society as a whole. When the amoeba (or off-shoots from it) evolved into a multicellular life form, it did so at the expense of a great deal of its freedom and potential. Likewise, a person who specializes in a particular job contributes to the higher possibility of the corporation, but has sacrificed a great deal of his freedom and capacity to express the fullest range of his energy. To specialize can, in a sense, mean to contract to a lower energy state. But this need not be true if we each partici-pate in the possibility of a higher energy that blooms through our collective (multicellular) endeavor. However, I suggest that nei-ther the average person nor the society in general is consciously aware of the potential to incarnate the highest possible energy. Like Laura, we grow up and literally crystallize in identity.

Now a cancer cell is highly metabolic and rapidly dividing, and therefore it remains immature and poorly differentiated. If we con-sider that higher energies (the transformational impulse) are seeking to be expressed into incarnate aliveness, then perhaps this im-mature cell is more capable of responding to the awakening energy than a mature cell which has lost most of this freedom. The range of energies to which a mature cell can respond is strictly limited or it could not play its special role in the functioning of the whole.

Perhaps the cancer cell does not differentiate because to do so would mean to become stultified within a lower energy system. In other words, the higher energy only has freedom to express at the primitive cellular level because aliveness is so bounded in the body as a whole. We can imagine this as a dimensional bar-rier between the cancer process and the so-called normal body. The cancer won't differentiate because to do so would mean to step down in energy. This is not possible. It would be like trying to have heat flow backwards from a cold object to a warmer one. Thus what is needed is for the whole body to move to a higher energy. When this occurs, the high energy body quickly absorbs and expels the aberrant tissue, and the impulse for further aber-rant growth has ceased because maturing is no longer stultification.

We can further measure the energy of the cancer process by looking at the amount of energy it takes to challenge it from our conventional perspective. Because we refuse to see that cancer is our own aliveness seeking to find expression, we keep attacking it as though it were something else. Consider the billions of dollars spent, the high-energy physics, the biogenetics, the complex chemistry that has been brought to bear on this "disease" with only minor progress. This is evidence of the tremendous energy necessary to influence the cancer process only slightly. And if we continue in this approach, our influence will remain minimal. We are using more and more energy from the outer collective consciousness (consider how many people it takes to develop biogenetics, or high-energy electron beams to shoot at cancer) to fight a disease which I believe is the inner expression of our growing collective aliveness. We are fighting ourselves.

Schizophrenia is also a transforming process, but one occurring at the level of the mind. The boundaries of the mind are being stretched. While in cancer the physical transformation is not referent to the larger wholeness of the total organism, in schizophrenia the mental transformation is not referent to a fixed sense of identity. The cancer process is transformation confined within the egoic body without the divine body to give the energy space and a context of wholeness. Schizophrenia, on the other hand, is transformation in the divine body without the egoic body to give it boundary and form.

Schizophrenia is also a high-energy disease, and we have had equally little success treating it. To the degree that we can suppress the disease with drugs so that the individual can function minimally, we have nominal success. But to treat a schizophrenic without any medications or with the absolute minimum, as they do at St. George Homes, requires an enormous amount of energy, organization, foresight and planning. One literally has to create a structure that can contain the patients and creatively direct them. At the end of the day, most of the schizophrenics have been barely influenced while the staff is exhausted, scattered and struggling with their own sanity.

If cancer is merely a molecular process sometimes carried genetically or triggered by a sequence of chemical, viral or other stimuli, then why do schizophrenics have one-fifth the incidence of cancer? Schizophrenics are exposed to the same toxins, pollutants, and radiations that we believe trigger the cancer process. Do we presume that Nature built in a special kind of immunity to these very new dangers when implanting the aberration that triggers schizophrenia? When we speak of a carcinogen, we must also speak of an individual's level of conscious integration. Here we come to the old argument of disease potency versus host resistance, but with a whole new sense of what host resistance means. It is interesting to note that paranoid schizophrenics have a somewhat higher incidence of cancer than other forms of schizophrenia. Is it possible that paranoids, who also have a more intact ego boundary (egoic body), are approximating the general energetic boundedness of individuals with cancer?

CIGARETTE SMOKING AND ENERGETIC OPENNESS

Of course there will always be physical expression of any illness, but that does not necessarily mean that the cause resides in the physical realm. Consciousness is not just energy, or some subtle ether; it is all levels of Existence simultaneously. Physical reality is one level of expression, mental reality another. The level from which we recognize an underlying cause depends primarily upon our level of realization. For example, cigarette smoking is definitely proved to be related to cancer. At the physical level, this is thought to be the result of the tars, heat and other products of tobacco combustion. From this point of view, the best "cure" for lung cancer, emphysema, or oral cancer would be to stop smoking. Obvious and logical.

However, I have observed another dimension of cigarette smoking. In my work we are exploring higher states of consciousness and moving into greater energetic openness. In a heightened state I can stand next to a person and feel the degree of energetic relationship that occurs. This relationship deepens as each person moves into greater conductivity and openness. Invariably, when smokers step outside for a cigarette, they return somewhat closed down once again. It is my observation that tobacco smoking tends to create a greater energetic density, that it helps one to sustain a sense of boundedness or separation. But to do so is to decrease participation with those levels of energy that are a direct reflection of our communion with others and our own larger wholeness. In this sense, we are cutting ourselves off from deeper aliveness or perhaps letting that aliveness express without direct connection with the larger wholeness that is the integrative context for healthful growth. The very root of the word *health* is "whole." I suspect that people who smoke are already fairly sensitive and employ the cigarettes to ground themselves, especially when they are in a space of diffuse social energies. It is this habituated dynamic of being in a heightened state, but continuously closing down or containing the energy, that represents another level of the "cause" of cancer. But from this point of view, the solution is not so much to intimidate people to stop smoking by promoting fear campaigns. Rather, we face an inspirational choice, to stop for love.

To smoke is to deprive ourselves of our inheritance of higher consciousness. In doing so, one is slowing the potential for communion in which all human beings are uplifted. Many people stop smoking during the conferences because the group energy becomes so coherent they no longer unconsciously need to defend themselves from it. Once people realize that they never need to defend themselves, at least not habitually, from the larger collective consciousness, they can allow some of the discomfort that smoking protected them from. They realize that, through their availability, they are contributing to the refinement and uplifting of all people. Smoking stops voluntarily from a sense of inspired purpose rather than fear. If necessary, smoking can be used consciously, though infrequently, when one wants boundary. But it is no longer a basis for an habituated ritual of separation. It is the irony of cigarette smoking that it is seen as both a sign of individuality and of social relatedness. Yet, it actually diminishes the possibility of knowing the sacred meal of real human communion.

THE ASYMMETRY OF SCHIZOPHRENIA

Tremendous energetic availability with little or no psychic defense often occurs in schizophrenics. The difference between the schizophrenic and the mystic is that, while both are multidimensionally open, the mystic has already established the sense of personal "I." This allows the mystic to maintain a relatively stable personal reference point as he or she expands into larger realms. The egoic structure is sublimed, giving birth to mystical aliveness. Without a strong and integrated sense of "I," the larger continuum overwhelms and fragments the weak egoic consciousness. Schizophrenics lack this integrated "I" sense and are defined in accordance with the ever-changing psychic milieu. They are like spheres without fixed centers. They approach the mystical state where no emotional or intellectual process is truly real with regard to the Self. But fluctuations of the perimeter (the psychic milieu) are not symmetrically conveyed to the rest of the sphere by the continuity of a central point of reference (a strong self-consciousness). Instead, the center is constantly moving and the energetic structure—the basis of identity—is constantly forming in highly asymmetrical patterns.

I actually felt this asymmetry the first time I scanned the energy field of a schizophrenic youth at St. George Homes. The field was extremely responsive, but it seemed to have pieces missing. Instead of expanding more or less symmetrically around the head, as I had previously observed with many other people, it was highly irregular. In contrast, mystical consciousness expands far more symmetrically, maintaining a relationship to both the center and the perimeter. The average individual is more like the mystic, responding fairly symmetrically, but only available in a limited way. The grounding in basic consciousness is so strong that he or she remains relatively impervious to energetic influences.

❋

On the several occasions where schizophrenic individuals were guests at conferences, I would ask them how they felt as they sat with the group. By that time, the group would have been together for eight or more days and have already moved into an expanded and highly coherent energy field. Invariably the schizophrenic guests would describe feeling as though they were in a warm bath, that the room was fluid or molten and filled with energy. They all liked it. (Now this kind of sensitivity is natural to me since the opening, but for the average individual it usually takes the majority of a conference or several conferences before they have reached a state where they can directly sense the energetic presence of the environment acting upon them.) Because the group energy is so coherent, the energy field itself provides a sense of continuity and boundary for the schizophrenic. One likened it to being it in a womb. I believe it is a womb in which schizophrenics could be helped to individuate. In such an environment they would be able to sustain a consistent sense of personal self, perhaps long enough to develop a stable point of self-consciousness. At the same time, the very consciousness of those creating this environment would already exist at a level that naturally honored the innate sensitivity of the schizophrenic.

However, to maintain such a coherent psychic milieu is extremely difficult in our culture. In smaller societies the collective energy is more integrated and self-contained. In these societies it is not uncommon to integrate schizophrenic individuals into the culture, often as spiritual teachers or artists. By contrast our larger society, in its multiplicity, is highly diffuse and disjointed, and thus represents a continuous stimulation of new and poorly integrated states of being. To compensate for this, the schizophrenic tends to require intensity, usually in the form of physical and emotional pain, to create identity. In general, he or she invites resistance and forces the environment to set limits, often in the form of suppression and confinement. Massaging a schizophrenic, one can't help noticing the heavy muscular armoring. The muscles are tensed continuously. In this way, the relatively unbounded schizophrenic receives feedback from the body that helps to provide a reference point for a sense of "I am."

Because their psychic boundaries are so transparent, some schizophrenics are capable of tremendous intuition and empathy. Yet without the centering "I," they cannot accurately distinguish themselves from their intuitions or use them in a balanced way. The same transparency conveys an immense creative potential, carrying with it at times a sense of the numinous. The children of schizophrenics seem to be beneficially affected by their encounter with their less-bounded parents and tend to be unusually gifted. The relationship between genius, creativity, mystical experience, and schizophrenia has been noted for a long time; it is the positive side of their energetic openness. The negative side is, of course, their fragmented and often tormented personal identity. I believe this openness gives them a relative immunity to cancer. They are in a relatively unobstructed connection to Wholeness and what they lose in fragmented identity, they gain in the regenerative harmony of such contact.

In contrast, the people with cancer with whom I have explored can be characterized as being far more bounded and stable. As a rule, the kind of sensitivity to subtle dimensions that characterizes the schizophrenic is not present. In these individuals the sense of "I am" is well-developed. They are oriented to the content and structures of their lives—to ideas, family, career, and so on. Most do not unconsciously utilize their bodies as the locus of their identity in the way the schizophrenic does with muscular tension and self-inflicted injury. Often they have no real awareness of their bodies other than as instruments for their particular interests until the time of their illness. In fact, people with cancer generally have been remarkably free of other kinds of illness. If the schizophrenic has difficulty discriminating internal from external reality, the individual with cancer has no such difficulty. These dimensions are seen as quite separate, and there is a strong tendency to hold energy inside and not let it express outwardly. Thus they rarely become nonfunctional due to psychic overwhelm in the same way a schizophrenic does. To me, this represents a degree of imperviousness to the deeper energies of consciousness that tend to dissolve our boundaries and thus destabilize our identity. The unavailability of the energetic field helps to maintain a stable identity or "I" sense that is not easily perturbed.

✻

On two occasions an individual with cancer and a schizophrenic were simultaneously guests at a conference. Both individuals were interviewed in front of the group and afterwards the energy-sharing ritual took place. The verbal interview provided one way of experiencing the guest and the energy sharing another. These were the only times that such a sharing occurred back to back, and the contrast was quite dramatic. In both instances, the sense of vastness and group communion was tremendously enhanced in the presence of the schizophrenic. They seemed unable to erect even the slightest boundary to resist the energy sharing, and in fact their openness actually inducted the group into greater spaciousness. This was true during the interview, even though the content was far from linear and certainly not of the sort to create a sense of personal identification. Nevertheless, while in the expanded state generated in the conference, the participants found the schizophrenic inexplicably inspiring. They spoke of feeling a deepening sense of love during the interview and a sense of effortless and immense expansion during the energy sharing. When I asked what people meant when they used the word *love*, they described it as feeling less separate, more At-One, more in communion.

With the cancer guests, the verbal sharing was also very rich, but in a different way. The conference participants invariably become quite identified with the guests with cancer. They moved into discussing their personal histories, the things they had learned from their own suffering. They felt inspired by what they perceived as the courage of these guests. If the schizophrenic reflected the spaciousness of their being, the cancer guest became a mirror for their psychological issues. The schizophrenics seemed to open the door into the timeless immediacy of the moment, while the cancer guests generated a space of deep self-reflection in which the participants looked at their lives through their memories and turned toward the future with new determination. In the formal energy sharing, the energy field seemed thicker. With the schizophrenics, the field is already open and one simply joins it and expands. But, with the cancer guests, there was more a sense of having to work to enter the space of communion and the field would get intensely hot, as if the energy were meeting resistance or contained in a smaller space. The participants described a sense of love and beauty in these sharings too, but it was far more emotional or sentimental in character. I noticed that the participants, while definitely in an expanded state after the group energy sharing, nevertheless tended to be more withdrawn and personally self-involved after being with the cancer guests.

CANCER, SCHIZOPHRENIA AND
COLLECTIVE TRANSFORMATION

Some years ago, I reported these observations at a conference on transpersonal psychology. A psychiatrist approached me to say that I had helped to elucidate a painful problem that he had been pondering. He told me about one of his schizophrenic clients. They had been in therapy together for quite a while and he stated that he had "cured her." However, not long after the cure, she developed cancer. What troubled him the most was that while his client was schizophrenic, they had a beautiful, loving relationship. After the cancer appeared, the woman seemed to withdraw from him, even to hate him. Here, in this poignant image of oscillation between schizophrenia and cancer, between unboundedness and boundedness, between love and hate, there is a vital message for modern man.

The afflicted unboundedness of the schizophrenic is not simply a disease, it is the transformational impulse taking a particular presentation in the psychic milieu of our time. It is, I suggest, one of nature's ways of injecting new possibilities, greater space, and greater room for love into the collective human experience. In this sense, we are speaking of love as that force that already unites all that seems disparate or even in conflict. It breaks down relative distinctions that become the basis for separation and restores a sense of wholeness and continuity. It is a principle of life, not the sentiment we know from a very bounded and personal human level. To know love, to be a presence in which deeper love thrives, is to stand as a door between the personal self and the vast uncreated consciousness. It is precisely this potential that schizophrenia represents. It is the very sensitivity that places our world not merely outside us to be used and modified, but inside as well, to be hallowed.

In contrast, cancer refers to the stabilizing forces that prevent change from happening too quickly. The transformational impulse is not only realization of oneness. It is also the return from that state into a new level of incarnation. It is the egoic boundedness that allows the statement of "me" upon which that incarnation builds. Thus, identity is also sacred. There is a wisdom in every form of life. When change occurs too quickly, it too, just as surely as rigidity and crystallization, is a disease. Built into the deepest roots of life are those forces that slow the process of change, that demand that all change, if it is to be wholesome, must be referent to the greater whole. If there is to be transformation of one cell, it must be connected in some way—energetically—to every other cell. This is the radiance of life, not merely shining out, but shining within and uniting every part to every other part. But the price we pay for this stability, so that we aren't deformed by every transient force that alters our milieu, takes the form of over-exaggerated individuality and separation. It disconnects us from a deeper sensitivity, and we begin to regard change as something we can do in our own time frame. Thus we attack our world, conquer it, dam the rivers, utilize every energy source, and fill the environment with triggers for a level of change we are not ready to pass through, as it is not referent to the whole. The price of the forces that stabilize identity is an intrinsic insensitivity. The individual is locked inside himself and the world is outside. Only at the moment of discontinuity of realization is it possible for the energy to realign so that all the forces, inner and outer, become referent to a larger continuity.

How we regard cancer and schizophrenia says much about our society and its values. Schizophrenia breathes a special gift of non-rationality. In simpler societies, it brought people closer to a fundamental spirituality. It brought mystery into the ordinary, connecting the status quo to an underlying numinosity. But in our world, the emphasis is on the rational and on individuality measured in personal achievement, rather than on effective relatedness. Thus the sensitivity of the schizophrenic is a pathological and misery-ridden dynamic. Conversely, cancer points toward the rapidity of change in our society and the natural resistance to it. It shows the creative force unfolding, but disconnected from the larger spiritual wholeness that unites humanity to itself and the surrounding world. Cancer reflects the gravitational force of identity and structure without the Grace of transcendent vision. Schizophrenia reflects the Grace of transcendent vision without the gravity of identity and form. Both reflect the higher energies moving through our world and the basic imbalance of our time. Cancer asks for greater conductivity, for softening the identity-creating boundaries so that each individual can function with a more direct sense of relationship to the whole. Schizophrenia asks for decreased conductivity. It calls for identity that we build from contact with and reverence for the transcendent. The schizophrenic approaches the transformational door but cannot pass through because he or she lacks the capacity to define a relevant identity in our current collective milieu. The person with cancer is also approaching the door, but the energy is imprisoned within the body. He or she cannot pass through to new aliveness because the energetic structure is held too densely. To the person with cancer, madness may seem even more like the death space than all the rigors of medical treatment—whereas structure and rigidity are the death space for the schizophrenic dynamic. Unless both are seen in the light of the transformation of consciousness, we will continue to regard them as pathologies separate from the larger collective pattern and miss their real significance as mirrors of ourselves.

There is a suggestion in all this about the way we approach these two dynamics in medicine. Invariably, because cancer is approached mechanically and the accompanying problems require more and more technology, these patients are often isolated or surrounded by others with similar problems. For different reasons, the schizophrenics are also isolated. But the natural induction of each might be beneficial to the other. I am suggesting that the treatment of cancer represents a movement by the individual and society as a whole toward the unboundedness and conductivity demonstrated by schizophrenia. Similarly the treatment of schizophrenia can be likened to a movement toward the boundedness of cancer. But these processes are not conscious. They are prior to conscious dynamics and are not adequately reached through conscious efforts. A more direct approach might be to allow these individuals to interact as much as possible. Rather than keep these people on different wards or in entirely different facilities, bring them together. Perhaps this is unrealistic when the schizophrenic is acutely disturbed or the cancer patient is very ill and weak. But in other circumstances, I suggest that the two are a natural medicine for each other.

ANOTHER LOOK AT THEODORA

We can now return with greater insight to Theodora. It is possible that when Theodora's functional identity became strong enough, her ego-boundary became sufficiently impervious to the radiant, ego-dissolving forces of the larger consciousness. As her career brought her into the world, she withdrew further from the deeper Self. Her existential fear receded, but this may have been a swing from a state of too much openness to a state of less openness. Still, the deeper energies continued to demand expression, and the cancer may have been the result. Her whole life had existed at that razor's edge between too much openness and too much density. In a sense, her singing career became a nearly perfect resolution because it provided discipline and purpose (which help create the ego boundary) while allowing her to enter an expansive space of pseudo-oneness that she could tap while performing. Her career had opened so quickly because she not only had a fine voice, she also generated a presence that tended to capture and unify an audience. I'm sure the collective energy of the audience provided such an empowerment that at these times she could really expand safely; the performance itself provided the structure that grounded the higher energy. (The heightened energy of performing can actually addict artists to their work. They only feel alive and real when performing before a large audience and when they are focusing the energy to a higher potential. If the energy of performance never resolves in a general expansion of consciousness toward genuine humility and the capacity to be in ordinary relationships, it can burn the performer out. Then drugs and alcohol begin to enter the picture for stimulation to maintain the edge or to shut down the sensitivity.)

THE MYSTERY OF AWAKENING

The question arises as to what specifically initiates the awakening process toward the moment of discontinuity. To this, I must answer with speculation. First of all the awakening process is not unique to one person; it is happening all the time in all of us. Yet, in a given lifetime and across a given population, relatively few actually move into the deeper mystical opening. There is a line in *The Gospel According to Thomas* that says, "I shall choose you, one out of a thousand, and two out of ten thousand, and they shall stand as a single one." This speaks to the infrequency and the universality of the process. Realization itself, and the realized consciousness, are very similiar from individual to individual. In my experience the level of energy of the individual positively correlates to the likelihood and depth of opening. Generally, this means a life of intensity, creativity and service, with the ability to stand in one's own light and simultaneously enter into deep rapport with others. The conference process taps group energy and clearly accelerates the awakening potential for each person. This phenomenon of collective energy heightening the transformative potential for each individual shows us that the overall rate of awakening is definitely connected to the collective consciousness. The energy of society is heightening as we grow larger and more interconnected. Simultaneously, more and more people are being carried toward the moment of jumping to a new energy level. The increased size and interconnectedness of society is largely the result of the scientific revolution. One can image the whole scientific process as a huge hand bestowing Grace upon humanity, raising the overall energy and consciousness. However, like all Grace, the energy is neutral and can be expressed equally in creative or destructive manifestation. One of the consequences of this generally heightening energy may be that individuals who are poorly grounded in the egoic self may be pushed toward schizophrenia. In contrast, those who are strongly bounded within egoic consciousness force the energy to express as cancer.

But this still does not explain why only some are "chosen" to the deeper awakening. I suspect that it has something to do with our innate sensitivity. I also observe that suffering—in the existential sense, not mere self-inflicted pain—seems to correlate with awakening. It is not only that suffering may drive us to search more deeply, but also that our suffering reflects the underlying depth of sensitivity. Such suffering implies that we are fairly open and conductive; we resonate in energies beyond the egoic structure. However, one must also be fairly well grounded in the structure in order to have a personal relationship to the suffering. In any case, I don't believe that the kindling of the transformational impulse is completely random or uninvited. As we look toward these areas of human experience, it becomes hard not to conceive of a soul, some deeper aspect that has its own timetable of unfoldment and its own deeper longing. Perhaps that timetable is being accelerated as technology turns our world more and more into a global society. I also suspect that the timing for opening can be dangerously accelerated by misguided spiritual efforts, severe life trauma, or the use of drugs. But even if we attribute greater wisdom and benevolence to the soul, so that these provocations are never considered wrong, when the opening befalls us, there is, at least, a temporary devastation.

10 ∗ PERTURBATION VERSUS TRANSFORMATION

IN THE EXAMPLES OF LAURA AND THEODORA we have two different degrees of apparent physical transformation. Why? Why did Theodora's cancer resume after the brief remission and then seem to be even more virulent? Why do people have unusual success the first time they try something and much less later? What is beginners' luck? Why are medical treatments often initially effective and later less so? While I do not think these questions can be completely answered, a partial explanation can be offered by examining the difference between fundamental transformation and what I call *energetic perturbation*.

Fundamental transformation is a radical shift in the energetic structure; it is the new note that eventuates when the old system makes a quantum leap to a higher energy level. As we have seen, such an event can be followed by major changes in the bodymind: healing that is both physical and psychological, a whole new order of dawning creativity, and the awakening of mystical consciousness. Transformation produces a new energetic system of broader sensitivity that in turn radiates greater love. In this sense it can be said that the new system reflects a larger wholeness. Yet, while it is more sensitive, it is also far more stable. And this is significant because the transforming individual is capable of facing very challenging situations while at the same time being exquisitely open and compassionate. Most significantly, it is not superficial change that is simply added to the previous life dynamic to result in some modification of perspective or values. It is a change that initiates a whole new life dynamic.

In contrast, the concept of perturbation describes a different category of change. Perturbation is a temporary change in consciousness, so that for a while the bodymind demonstrates different capabilities. When our energy system is perturbed, we may briefly experience all the phenomena that occur with fundamental transformation. There may be rapid healing, new insight and understanding, and even a deepening of mystical values. When we are raised to a higher energy through an outside agency, such as a transformational conference, an inspirational book or person, or an intense life crisis, the basic egoic consciousness is temporarily perturbed, thrown out of equilibrium. While in this "altered" state, the individual handles energy in a different way and thus may not empower old dynamics. At this point, a problem may become irrelevant or a disease may go into remission or dormancy.

However, without the fundamental shift, we eventually return to the familiar equilibrium and the old note of being. This is an essential homeostatic mechanism of the bodymind that ordinarily protects us from excessively rapid change. But this mechanism also indiscriminately resists all transformation and will restore us to a condition of familiar energy even though, once restored, we are dying or miserable. Rather than a new note of consciousness, we find a crack has been opened in the old structure that allows the light of a deeper possibility. For a while there is openness and vulnerability. For a while there is new or renewed discipline and conviction. For a while the knot of self-control has relaxed and one is available to greater aliveness. Depending upon the commitment of the individual, the crack may be enlarged until there is fundamental change, but more often it gradually closes as the old system becomes familiar with it and learns to accommodate the change.

A poignant example of this is the chronic dieter. On the first attempt, he or she is successful in losing weight, but then gains it back and finds the new weight even more difficult to lose. At first, the basic system is not adapted to the perturbing factor of decreased calories and to the heightened psychical energy that comes with the focused will and the ritual of dieting. But this energy must be sustained by will because, after a while, the dieting ritual is no longer new and exciting. At this point, the psychical energy has been neutralized and old habits become literally irresistible. In the meantime, the body has adapted and is much more calorie conserving. Thus weight returns even faster and becomes even harder to lose. This is a classic example of the change due to an initial perturbation that has been accommodated by consciousness at physical and psychological levels. In fact, efforts to repeat this kind of perturbation will be unsuccessful; a new way of perturbing the energy must be found.

The possibility that a perturbed system can move on into fundamental transformation is crucial. The moment of radical discontinuity is unpredictable and fairly rare. Far more common is the process of perturbation. In fact, the vast majority of all efforts toward transformation tend to fall into the category of perturbation. This includes everything from altered states of consciousness to the effects of chemotherapy. Forces of various kinds, invited and uninvited, cause varying degrees of perturbation. Many are beneficial (i.e. a medicine that overcomes disease perturbs in favor of the basic energy system). Yet most perturbations do not lead to the possibility of transformation. Obviously, we do not want every bacterium or chemical to cause a permanent transformation. If they do, then usually the effect is death. Thus the capacity of the energetic structure to accommodate perturbation is one of its strengths. It is also, from the point of view of the transformation of consciousness, the basic force that we must learn to overcome. There can be no new note without a radical discontinuity of consciousness. However the value of perturbation is that the cumulative effect tends to produce a more fluid and open consciousness. With each perturbation that produces a glimpse of the higher, our consecration is subtly changed, and a gradual turning toward the higher is effected. This, I believe, is a favorable condition for realization.

＊

A perturbation of consciousness accompanied by some degree of bodily healing and/or psychological change rarely will be sustained when we re-enter our familiar lifestyle. We do not even realize the moment we step into our home, face our family and friends, and resume our familiar roles, that we immediately are cued into the old consciousness, and the induction of higher energy is soon dissipated. This is one of the fundamental dilemmas for all of us pursuing the transformational impulse; one's whole life must participate. If not, a deep conflict is set up, and whichever aspect receives the most nearly continuous reinforcement is likely to win out. Invariably it will be the collectively reinforced values, the conditioning that we have undergone throughout the vast majority of our lives. How can the new energy ever hope to overcome this?

I have seen people leave a conference where they were lifted to greater aliveness and later fall into a reactive depression because they couldn't sustain the energy in their familiar life context. Sadly, we invalidate our glimpse of greater possibility or attack ourselves bitterly for failing. There is no failure here, just the age-old interaction of "Gravity and Grace" as Simone Weil put it. I define Gravity as the pull toward basic consciousness reinforced by the very structures (family, job) in which that consciousness evolved. Grace is the pull to the higher consciousness that comes as we learn to develop attention to the higher possibility and engage our relationships with a new degree of communion. Christ spoke to this very process when he said, "All those who obey my Father in Heaven are my family." In making this remark he was saying that the higher energy does not make distinctions like the basic consciousness. Relationships personalized as "my wife, my child, my mother" originate with ego development in an earlier energetic potential. In the higher consciousness we understand our family is not necessarily our kin, but rather all those with whom the deepest sense of aliveness is honored and invoked.

A new level of energy generates a new life with a radically different awareness that emphasizes the quality and consecration of all relationships. Granted, there is no formula for this and it usually evolves spontaneously. Often it seems to be contrary to many deeply ingrained feelings and needs. These simply cannot be ignored. Thus I am not speaking of a calculated renunciation of family and old friends, but an inspired commitment to pursue behaviors that intuitively honor the highest energy moment by moment. In practice, this embraces a dynamism of polarities (personal space as well as family responsibilities, individual needs as well as the needs of the multitude, taking responsibility for one's energy level as well as social and job commitments, discipline and will as well as allowing and surrender) and not a simple resolution attained by truncating one or another of these dynamically opposed forces.

After my opening, I immediately knew that the woman with whom I was living was no longer compatible with me. I couldn't cut the relationship off completely, so I moved into another bedroom and let a new quality of relationship unfold. It required a continuous juggling of the tendency to re-immerse and attach versus withdrawing and cutting off, but our relationship remains today a creative friendship. Clearly there are infinite possibilities one might pursue. But eventually we realize that it is fruitless to throw away a personal relationship on the basis of some imagined alternative. Following our energy is a radical aliveness that carries us to the edge of what is happening in the moment, and to staying present no matter what occurs. However, over and over the gravitational pull of familiar patterns will overwhelm the movement into the larger possibility. We may have learned to access a higher energy, but now we must discover a lifestyle that matches it.

I believe it was this very issue that Theodora faced. Her breakthrough was a deep perturbation, but not a new note. Nevertheless there was a distinct possibility that she could have pursued and deepened her opening. She acknowledged having a fantasy of buying a red sports car and traveling across the United States. She saw herself taking part-time jobs, waitressing, singing in churches. It would be a life lived one day at a time (precisely the kind of process that tends to bring one into the immediate moment and thus into a generally higher energy). However, she never let this fantasy become a reality. As we know, she went home and married her fiance and her disease aggressively recurred almost immediately afterward.

Now we come to the question of why Theodora's cancer resumed with increased virulence. The very shift that had led to her transient healing subtly opened her, increasing her capacity to access more energy. In the perturbed state the disease process was no longer necessary because it was channeled into her larger, more coherent wholeness. However, when she returned to her old life, the disease, part and parcel of her former "wholeness," resumed activity with even greater potency. I suspect her increased openness was now feeding the disease configuration.

I must reiterate that there is no way to know whether Theodora made a wrong decision. She could have followed her sports car fantasy and the disease might have recurred anyway. The point is that the potential to kindle and sustain a new energy often requires, at least in the beginning, a special space in which it can be nourished. In my observation, the further we can get from our familiar conditioning the better. It is not so much a process of withdrawal as it is an engaging of something new. This is why people traditionally ritualize their new spiritual affiliations by shaving their heads or wearing special robes. In a sense this is just substituting one level of identity for another. However, for many people, a new and strongly defined identity that symbolizes and invites the new orientation is very important. Yet, even with this, it must be acknowledged how difficult it is to overcome our familiar patterns of attachment and self-identification. The old structure is more than capable of reasserting itself despite changes of costume and habitat.

TRADITIONAL MEDICINE: PERTURBATION

The temporary benefits of perturbing consciousness are not unique to my work, but accrue to all work, including traditional medicine. Just as the energy of a group of people can become a force that perturbs the basic consciousness, so too a drug is a perturbing agent. The drug may be specific, such as an antibiotic that perturbs the bacteria sufficiently to cause breakdown, or it may be directed at enhancing the body's natural biological response. In either case, the drug's capacity to act in an appropriate and predictable manner reflects our scientific understanding, which in turn bespeaks a degree of realization. It is an understanding, however, that is still relative, still limited to the idea of human identity as comprised of separate bodies, with disease as something outside or other.

Some diseases, such as cancer, are not easily understood by examining only the individual human being. In *The I That Is We*, I suggest that cancer is a disease empowered by a collective energy. It is a potential for growth in the individual that is activated when we heighten more energy without a sense of the wholeness of life. As has been discussed, we are collectively heightening our energy as the complexity and interconnectedness of our society grows. But most people are unconscious of this dynamic and remain in life orientations that are fundamentally too personal and too small—such as believing that strength lies in protecting our territory (family, nation) rather than opening to communion with more of humanity. Without an accompanying refinement of our spiritual and social interrelatedness that would allow us appropriately to handle this heightening energy, we are creating a high-energy growth in a low-energy system. The epidemic of cancer reflects the collective dynamic where more energy is moving through people than many individuals have the capacity to conduct.

We are only limitedly successful in perturbing the cancer process within the individual, and such efforts invariably interfere with the basic integrity of the body rather than inviting a whole new level of integrity. This suggests that as we approach challenges such as cancer we are operating from too small a realization of what it means to be human. To interrupt the equilibrium state in which cancer is a natural corollary (not a disease that is separate from our basic humanness) requires a fundamental transformation of all humanity and not mere perturbation of individuals. It requires a cultural realization, a cultural transformation—put simply, a new way of life.

Actually, my phrasing is inaccurate. It is not that anything is required, for our inquiry into this disease is already revealing how our habits, values, industrial processes, are harming us. As a society, we think we can mitigate cancer through prevention (i.e.

by stopping those behaviors we recognize as causative). In this, I fear our perspective is too small. These "causes" are the by-products of our current level of realization, which refuses to acknowledge the interconnectedness of everything. The newspapers proudly announce the GNP annual increase, or the population growth of Los Angeles, but living as I do in the Owens Valley where water is ruthlessly pumped from the ground and diverted from the streams, drying the lakes and killing the wildlife, I am appalled by such blindness. One begins to suspect that cancer is a blessing that forces us to look at ourselves. I fear that nothing but growing human misery will awaken us.

In the end, our medical efforts to prevent cancer are only acting at the level of perturbation because we will not (I must believe we can if we choose to) look at the larger picture. We keep trying to juggle our behavior in order to achieve short-term goals. We keep thinking that cancer and most diseases happen in individual bodies and we focus primary attention on each person rather than equally on the whole. This is equivalent to being immersed in the content of consciousness without ever realizing Consciousness itself.

Let us consider a far deeper understanding of what prevention really means. It means literally "to come before." In this sense, prevention means to realize the more fundamental consciousness that "comes before" our present level of realization. Thus, prevention is actually Transformation or Realization. Cancer will not be cured out of our fear, nor through any amount of perturbing efforts. We will change (are already changed) when we realize as Laura did our fundamental oneness.

Now, a drug can perturb the individual consciousness or body-mind, but separated from the total response of the individual to life as a whole, no drug can totally shift the basic energy state. Yet, as discussed in *How Shall I Live* (Celestial Arts, 1985), drugs such as those used in chemotherapy are so potent in the way they affect our sense of well-being that, like surgery, these drugs can become a door with deeply transformative potential.

I have no objection to the use of chemotherapy or any of the other highly invasive procedures that mechanical medicine is capable of performing. Rather, my concern is that we are employing

an extremely powerful force without adequate spiritual preparation, without tapping into the full transformative potential that
such an experience can carry. Chemotherapy is a major intru-
sion into the temple of our being. It could be seen as an initiation, a socially recognized rite of passage where people using such
medications become honored as adventurers into the Unknown.
Rather than reading the drug and dosage off a chart, based on
statistics regularly updated by the medical community (a giant
physiology experiment), the physician could be the heart of a profoundly transformative ritual. The patient could be celebrated for
the experiment in aliveness that each one is making, not merely
for himself, but for everyone. We could be celebrating the full spectrum of change that can be initiated by these powerful agents.
We could be ready to tap and amplify every aspect of new vulnerability and openness so that it might become a source for new
awareness, new aliveness. In such a context, the drug becomes
an aspect of a ritual of social and spiritual transformation and
would invariably be more effective. We would have in large degree overcome the assumption of separation. At the same time
we will have tapped a means of enlivening the whole body and
the use of such toxic agents might well become unnecessary or
quite rare.

PSYCHEDELICS AND TRANSFORMATION

There was some hope that the psychedelic drugs might lead to
the awakening of greater wholeness. For many people, this *has*
been the case. There is even some evidence that breakthroughs
experienced under psychedelics have resulted in healings—but they
have also resulted in psychosis. In my observation, the transformation evoked by these chemicals, while valid, is not of the same
order as that which comes through spontaneous realization. One
can go through a door with these drugs. Many have. As with
surgery, chemotherapy, or any profound life crisis, each person
grows in accordance with the consecration in which he or she
undertook the experience. But I have never met anyone who has
been "transformed" through use of psychoactive drugs who carries the capacity to awaken others by the radiance of his or her

being. The discontinuity caused by the drug is not the same as that of Realization. There is new vision, new insight, but it doesn't seem to penetrate much beyond the mental, psychological, and emotional dimensions.

I feel that the use of psychedelics in the transformational process has, at best, very limited application, and I strongly recommend that they be avoided. There *are* points at the beginning of the adventure when these agents may have their place on one or perhaps two occasions, but after this we begin to get involved in an addiction to intensity as well as to the idea that there is a goal to be attained. Furthermore, I have observed thousands of people in transformational exploration, and those who use or have used lots of drugs generally are less able to integrate and support a higher energy. It is as though they have burned their psychic structure and it won't hold a higher energy any more. My sense is that a few experiences do not have this effect, but that frequent use does. As far as I am concerned, psychoactive agents used without a disciplined awareness are a foolish risk. With awareness the risk is reduced, but a disciplined awareness, one that is simply attentive in the moment, of itself leads to a naturally heightened consciousness that obviates the desire or need for any drug.

It is far better to remain ordinary and untransformed than to continue to seek the intensity of drug experiences. Such seeking, unless very consciously recognized and consecrated, is often a subtle form of rejection of the simple ordinariness of life. Perhaps this is inevitable in our world, but it reflects not only a basic immaturity, but also our collective obsession with getting there faster. There is a subtle distrust of existence hidden in the urge to use drugs. And with this unconscious consecration, the degree of perturbation produced by these drugs is too rapid, potentially destructive, and insufficiently referent to a deeper wholeness to produce a lasting transformation of consciousness.

Different psychedelics have different dynamics and some (like the currently popular "ecstasy") are less likely to produce psychosis. They often produce extraordinarily pleasant encounters and thus become all the more attractive. Some therapists argue that these drugs can be used beneficially to improve relationships. Here I step back with great skepticism. While the drugs can produce an illusory sense of mystical love, I have observed a gradual diminishing of the capacity for deep relationship in frequent users. The love is somehow immature, regressing easily into romantic attachment or even *detachment*. There is nothing in it that speaks to the suffering and paradox of mature relationship, the sacrifice, the letting go of what used to be, to really meet what is. Rather, it tends to produce a consciousness caught up in the need for intense feeling and immediate gratification. It is this very bias toward intensity and feeling—making intensity equivalent to meaning or profundity or love—that is the greatest limit to the transformative potential of any psychedelic. It is a consciousness that has failed to accept its own ordinariness. The use of these drugs would be rare indeed in a society where the source of the higher human potential is seen to be our overall relatedness, our capacity to come together in an energetic synergy that creates the heightening of consciousness naturally. Still, in our present world, under very specific circumstances and allowing for Life's own mystery, the use of psychedelics can have value and has been part of the force that began the acceleration toward world transformation.

ALIVENESS AND SUFFERING

Chemicals such as those used in chemotherapy and the pharmacologic armamentarium of modern medicine perturb the basic energy of the bodymind. They effect the relief of symptoms, and this is a temporary blessing. However, from the perspective of transformation, they often allow us to tolerate our basic state; they do not, in themselves, shift us to a new level of aliveness. In fact, by helping individuals tolerate their basic states rather than transformatively challenging them, we are, I believe, potentially interfering with transformational impulse. Perhaps in this way we invite more insidious and universal illnesses such as AIDS or the disease of thermonuclear annihilation. There *is* a natural compensation, so that the price we pay in suffering or uncertainty often yields an increased capacity to share and interact with others with greater reverence and love. In *How Shall I Live*, I point out that when we diminish the natural transformative potential of illness, we rob society of one of the mechanisms for developing a higher spiritual awareness. We are restoring the old equilibrium again and again and thereby inviting an even greater destabilizing or transformative force to surface in some other dimension. Because our sense of treatment focuses too narrowly on the problem of a disease rather than transforming the basic consciousness, we are creating a humanity whose fundamental illness—the illusion of separation, of "me-ness"—faces us with the destruction of our world.

Obviously, medicine is not solely responsible for this. This is our approach across the length and breadth of human activity. Our freedom to push toward the next frontier, to expand outward, decompresses the transformative tension whenever the energy becomes too intense. In this way we have grown technologically and scientifically, we have conquered more of observable reality, we have created greater interconnectedness and thus a greater overall level of social energy, but we have not grown proportionately in our capacity to love or to live together as a whole. This capacity is the by-product of egoic death/rebirth, the transformative shift to a greater realization. Thermonuclear extinction is, in a sense, the collective metaphor of death/rebirth, the accumulated and exponentially heightened denial of fundamental change.

Thus, as long as the basic egoic dynamic is not understood, and our emphasis is always on perturbation, the wholeness of life will elude us. We walk around feeling strangely uncomfortable and dissatisfied and keep trying to remedy this. We confuse transient perturbations and alterations at the level of this discomfort with true change. But soon the basic equilibrium is restored and the old dynamic resumes. With medications we see this all the time; we call it "tolerance." This is a good word because it means that the basic consciousness, though perturbed and thus helped to function differently for a while, has learned to tolerate or incorporate the perturbation. What we want is not a force that perturbs and then is tolerated, but rather a force that perturbs and, in combination with a reorientation toward life as a whole, invites Transformation. We must go deeper into our existential pain.

This is the medicine for the future. It will no longer be a medicine unconsciously designed to get the warrior back into the battlefield of life, but rather a spiritual force through which Life's lovers become more whole. It is a medicine that will recognize the important health value of uncertainity, vulnerability, and our capacity to face paradoxical tensions and stresses. Medicine that leads back to the basic egoic energetic state is doomed to failure for, in so doing, it loses contact with wholeness and fosters disease in more subtle dimensions. Medicine, as with all human endeavor that respects wholeness and invites radical aliveness, must empower a larger consciousness. Thus even as each person's life is made more comfortable, there must be a compensatory stress, a demand to transform and assume one's role as a spiritually aware individual, capable of sustaining the heightening energies. We must come to know Life as Lover. To know this option and to help prepare ourselves and our world for this step is now the greatest single prescription for health for the whole of humanity.

11 ∗ THE TRANSFORMATIVE POTENTIAL OF POPULAR THERAPIES AND SPIRITUAL TEACHINGS

For the good man to realize
that it is better to be whole
than to be good
is to enter on a straight and
narrow path compared to which
his previous rectitude was
flowery license.
JOHN MIDDLETON MURRAY

The right tool in the wrong hands leads to wrong
results.
FRANKLIN MERRELL-WOLFF

I HAVE TALKED A GREAT DEAL about ways to perturb the energy without mentioning some of the methods and techniques currently offered by alternative and holistic medicine. It is not my intention to compare or discuss these contributions thoroughly. Rather I want to comment briefly on their potential for inviting radical transformation.

When we enter a program of self-discovery and emotional opening as part of a self-healing approach, like those pioneered by Drs. Carl and Stephanie Simonton and since spread by many others, we are perturbing our basic consciousness. The methods used to accomplish this are meditation and visualization exercises in conjunction with psychological therapies to free "blocked" emotions. These programs have been broadly successful in helping to create greater well-being and, at least in his early cases, Simonton reported an increase in disease remission as well. At first many people reported success in healing themselves with these techniques. Yet frequently, as with other treatments, the disease later reappeared. Using visualizations to cure the disease no longer seemed to be effective. As with drugs, tolerance had developed.

The transient physical success of these approaches for some people may reside in the degree to which their involvement temporarily altered their basic energetic pattern. The newness of the approach was stimulating, and a strong faith in the effectiveness of the techniques provided a way to focus awareness and generate energy. In addition, new relationships, group support, and new behaviors and values created a high-energy community for a while. I believe that the combination of these factors, complemented by the increased availability of the individual opened by the disease, tended to bring about a new note of consciousness. This heightened energy triggered the symptom remission.

However, the context in which any new technique is explored is as important as the technique itself. And the context of these approaches is a "fight the problem" dynamic where visualization and psychological awareness are used against disease in the same way that traditional medicine uses drugs. Thus the context is the old subject/object consciousness, and one can only transiently perturb a disease process which itself is an outgrowth of that consciousness.

For example, we are told to visualize the good cells fighting the bad cells or the good drug fighting the evil sickness. Energy is generated by splitting the psyche in half and pitting one side against the other. One team competing with another will generate a lot of energy, but the greatest energy comes from knowing how to unify the two in a new dynamic. When we send the good cells out to conquer the cancer cells, we create a sense of power and control that mobilizes us briefly to a heightened energy. But this energy is predicated as much on the existence of the disease as it is upon the potential to overcome disease. So we miss the whole point of a disease such as cancer, which from a larger perspective can also be seen as a healing force. The cancer is asking us to realize our wholeness as Laura did, rather than continuing to go to war within our psyches to generate a sense of aliveness. Thus visualizations of this nature can only transiently perturb the basic system; they can't be genuinely transformative because they are methods that essentially reduce the whole to competitive parts. Eventually, when we relax the effort to empower the positive force over the negative, or we stop affirming the positive ideal, the excluded half returns, either at the same level or (as with Theodora) with more energy and at a more pervasive level.

Employed here are the transformational vectors of Creative Involvement and Intensity (will), yet lacking is the third, Unconditional Love, where patient, disease, and therapeutic context become a single whole. Utilizing visualization techniques to harness the body's natural healing capacities in the way suggested by Simonton and others does not recognize the larger context from which these practices originate. They are part of yogic discipline and are involved with mastering every facet of the bodymind. Of course, such concentration generates energy, and this energy alters bodymind dynamics. But generating this energy through visualizations that employ traditional medical understandings about bodily defenses once again represents the old consciousness. I believe that problem-oriented therapy can never really be transformational or holistic. By its very focus, it has narrowed the definition of life. If anything is truly holistic, it is life itself, lived fully for its own sake. This is what the will to live is all about, an embrace of life, not a war against disease.

During a recent lecture, a man, on hearing these principles, argued that people who could harness the will to fight their disease often improved. He was treating a woman in precisely this way and wanted to know what I would do for her. I told him I would do nothing but be present for her. Why, I asked him, did he need to get her to fight death? Had he looked deeply into his own death? Had he looked at all the death we create in willing ourselves into life without having first faced the existential void within? I suggested that in all things there is a compensatory relationship, so that if he as healer pushed her toward life, then in order for life in its totality to be honored, he would have to go deeper into his own death. Not that he should take on disease from her, but rather face his own egoic death. In this way he would join her. In their unobstructed relationship there would be greater love (not necessarily healing) for both. There is a violence, I suggested, in the relationship that grows from his inability to face death that takes the form of making her fight for life. This is not love. Man has always fought for life and the potential for death grows greater every day.

TRANSFORMATION AND THE NEED FOR RESULTS

The need for results or for practical, easily defined and executed techniques is one of the greatest shields against the unknown and the exploration of new possibilities. It is the shield I encountered when I spoke about new ideas in transformation and health during "grand rounds" at a major medical center. Evaluations of my talk were high for stimulation and interest, but much lower when it came to practical application. The bottom line for most doctors was, "How do I make it work? How do I apply it to my patients?"

This cry is echoed by many healers today. It has its roots in our compassion, in our aspiration for wholeness. Doctors, therapists, chaplains, everyone in the service community is asking, "How can I help?" There is a need to reach beyond the bounds of formal training. Yet for the most part our concept of help is based on some new technique, some new insight. We think our ignorance of the facts, whatever they might be, is holding us back, so we ask for more research. We wonder if our approach is too narrow, so we add more techniques. Even traditional physicians are augmenting their usual methods with counseling, vitamins, meditations, herbs, and even fire walking. Although each addition fills a certain gap or creates a subtle new possibility, and the impulse for practical tools is very sincere, the very *idea* that some external remedy will make the difference avoids the fundamental truth of unknowing.

We want to help; often we don't know how. Here in this sense of incompleteness is the truth, something substantial, for this is what brings us into the immediacy of the moment. The notion that more knowledge is needed is a concept, an inference. Thus again and again we turn toward the inferential—the unreal or partially real—rather than stepping through the door of our immediate truth. There are many healing arts, traditional and nontraditional, scientifically based and intuitively based, but the real truth is our caring and the eternal question, "How do I apply it to my patients? How can I do more?" It is this very unknowing, not our attempts to resolve our uncertainty, that is the profound and neglected door into a deeper dimension of our humanness, a dimension in which vulnerability, compassion and humility draw us together. This is not to say that we should turn our backs on science, herbs, intuition, or energy channeling. Certainly they are part of our inquiry into life. But facing this question, peering into the abyss of our unknowing, illuminates our souls and becomes the radiance that permeates our sharing.

Transformative understanding cannot be "applied." We must work on ourselves, work to awaken deeper aliveness in the immediacy of our own lives. When we understand this, the healing arts that we practice become sacred scaffolds by which we are able (and privileged) to externalize the awakening consciousness, allowing it to incarnate in ourselves and in our world. When we understand that health is simply the enhancement of consciousness and begin to change the context of the practice of medicine, work becomes worship and we are no longer blinded by our sense of inadequacy, our desire to do more. In humility born of expanded awareness we do our best; yet the unknowing remains and carries us more fully into the immediacy of the healing relationship. From this comes the unexpected, the true art of healing.

In contrast, the unawakened consciousness is epitomized by a sense of separation between the technique and the practitioner and the inability to see that the effectiveness of any technique resides in one's own radiant presence. This same consciousness sees disease as separate from the wholeness of the person. Thus, it tries to modify the disease instead of empowering wholeness. Similarly, the person who just wants to be shown methods to heal himself and follows any regimen if it leads to desired results is unwittingly combatting a disease instead of empowering wholeness. Such a battle can only bring temporary victory because it is waged from the same level of consciousness out of which the disease evolved.

The myth of practicality and measurable results that motivates the modern health care and research world must finally be balanced with a sense of life's mystery. It must be combined with a willingness to play with new ideas and behaviors that are difficult to measure or even evaluate. As an example, Reimean geometry was considered clever but unimportant by most nineteenth-century mathemeticians; yet this "cleverness" was utilized by Einstein in his work on relativity. Likewise, in our exploration of health, we must be willing to take the next step into life without knowing where it will lead.

This is precisely what Norman Cousins did. In his book *Anatomy of an Illness* he reports healing himself of a serious illness by watching films that made him laugh. He also followed his own diet regimen, had an excellent working relationship with his physician, and received tremendous love and support from his family. But Mr. Cousins spontaneously and completely followed his intuition. Throughout that process, he acted without ever really knowing what he was doing, why he was doing it, or whether it would work. This is the essence of Creative Relationship and Intensity in the healing process. His methods allowed him to access and express a lot of energy. His obstinacy and perseverance were expressions of his innate being. He was not so much fighting disease as using it as a springboard into life.

But now, as a result of his success, whole conferences have been organized recommending laughter as a healing technique. This I feel is a mistake. It would be wonderful if we could teach Mr. Cousins's admirable uniqueness, his ability to be himself and tap his deepest resources. But I don't believe this is something that can be taught. Rather, we can radiate and inspire this possibility if it is alive within us, but ultimately each person must find the equivalent in himself or herself. To think that we can tell others how to do what spontaneously occurred for us, with its own Grace, and expect it to have the same effect on them is once again reducing the whole to a manageable process and simultaneously losing the energy which was the deeper healing force.

EMBRACING PARADOX

Radical aliveness is not something that we do—rather it is a way of being that honors life's paradox. In contrast, today there are many pseudo-spiritual teachings that are unable to embrace paradox. They are concerned with learning to reprogram the mind and thereby come to a sense of empowerment. To solve the dilemma of suffering, we are instructed to think positively and to envision the world we want to create. There are churches built around such teachings and there are courses that you can do on your own at home or with study groups. In this way, we can learn to exercise subtle powers of mind, and this is how the world can be made whole. While I cannot deny the value of these teachings in improving one's self-esteem and well-being, I feel it is important to see how these so-called transformative approaches can, like all beliefs, obstruct radical transformation.

I am inherently cautious about taking "truths" that originate from states of higher consciousness and applying them rationally to life at lower levels of consciousness. Realization gives birth to new understanding and wisdom; it is not a method for attaining that understanding. The moment we return to ordinary consciousness and attempt to apply "higher truths" we are normalizing reality (as in the mathematics of electrodynamics). To some extent we can exercise new powers to make life work, to make it fit, to get it right, but underlying this is a consecration rooted in fear. Our powerlessness is seen as wrongness, rather than an acknowledgment of the all-pervading Divine. Thus at this level of development we are exploring power—in a sense, learning to play God. For a while there is a sense of security; we are manifesting our needs more capably. But this all too easily becomes an escalating need for control instead of the peace that one might expect from having glimpsed the inherent coherence of Existence. There is no sense of inquiry into life, just a need for tools to make it work. It is as if life is wrong until we have seen the "law" that shows us how to do it right.

Usually our fear shows up the next time we approach the transformational door and must face the "no mountain" space of existential undoing. At this point those who have programmed their minds with affirmations instead of birthing the capacity to stand in their own light will recoil from the Grace of transformation.

Individuals who are attracted to positive-thinking and affirmational approaches are often people who have never felt powerful enough—as if there is ever "enough" for the basic ego! For some, the value of these techniques as external tools that trigger Creative Involvement cannot be overlooked. Yet many people, after some exposure to these approaches, feel the need to move on, recognizing that their lives were only transiently enhanced by the contrast with their usual ideation. Others become caught in them and, as soon as there is stress, rather than growing in their capacity to love, they use their teachings unwittingly to escape deeper relationship to themselves and others. I find an eerie unrealness in so much of this, a denial of the body and of the negative pole of existence, a denial that creates superficiality, rigidity and defensiveness. Why are we so afraid to go deeper through the door of the Unknown, trusting our own experience?

Deeper knowing is not learned as an outer subject; it is born out of radical aliveness, an aliveness wherein it is more valuable to not know how to go forward than it is to follow a premeditated program.

There is a world of difference between the conscious mind, understanding and affirming so-called enlightened ideas and then believing they are one's own, and the state of radiant aliveness that can only come through direct experience. There is no question that reading inspirational thoughts each day produces a new ideation that has the power to alter the quality of attention. It helps people to respond in new ways, to open to life as they desire it to be. But the sense of well-being and new potency is only a transient perturbation, not a full embodiment of higher energy. There is a great illusion in the sense of awakening that comes from our success in modifying reality through changing the orientation of consciousness. There is an arrogance in this stance that does not surrender, for surrender implies no choice; there is no certainty. It is this uncertainty that births faith, humility and the inner strength so essential for approaching fundamental change.

Love is the great prescription, the great remedy of the many popular spiritual teachings that claim to be new revelations of

Christ's message. They say we must learn to see love everywhere and in so doing redeem all our relationships and bring harmony into our world. Who can argue with this? Yet the implication is that love is something we can and must do, and it becomes once again an assault on how we are, on our pain, our doubt, our questioning. We are once more dealing with the confusion between higher realization and basic consciousness. Love *is* the nature of Reality that makes it possible to find wholeness as we enter and pass through the door of any experience. In fact, to try to make love happen is antithetical to love and must result in splitting life force apart. Perhaps this is why, the more we "try" to be loving, the angrier we become or the more our aliveness is repressed.

Actually these teachings do say that God's love and human, ego-based love are different and that at the moment of awakening we will see the reality of God's love in all things. It is the promise of Christ's life (indeed of all radically awakened lives) that each of us can, and eventually will, know this and be made whole in that moment. Now if the teachings stopped here, one could agree that they were accurately reporting the phenomenon of transformation. But they go a step further and suggest that we can begin to live that love now and thereby release ourselves out of the pain and struggle that the ego-based illusions create. Since, according to these teachings, none of this is real (only Love is Real), we can take the road of peace and joy, or continue on the road of struggle, disease and suffering, for both will get to the transformative moment eventually. If this is really our choice, then wisdom dictates we take the road of peace and joy.

Now, this sounds like wisdom; however, it does not confirm my experience of the process of transformation. My experience is that when we try to split joy and peace from pain and struggle, we sacrifice an important part of our aliveness. We may temporarily relieve discomfort, but this is not the same as transcending through a process of understanding and Grace, a process that inevitably involves having no answers. Again and again I hear students of these teachings speak of spiritual truths and how they are growing, but I don't sense the reality of this as I stand in their presence. It is not incarnating. However, following these teachings does not automatically diminish aliveness. Intuiting toward the mystical cannot help but serve our collective awakening. Yet when we turn toward disincarnate spiritual teachings, we must also become aware of our hidden desire to achieve fundamental change on our terms. We believe that we are embracing the Divine; yet unwittingly in our very approach we deny the Divine action of Grace that acts in us when we are empty, when we are uncertain and unable to proceed on our terms.

Any genuine mystical or spiritual revelation is true and consistent at the level from which it is channelled and received, but may not be true or consistent when interpreted from anything but the same level of consciousness. It does not matter how enlightened the source, we must understand that such teachings rarely translate directly to the ordinary levels of consciousness when we attempt to live them.

Once a person has developed the capacity to move into a depth of silence that transcends ordinary mental and intellectual functioning—a natural stage of development along the path of self-realization—it becomes possible to utter wondrously poetic and profound statements. There is an ecstatic dimension to this level of expression and it has wisdom, a deep level of integration and synthesis of aspects of life that ordinary consciousness does not perceive as integral and united. But there is no suggestion in this wisdom that it is easy to live these truths at ordinary levels of consciousness. The very attempt to live the ideals of love, wisdom and compassion brings forth the contrasting elements of anger, despair and selfishness. This is why I allow the full spectrum of my personal life to be visible to people. There must be no attempt to separate the higher teaching and the daily life. If I cannot yet live these truths even as I utter them, I must simultaneously acknowledge the distance between higher mental and intuitive realization and that which has been fully incarnated as ordinary living. This is why it is so valuable to have an immediate and ongoing relationship with a person who does access the higher levels of consciousness directly. This allows us to see, not only the transcendent embodying, but humanness also (what I often irreverently call ass-holiness). Spiritual teachings not exemplified by a living being do not engage the student in the immediate paradox and challenge of real relationship. But since such a relationship will not be possible for all people until we are genuinely able to see each other as Divine, most will get their first taste of mysticism from books. In doing so it becomes very important to examine the whole context of the knowledge we find in books and approach these revelations with thoughtful discrimination. Without this discrimination, I fear that recently channeled revelations like *A Course in Miracles* will become New Age fundamentalism. Many people already speak of these book truths as though they were Gospel, at the expense of learning through the process of facing the Unknown.

There is rich insight in *A Course in Miracles*, but it is not grounded in life as we experience and live it. The teaching was channeled by a woman who, after a lifetime of spiritual quest, became clear enough to serve as a vehicle for higher understanding. Yet she could not channel this out of the fullness of her nature, but only after splitting away from her personal consciousness. In her own right, she did not accept or live the teachings. It would have stopped there, but her colleague, who himself could not access such insights, was inspired by them. He became the vehicle to record them for eventual publication. Thus, a second split. *A Course in Miracles* is a teaching that required the synergy of two people, neither of whom could embody the teaching. It is, in fact, a teaching without incarnation. This says something of the heights from which it was received, but also forewarns us of the problems the average person faces in attempting to live the teachings. This purported message from Christ lacks Christ's suffering, the dynamic tension between humanness and divinity. It fosters the same splitting of humanity and divinity in the student. Human suffering, struggle and so-called negativity is denied (it is called unreal, which is true from the perspective of higher realization) rather than recognized as part of the incarnating principle. The effect is again a transient perturbation based on a valid expansion of perspective about one's nature and relationship to life. There is a temporary sense of lucidity and freedom because the center of consciousness has been moved toward the transcendent and removed from the material reality. But incarnation is inherently a process of paradox and tension that occurs at the intersection of these forces. Thus invariably the student is returned with a vengeance to the domain of the suppressed or unexpressed paradoxes.

Because teachings such as *A Course in Miracles* remain in a mental or theoretic spirituality, students of such approaches know little of the living current, of the forces of energy and the process of aliveness as higher consciousness awakens in the body. Disease is a tragedy or lesson to be met with prayer, love and attitudinal change. This is noble, yet it still splits the spirit and the body and does not consciously bring us any closer to radical transformation. Nevertheless, I witness a natural progression from these teachings to a more immediate participation in the transformational impulse. They can be, if pursued deeply, an excellent preparation for profound transformational work because they have already set the stage for a new perspective about oneself. They have allowed our usual emotional reactivity to be seen from a larger perspective, and thus contribute to the self-mastery necessary for deeper mystical exploration.

The power of any channelled revelation that we can study on our own resides in how thoroughly we try to live it. If we follow it impeccably (that is, if we adhere to the teachings at those moments when we don't know how to, or feel it is impossible to do so), then they too have brought us to the door of transformation. But the potential is only minimally in the teaching; it is in the student. Only half-hearted curiosity is a problem, for then we turn to these writings when we feel low, or unclear, or desirous of inspiration, and use them again and again to restore a sense of control or clarity. In this way we console ourselves, and the growth of awareness is minimal. It is usually easier to keep searching, keep modifying our awareness, keep following the program in the hope of becoming more, than it is just to *be*.

The power in any spiritual teaching awakens, and even takes on the potential to transcend itself, as it becomes a way of life—particularly when it becomes the focus for community. Hence certain processes, such as Alcoholics Anonymous go a good deal beyond affirmations and positive-thinking approaches, although they employ these methods extensively. It is how the group meetings are conducted that represents the major transformative force, for people are asked to open their hearts and stand naked before the group. Such a process is a powerful energetic invocation and, combined with the structure of the Twelve Steps, empowers the capacity to overcome alcohol addiction. It is not merely "getting oneself together," but includes bringing spiritual wholeness and dignity to life for the sake of oneself, one's family, and society.

A.A. embraces all three of the transformational vectors. It is one of the most successful examples of religious principles applied to a social issue. Alcoholics themselves are very sensitive people; that is why the numbing effect of alcohol becomes so necessary. This sensitivity has another side, an unconscious spirituality, an openness and availability to higher dimensions. The vision of A.A. (what some consider dogma) taps this submerged religious or spiritual inclination. It gives a structure upon which to embrace the transformational impulse. It provides self-examination (Creative Relationship) in front of and invoking a group energy (Intensity). And it does so with every member willing to be lovingly present to affirm the underlying wholeness that always emerges as the oppression of alcohol lifts off. This love is both supportive and ruthlessly directive. Thus it is a balanced love.

If I have a criticism of A.A., it is that the power of the process becomes addictive itself. The follower becomes addicted to the very definition of being an alcoholic and this remains as a kind of boundary necessary to continue to rationalize participation in the A.A. community. In fact, for the fullest development, I suspect that this continued self-definition must be released and one must be able to see alcohol as an occasionally useful part of life. There is another aspect of A.A. to which we can be alert: Spiritual development for some becomes the next addiction. I have worked with several people who, after successfully overcoming alcohol, became so addicted to excessive meditation that they began to disincarnate. This proved to be almost as destructive as the alcohol had been.

A.A.'s success is also its weakness. It is spiritually focused on attainment, albeit the attainment of a healthier state. But it does not go beyond this to a larger inquiry into the whole process of consciousness. Thus from the point of view of radical transformation it is a stepping stone.

✱

Wherever spiritual teachings become the basis for social action, a higher-energy life is being incarnated. For example, *A Course in Miracles* inspired Dr. Gerald Jampolsky's work with dying children. While I have already discussed what I feel are the limits of this teaching, I don't deny its inspirational value, especially as we are helped to look more closely at life and death. The arena of death truly is fertile territory for personal growth. Here at last is a face of undoing, a face that is a little easier to look into in another than one's own psychic death/rebirth. First we face the undoing process "out there," in someone else, then gradually in ourselves. Even to be in such a setting is to be undone if one is willing to be truly honest, to look at the subtle glamor that surrounds such work and to deeply examine one's own motives.

Finally, if we can set aside all the teachings, stop proselytizing for any belief system and simply be, we find that we have brought ourselves to a place not merely to serve, but to be undone and reborn as well. There are few greater opportunities than to see ourselves in the dying countenance of another and to realize that what we ask of them we must be willing to live for ourselves, that if we ask them to try to change or to embrace new hope, even if it is not the hope of being healed, it may well be that we are denying our own sense of helplessness, our own fear of undoing, our own fear of death/rebirth. Thus such moments invite us to fall into the abyss of what is, to let go of control and all knowledge, to just be, and perhaps to know the unutterable acceptance and peace that is the gift of death.

12 ✳ UNOBSTRUCTED RELATIONSHIP

Because God's love is in me it can come to you from a different and special direction that would be closed if He did not live in me, and because His love is in you it can come to me from which it would not otherwise come. And because it is in both of us God can have greater glory.

THOMAS MERTON

TODAY, THANKS TO WHAT I HAVE LEARNED from Theodora and others, whenever I share with another person I try to remain neutral. If there is even a hint within my consciousness that I am acting from desire for their attainment or any assumption about who they are or how they should be, I know that I cannot serve them. Rather than withdraw, I simply witness my involvement until once again the interaction is spontaneous and unpremeditated.

Whenever there was a radical healing or an awakening in my work, the higher dimension seemed to open spontaneously. These events have deeply changed my vision of life. They occurred without intent on my part. Even in the energy-sharing ritual, where there is an intent to enter the deepest state of communion with another individual, my subjective experience is hardly a good barometer for evaluating the depth or richness of what occurs. Healings have occurred, and I have not been consciously aware that anything has happened. And whenever I am aware that some-thing unusual is happening, that process is taking me; I am not doing it. Whenever I try too hard, want something to happen, or "do" something to another, I know that I am personally in-volved. At such times I have seen results, as if the deeper process operates despite my arrogance and hubris, but on none of those occasions has the door to the great mystery of relationship been opened.

The only single consistent pattern when profound change has occurred has been a deep, impersonal attention on my part. Prior to this, I have felt a sense of appreciation and even affection for the individual; often this feeling was returned. But this need not be the case, as, for instance, there was no such outer relationship between Laura and myself. When the healing or transformative alchemy is greatest, all personalizing has fallen away. Whatever the interaction, it is totally spontaneous. And during the con-tacts of greatest potency, my sense of self has been so ordinary that I might as well be doing the dishes. In effect, the egoic sense becomes inactive or subsumed, as it does at the moment of reali-zation. There is full alertness, but the personalizing, judging, characterizing, intending functions of consciousness are not oper-ative. If there is even a need for trust, the interaction has still not reached its full depth.

In this relationship, it becomes irrelevant whether anything at all happens because the part of consciousness that is normally concerned with results is not directing the experience. One may ask, how do I get to this state? Although the question itself is already an obstacle to the state, we must look to the whole of one's life to try and find an answer. This kind of attention de-velops gradually as we learn to release preoccupation with the need for meaning through our subjective experience. This attention is a by-product of deepening in the transformational process, and not something to be attained as a power or an end in itself.

Involvement or motive implies that relationship is being held at the level of subject to object (i.e. teacher to student, client to therapist). Energy can transfer, consciousness may change, so may symptoms; the possibilities for modification of experience at any level of consciousness are infinite. But I have never seen fundamental transformation occur at such times.

The moment of fundamental transformation is a moment of unobstructed relationship. There is no self-consciousness mediating between self and being. Self-consciousness is only present as a purely detached witness, but not as the predicative force. When unobstructed relationship occurs between individuals, both people have released subject/object consciousness. This is the most remarkable of all relationships. One can call it archetypal because in that moment each person sees the other as themselves and simultaneously whole. It is the nonverbal, ineffable experience of loving thy neighbor as thyself. It is God seeing God. It is the deepest relationship of Guru to disciple, where lover and beloved become a single One.

I doubt that anyone, no matter how adept, can know in advance when such a relationship will occur. Yet the possibility exists in every relationship. Those who have penetrated deeply into themselves know this possibility and often function as awakeners or uplifters for others. They are doorways between dimensions. An adept is simultaneously present in the immediate play of life and the deeper space of consciousness. Even while interacting with another, he or she inevitably inducts the other individual toward a heightened awareness. But this induction is not intentional nor willed in the sense of an obligation or capacity that should be exercised. It is simply a function of a more awakened condition.

In only the rarest of moments do we touch into the archetypal state of unobstructed union. The vast majority of relationships are contained in the shell of subject/object consciousness in varying degrees. It is the extent of our transparency to the deeper dimensions in any moment that determines whether we will share the sacred food of radiant presence. From one relationship to the next, depending on our mutual availability, we expand and contract. We experience varying levels of consciousness, and various possibilities for communication, understanding, and the empowerment that also conveys healing. Yet no matter how enlightened one individual may be, if the other person is not open to her or him, a degree of self-involvement bounds the energetic possibility of the relationship. And, since we are really mirrors of each other, if one person has still not released self-involvement, the other individual will also experience some degree of limitation. When this is the case, it is beside the point to blame or judge the unopened person. What is in one, is in both.

Take for example the relationship of healer and patient. The healer's identification as healer (or vehicle through which healing occurs) coupled with the patient's desire for healing represents mutual self-involvement, an already obstructed form of relationship. Often, in the act of healing, the healer's attention may briefly transcend this, but if the patient remains bounded in his desire for healing, the transformative (and thus healing) potential is limited. I have heard some healers say that if the "healing" wasn't successful, the patient just wasn't ready, that at some deep preconscious level the person doesn't want to change. Other healers may accuse themselves of being unavailable or impure. While the former seems arrogant and the latter pious, to say either means that the healer doesn't really understand the nature of unobstructed relationship. This is the paradox of the healing relationship: The inevitable definition of roles and goals both makes possible the relationship and yet binds it in separateness. Even when some healing occurs, this is still the fruit of an obstructed relationship, albeit a far more unobstructed dimension than ordinary relating. Healers and healings, as wondrous as they are, are relatively plentiful compared to the rare flower of awakening in each other's presence.

For myself it feels like a crucifixion to come to another and offer energy for healing. I am drawn to the other in love, yet feel a subtle violence to my deeper nature in the very splitting from the other that this gift may be shared. This is precisely why I no longer let my work focus on healing or transformation as an end in itself. The work is to develop self-reliance and mutuality of awareness so that we can see deeper and deeper into the illusions that bind our aliveness. As each grows conscious of these, we heal each other.

AN UNOBSTRUCTED RELATIONSHIP

It is one of the greatest miracles in life when two or more individuals come together in a state of fully unobstructed attention free of self-involvement. I eventually understood that my self-involvement during the interaction with the depressed cancer patient prior to the first awakening allowed me to take on his depression. In contrast, it was precisely the opposite kind of relationship, seven years later, that preceded a deeper realization which I termed, "Before Abraham or (Jesus), I Am."

It was a subtle shift from "me" doing the work of a teacher and hoping (or covertly requiring) that others grow, to knowing myself as the Principle of Being in which life is forever transforming. At that time I was in conference with a small group of students with whom I had worked for an extended period of time. One morning, the group was involved with whirling, a practice popularized by the dervishes of the Mevlevi tradition. I consider this practice very valuable, for it involves the whole body in the process of letting go into deeper consciousness. When individuals are energetically well balanced, they generally can whirl quite effortlessly. This is not always the case, for some people can use a great deal of will or have through athletics learned a certain kind of focus that makes whirling relatively easy. However, for most people the process of whirling is not natural, and they lose control and may become ill. I have observed that when a person does lose control in this way he or she also becomes quite energetically open.

While the group whirls, I remain present and attentive. On this occasion, one of the women who naturally tends to engage experiences very wholeheartedly quickly lost control and fell. I encouraged her to get up and find the balance between control and loss of control. She became irritated with my interference and got up to "show me." She soon was on the ground again, this time vomiting. I asked her who she was doing this for, and she got up only to fall down again. This time she fell several feet from me. I was regarding her with no particular thought. She began to crawl along the ground toward me and I could see she was crying. Then, even as I realized what she was doing, she was wiping her tears on my feet and kissing them.

It was the most natural and appropriate thing in the world. Her eyes looked up to meet mine and we just stared into the infinity of one another. I realized that this was an archetypal moment,

I was playing Jesus to her Mary; I was Ramakrishna to her Vivekananda. It was a timeless moment, a moment of pure being. Yet, it was also a most ordinary moment. There was no emotion, no judgment, no revulsion or embarrassment. And it was over as simply as it began. She rose and resumed whirling. But this time she was another person entirely. There was an arch to her back. Her head was held high, her arms extended gracefully and her hands perfectly poised. She rotated very rapidly on an irregular, textured lawn with a slight downhill slope. Yet she never staggered, never lost balance and never even varied over more than about a square foot area. I have seen Baryshnikov and other great dancers perform, but this was the most radiant movement I have ever witnessed.

I do not want to get involved in another "miracle" story, but this interaction, more than any other, showed me that attention—rather than desire or intention—is the heart of all relationship. This woman awakened at the moment of unobstructed relationship between us. Over the next few days the awakening blossomed. Her realization penetrated deeper and deeper into her being, until it finally redeemed the deep childhood shock that had crippled her physically for life. At this point, her experience became a state of Enlightenment that carried several other people into transcendent states. With this, the current awakened and she too began the difficult process of integration and building a new way of life.

Her greatest gift now is the capacity to connect people to the play and irreverence of life. I observe individuals once she has turned her attention to them. She dresses them up in costumes and challenges them to look at the boundedness of their self-image. Within minutes they are moving differently, animating the space around them with new confidence and vitality. Without any religious overtones she creates an aura of irreverent but profound religiousness, a love of life.

THE FUNCTION OF AWAKENER

A moment of unobstructed relationship awakens the deepest transformative potential. If the therapist in my consciousness had told her when our eyes met to own her own power, or had responded more traditionally, that relationship would have been bounded; it would have been therapeutic, perhaps insightful, but it would not have been transformative. *Our unobstructed attention is the greatest gift that we can share with anyone.* It is the development of the fundamentally nonviolent, nonintrusive, nonmanipulative awareness that is the heart of gifted psychoanalysis or any good therapy. It inducts space in which new possibilities for consciousness may arise. Yet it is beyond all psychological theories and therapeutic techniques. Freed and unobstructed attention is the force that produces the therapeutic results. The capacity to move towards unobstructed relationship is a corollary of the awakening process. And to the degree that it is alive in any individual, that person has the capacity to function as an awakener of others. I have served this function in varying degrees for many people, but the greatest joy for me has been to bring people to such a state of unobstructed attention that they begin to serve this function for each other.

The function of awakener or healer exists in every person to the extent that he or she has merged identity into the nontime, nonspace, noncausal dimension that is the province of Realization. One need not have spontaneously awakened in the mystical sense to serve this function; a shock, profound stress, or the induction of a high-energy individual can temporarily render one open. But always available is the capacity to enter relationships consecrated to a higher principle. Thus, when we assume the role of healer or participate in a sacred ritual with others, we simultaneously access higher energy. A person who has relatively little conscious self-awareness (i.e. is highly obstructed in day-to-day relationships) can temporarily step into a state of relative openness and be a fine psychic healer. In part this can be attributed to underlying capacities within all individuals as well as to the openness of the people with whom they share. But more important, I believe, is the Principle of Relationship itself. It is this dimension referred to in the scriptural wisdom, "When two or three or more are gathered in my name, there I shall be in their midst" (John 18:20). Whenever people gather, there is energy. It can be as minimal and diffuse as that which exists amidst casual socializing or as rich and profound as that between individuals gathered in the spirit of surrender to existence. Mob energy is the Principle of Relationship at one level; a prayer group in deep communion is the same Principle at another level.

Today many people are exploring all kinds of healing forms, including Reiki, Touch for Health, polarity therapy, and massage. In the course of their training, they learn how to enter altered states of consciousness and transfer energy. The popularity of these approaches represents far more than the desire to alleviate suffering. It is part of the collective impulse to find forms for exploring subtle dimensions of relationship. Many people are attracted to work with healing energies simply because it teaches them how to be open to higher dimensions. When we needed to learn physical mastery, we engaged in sports. But for mastery of subtle dimensions of attention, we require other forms.

The various healing forms are a step toward mastery, but they do not necessarily bring us into obstructed relationship. Invariably, individuals learning these healing arts are seeking depth relationships, but they simultaneously acquire new identity on the basis of these skills. Once again, the underlying Principle of Relationship remains obstructed and unconscious. As we already have seen, the fundamental sense of separation remains unsurmounted because of this paradoxical split between healer and healed. And this paradox occurs in another dimension as well. It exists in the very premise that a higher energy is being called forth. Thus, rather than the energy being a product of freed attention, it is the product of identification with a symbol. This symbol may be called God, Universal Source, or whatever, and there is no doubt that turning one's attention toward It invites energy. But it also promotes a continued illusion that the Higher Source is something outside of present experience. This is the ancient separation of spirit and matter, heaven and earth.

Today I realize that my greatest responsibility is to remain myself. The potential for unobstructed relationship is a principle that exists at all times. In practice this is paradoxical; even trying to remain open places a limitation on the innate condition of availability. Thus it took me seven years after the initial awakening to fully realize that I am that very Principle of Relationship that is always available. It is not a question of effort or doing. It is a matter of awareness, of self-knowledge. It is simply a state of detachment akin to what Franklin Merrell-Wolff has written of as "high indifference." All my own concerns with being more available, guiding others correctly, doing no harm—along with any impulse to act as a result of these considerations—have nothing at all to do with the innate capacity to be unobstructedly present. The degree to which others can partake of the awakening or transformational function then becomes completely dependent on their availability. I can point others toward fuller awareness and invite deepened attention in them while I remain present, but that is all I do. What each individual receives from me (or anyone else) varies precisely in accordance with their own attention. If that attention is rooted in subject/object consciousness and they see me as friend, they receive friendship; see an egoist, and they are trapped in issues of control and distrust; see a healer, and they receive healings; and so on. But if the person's awareness even momentarily transcends all this, then our relationship can serve as a source for awakening. And I am lifted as well, for there is no richer relationship than when others join me in the Current and we together partake of the great mystery.

Thus today I would almost certainly not intervene as I did with Theodora. If the sense of urgency and anxiety that I felt with her is present, as it sometimes is, I simply remain attentive. Certainly this does not mean I am passive. I do introduce exercises and other activities that intensify the energy and carry each person toward the edge of themselves. But I have a deep faith in the wholeness of each individual and in the natural timing that carries us each to the threshold of radical possibility. Thus there is no urge to push. I let myself go deeper and deeper into whatever I am experiencing, until quite spontaneously I find myself speaking or taking some action. But, like Laura's singing, the words or the action just happen and are not attempts to fix or change the situation. It is simply a creative relationship with the moment and it can lead, as it did with the woman who was whirling, to virtually any possibility.

13 ✶ THE DOOR OF ALONENESS

When night comes and you too are dark,
lie down and be dark with a will.
And when morning comes and
you are still dark
stand up and say to the day with a will,
"I am still dark."
It is stupid to play a role with the night
and the day.
They would both laugh at you.

KHALIL GIBRAN

THE EMBODIMENT OF THE transformational impulse so that we grow increasingly conductive of the higher energy is a lifetime initiation and adventure. There is no simple way through this dilemma; there are no easy formulas, behaviors or values to follow. The possibilities for embodying are infinite. To be radically alive requires no formal religious belief or code of ethics. What is required is the continuous rediscovery of the consciousness that gave birth to these beliefs. To me this involves awareness, endless self-examination, creative relationship, and growing love for the truth of ourselves (which includes our uncertainty). Fundamental to all this is one basic principle: We will not arrive at a new level of integration purely on our own terms. We cannot be passive; we must have a sense of purpose and vision, a deeper understanding of consecration. But the impact of life upon us is always just as valid as the dreams we have and the efforts we make. We have to learn how to learn from ourselves in the very areas where no one has taught us how to learn.

This understanding moves out of a win/lose, success/failure modality and returns us to the immediacy of life as it is. It creates a dynamism in which the goal we successfully pursue simply opens us to new possibility, and the goal we unsuccessfully pursue equally brings us to new possibility. There is no judgment here, only attention, only an ever-deepening creative relationship to the immediacy of life.

To this flexible and fluid awareness, ultimate success or feeling good is irrelevant. Attention will always bring us to places we do not know and thus alter our relationship to what we think we know. It does not make us secure or invincible. This is not a mistake; it is the next level of paradox. Here we come upon the door of frustration, of impedance of our desires. This door leads to a whole new conception of life and a re-evaluation of who and what we are. Here even the success of our efforts inevitably shows an even larger picture that intensifies an ever-deepening sense of uncertainty. We stand in this discomfort, knowing that it is not wrong, knowing that it is not a sign of error but the tension of paradox. It is our inability to grasp the largeness of life that creates greater conductivity, and helps to bring us more and more toward the capacity for unobstructed relationship.

It is a rare individual, indeed, who consciously recognizes the value of this struggle and, rather than resisting discomfort, takes the transformational road of self-surrender, so that gradually the structure of outer consciousness relaxes and becomes spacious. It is a radical understanding to face this necessity, to see it, and then to yield one's life toward unknown possibility without any assurance of outcome. Here we face the door of aloneness, for once we begin down this road the motivation will come less and less from external sources.

In the beginning, when the path seems to lead toward greater consciousness, increased psychical powers and wisdom, its value seems more apparent and others walk the road with us. But gradually, as the way becomes more and more an existential relationship with the immediacy of ourselves, we begin to greet life and do our work from a space of growing emptiness. That emptiness easily becomes despair if we do not go through the door of aloneness.

We want confirmation from others. We want approval and recognition. We want to look around and see who else is taking similar steps so as to assure ourselves that we are on the right way. But eventually this has to be surrendered. The journey is no longer being made for anyone or for any purpose and we cannot know if it is the right way.

The journey of awakening has unfolded from understanding to understanding, from consecration to deepening consecration. Finally we stand alone, often surrounded by loved ones and admirers who feel the radiance of our deeper relationship to life and want to believe that it arises out of our certainty or the values our words seem to communicate. Often they are afraid of the pain that is also plain to see at times, for the deeper we have penetrated into aloneness, the greater the burden of life we carry. Our simplest contemplation yields the fullness of unknowing and, with this, there is the call of our heart to the upliftment and fulfillment of all life.

This is the door of aloneness. We stand in our own light, in rapport with what is, and there is no place to turn, for it is all the Living God. It is a state of integrity so demanding that again and again we ask, "Why me? How did I ever get here?" This is the radiance that is also anguish on the face of the saints. It is the point when our understanding has surpassed our capacity to choose for or against. We live out of the immediacy of ourselves, no longer able to know if we are loved or if we love, no longer able to act with conviction of rightness. We act from the wholeness of ourselves, afraid even that our prayers are a rejection of God's immanent truth. Truly we see that we have never really been in control of our lives, that every effort to gain control and to direct life has separated us from ourselves. And herein is great freedom, the peace of aloneness. We yield ourselves freely into life. There is no more looking back, no more wondering whether we are accepted or understood. We remain open, unobstructed, and at peace.

Few reach the door of aloneness except perhaps in the moments before death. And even then few are ready to embrace the transcendent possibilities of this moment if there has not been conscious preparation. And what is the preparation? Does it come through books, or teachers who have attained some deeper realization? In this, there is a Catch-22 once again. Why have we sought? What is it in our experience that we distrust, that we feel unable to meet? If we have sought them out, then we must think we know where we are going, and more often than not, this still keeps things on our terms. How can such an approach help us to meet the moment of crisis, of fundamental discontinuity where we must always stand alone? It is like a healing crisis induced by a homeopathic remedy; it is often worse than the disease and, rather than trust to such a crisis, many people will seek another doctor or take some medication to suppress it.

I know this dilemma intimately. It is the dilemma of "my will versus Thy will," of self-love versus the love of God and one's fellow humans. Ultimately it is the dilemma of trusting that the development of the separatist ego has gone far enough and that now it is time to begin the journey toward Union.

Whatever I have achieved since the awakening has not come in the ways I expected. If someone had told me years ago that my work would organically unfold until I would be living in close association with a group of people united by a common vision, I would have scoffed. Even now a part of me is never at peace with our association. Our relationship is both inspired and very difficult. The boundary between individual and group penetrates into every aspect of our lives, forcing each of us again and again to examine our consecration in light of the needs of our multifaceted natures. Contradiction is the order of the day. There is immense creativity and inspiration, and there is deep and often painful questioning. The adolescent in consciousness makes its demands, the Gandhi, its. The personal space is forever breached by the commitment to a collective process. In our own way, in the issues that face us as a group of individuals linked by a common vision, democracy meets socialism, capitalism meets communism.

Perhaps the major understanding that keeps me with this process is that it unfolded step by step, while all along I felt I was honoring what was most real in my consciousness. If the deepest introspection and inquiry lead us in a certain direction, then why, when things become difficult, do we assume we have been misguided? Throughout this process, inevitably we find ourselves questioning the wisdom and the very basis of our association. People have come and gone, but we finally realized that we have no real choice. Eventually we see that all choice leads to choicelessness, and it becomes unnecessary to keep moving from situation to situation on the basis of our ever-changing feelings and needs.

I know of nothing that creates multidimensional openness and transparency faster than truly to offer our lives to each other, consecrated in a higher understanding.

I have long pondered the statement, "No greater love has a man that he would lay down his life for his brother." This is often construed as the willingness to die for another, and I suppose this is a possible corollary of deep love. But dying for someone is a relatively rare circumstance and, when it occurs, probably happens quickly from an impulse rooted in strong conviction. It seems to me that this final impulsive act is far easier than to face one's consecration to self and others repeatedly in the immediacy of daily life. Moment by moment, from one interaction to the next, we face the choice to contract and disengage from relationship. Again and again we face the decision to place our own comfort or values above those of another, to let beliefs and habits rationalize our withdrawal from unobstructed communion. This is especially true when things are difficult. It is precisely when we are in the most pain that we want things on our terms. Yet, as long as we want life on our terms, the old dynamics will continue to dominate.

I believe that to lay down one's life for a brother or sister has nothing to do with physical dying and everything to do with egoic death. It is the laying down of our choice to withdraw from relationship, the laying down of our freedom to pursue our comfort or needs without deep sensitivity and contact with everyone who may be affected. When we finally realize that each of us is unique, that we each have similar and yet differing needs, that our expression of ourselves must have room for diversity, that the division of energies and resources cannot simply be on the basis of power, and we begin to accept the consequences of our own pleasure and freedom on the basis of this understanding, then we have begun to lay down our lives for our fellow humans. We must each pass through the door of aloneness, so that no matter what the collective values and beliefs, our own understanding holds us to a quality of relationship to life that says, "I will not withdraw from open, honest, vulnerable relationship. I will always listen, always seek to understand the point of view of the other person, and to the best of my ability I will accommodate him or her even as I consider myself." Then we are involved with a way of life wherein the love of God and of our neighbor transmutes the very substance of our humanity.

We may say that this is noble, that these are the higher values, that this is how one should be, but this makes such behavior just another ego-driven goal. Humanity's selfishness is simply the reflection of greater density, greater separation. It is the natural expression of relationship at a lower energy level. The higher expression is not better, or more true, or even wiser; it is simply inevitable. The love of God and of our neighbors are not the greatest of the Commandments because they are the ones we must obey. Rather, they are the ones we are already obeying, the ones that are the most fundamental, that underly the gradual awakening of Consciousness.

A commandment is not an injunction for behavior, it is an expression of Law. The service to life that such commandments seem to affirm is neither noble nor a sacrifice, it is simply the reflection of the quality of relationship that at once sustains a higher energy and is the reflection of it.

To love God is to embrace the Unknowable and Uncreated. It is not something we do, but that to which we are called by the very nature of consciousness. It is the timelessness that makes time possible, it is the immeasurable that makes all measurement possible. In every action, every invention, every discrimination, every new discovery, we are loving God. To love our neighbor as ourself is to enter unobstructed relationship. It is to be propelled into expanded consciousness by the dissolution of boundary between self and other. It is the most direct and powerful way to reach an expanded aliveness—the very nature of all human endeavor that is slowly bringing mankind into greater neighborliness. Slowly, from every corner of the earth, each and every individual begins to participate directly in everything we do and are.

To face the door of aloneness implies tremendous devotion and will. Devotion is a feeling state that allows a closer approximation to the Unknowable than is possible through reason or conviction. It arises naturally as more and more we see our inability to maintain an unobstructed relationship to life. We see our own frailty, the brittleness and impetuousness of our own psychical state, the conflicts that arise within us due to the differing needs of various aspects of our psyche, and this troubles us. Being troubled in this way produces humility, which is itself a devotional stance. We are at once attentive and yielded. We step forth into life with our dreams, but we are pierced by life's reality as well. We take the road that honors our convictions, but we are not the champion, not solaced by the worthiness of our cause. The subtle arrogance and self-substantiation inevitably residing within our efforts wounds us. And, no matter what we may do, we know that ultimately we do not know. Thus we begin to touch life with devotion.

Will is the strength of commitment and concentration to stay present in the immediate moment no matter what it requires. One does not overcome the less conductive energy patterns by turning away from adversity, or by losing interest when one no longer is enjoying the play. All the work brought forth in the seventies, by est and other groups that emphasized personal responsibility, was setting the stage for a level of maturity in which we begin the deeper work of letting ourselves be digested by life. Instead of being ripped apart in the transformational process, it is possible to commit oneself to a way of life that itself begins the weakening of the egoic control structure. Facing our own aloneness, we become obedient to the transformational impulse that is the deeper calling of our soul.

All deeper spiritual exploration understands the immense value of obedience that tests the commitment of an aspirant. The great mystic Padre Pio, who demonstrated stigmata for almost fifty years, was adored by his parishoners and visited by millions from all over the world. But when superiors in the church hierarchy ordered him to withdraw from leading mass and hearing confession, which was his great love and a major aspect of his service, he complied without hesitation or complaint.

Obedience is only possible when we ourselves realize that there is something fundamentally wiser that we can know only when we are finally choiceless. In our world, very few will ever put themselves in the situation of such choicelessness. Yet transformation asks this of us at a certain point in our development. It is not merely obedience to some outside authority; what we really obey is our understanding that at some point we can no longer have life on our terms. Once this is understood, then the question of choice, of free will, is really the question of one's deepest relationship to life. It is here that one sees his consecration and, seeing it, has the choice to take that road that empowers the more superficial aspirations or the deepest. Because discerning one from the other is not easy, the very exercise of will is no longer a simple process of staying with something until its natural conclusion. There is no conclusion, and the will we must access to go deeper into being is not the same as the will that we can develop by pushing against life for our personal attainment. It is the actual giving over of ourselves to each other, in a way in which we cannot win in the egoic sense, that empowers the possibility for realizing a higher will.

(I do not mean to be absolutist in these remarks. I am all too familiar with my own limits, the points in my personal life where I simply need to turn away and rest. But I do this with an eye to balance and an understanding that, if I am to be sufficiently relaxed so that I may stand in unobstructed relationship with people, the body and other levels of my being must be given the space they require.)

It is a basic misconception in the Western mind that the ego must be eradicated to attain enlightenment. This is not the case, for if the ego were to be truly destroyed we could not function in the world and our enlightenment would be meaningless. The ego is not something evil or archaic; it is not a *thing* at all. It is the basis of subject/object consciousness, the locus of identity necessary for the development of self-consciousness. It is only because the ego becomes passive or inactive—not because it is destroyed—that one can enter the larger consciousness.

Everyone knows this experience in varying degrees. It is that state in sports or lovemaking where you are completely aware, but you are not controlling what is happening. For this brief period the egoic self is inactive. The proof of this is that, the moment you think "I'm doing great" or the moment you consciously try to affect what is happening, the magic stops. While one is in this state, the energies of the old self are subsumed within the energy of the larger, freer beingness. These refreshing moments of balance between doing and not-doing, between will and surrender, are in a sense mini-realizations analogous to mystical realization but on a far smaller, less multidimensional scale. Thus it becomes clear that the transformational process is not about destroying the ego, but about learning to let the ego become passive in a growing range of life involvement, so that we thereby remain conductive of higher levels of aliveness.

✻

The development of self-mastery is tremendously helped if one has a relationship with someone, whether living or not, who models a higher possibility. (This seems to contradict what I said earlier about the Catch-22 of such relationships. Actually, it does not; I merely invite us into the other side of the paradox.) It is not necessary for the model to tell you what to do. In fact, the best teachers never do. Of far greater value is that they become an object of love. There is nothing that quickens the transformational impulse more fully than to fall in love with someone whose very being acts as an inspiration to know oneself and not turn away at the times of great trial. But in the end we each must stand alone—and with no guarantees. No matter how deep our models have gone, during the time of unknowing it is not they, but the love and faith we ourselves have mastered, that is the key element.

They may symbolize that love, may even be the reason that we have opened our hearts so deeply. Undoubtedly they will have contributed immensely to our induction into greater aliveness. Their energy may even seem to be present at the moments of greatest trial. But if they are still present as objects of our consciousness, then the realization has not dissolved beyond symbolic awareness and reached its fullest fruition.

An example of this is the story of the great Indian saint Sri Ramakrishna, who had worshiped the Mother deeply. He had learned to see Her in such detail and with such devotion that She became the All to him. At any moment he would swoon into transcendent bliss filled with the vision of the Mother. Finally a yogi told him that he would have to release his beloved Mother if he were to go deeper, and Ramakrishna was very disturbed. "But how?" he asked. The naked saddhu picked up a shard of pottery and ground it between his eyes. Suddenly, the ecstatic vision of the Mother was gone and Ramakrishna attained a higher level of realization.

While one who has realized can act as an energetic template up to a point, at the time of realization we must stand alone. Here the love we have learned in relationship to the inspirational teachers whom we have elevated to highest meaning within our consciousness becomes their greatest gift to us. At the time of fundamental discontinuity of consciousness, it is this love in its essence—not as devotion or identification with a specific individual—that expedites the movement to the higher dimension. Afterwards, these beings may once again be models of inspiration and stability who help us determine the direction we wish to take with the new energies. But it is ultimately our capacity to pass through the door of aloneness and stand in our own light that determines the depth to which we will be able to share our realization, and the originality and appropriateness to our world of what we have to share.

14 * RESONATION CIRCLE AND THE SACRED MEDITATION

Softly falling inward,
    a field of warmth gathers,
    hands electric,
    breath alive,
    cycling awareness,
links inner and outer.
I and Thee.

And there the other waits
    and is myself.

We gather in silence,
    palpable, magnetic,
    ancient, timeless communion.
Knowing and not knowing,
Knowing now and forever
    but not here in particular.
Infinite interpretations,
Wonder is enough.
I rest with this. . . .
                                    RICHARD MOSS

THE POTENTIAL OF CONSCIOUSNESS in human beings will always be experienced individually, but the capacity for embodying will grow equally from the collective body as from the individual. The higher states of consciousness are not the property or the attainment of any one person. Such states grow in a field of consciousness that is ultimately comprised of all of us and more.

To begin to generate the unified energy in my work I use two basic modes: the resonation circle and the Sacred Meditation. Both ultimately involve the same quality of attention, but the resonation circle is not as formally ritualized. Visually, the resonation circle appears as a group of people sitting or standing and lightly holding hands. Everyone is asked to give their inward attention to the deepest sense of Being they can intuit. The word *resonation* speaks to the process of summating and amplifying the energies of individuals into a more coherent or unified quality.

Implicit in resonation is the willingness to release whatever is occupying our personal space (no matter how compelling) and let go into Being. At the usual ego-bound levels of consciousness, we are each so out of phase with one another that, when we engage at this level, we have a virtual cacophony of energies that tends to cancel out a higher possibility. It is impossible to summate the energy. It is like a team made up of stars who play only for themselves. But the unified energy of even the most ordinary group of people far exceeds the energy of single individuals, no matter what their caliber. In letting go of personal preoccupations, there is a natural tendency to fall toward a more universal dimension. The vibration of this space begins to build upon itself. It takes no special capability. All that is required is a little time and the willingness to trust in the deeper level.

The effect of a resonation circle is that each person begins to feel his or her body rapidly becoming energized. For some it feels like warmth, for others silence or peacefulness. There may also be an intensification of previously low levels of discomfort until, all of a sudden, one's back is screaming. For this reason it is advisable to sit as comfortably as possible. The amplified energy alters awareness and, under the guidance of a person who has some familiarity with these spaces, a group of people can quickly be led into exploring whole new dimensions of perception. The heightened energy soon dissipates after the resonation circle is broken, but I have observed that there is always a residual effect that is not immediately lost. In my conferences, resonations last from a few minutes to a half-hour or longer. They occur at the beginning and the end of every session and whenever the centering of awareness is desired. In addition we resonate before all meals. I have explored conferences in which the resonation circle is the only activity. The effect is profound, and after a few days everyone has moved into a heightened awareness. Over time the energy of the resonation comes into harmony faster and faster. In the period immediately following a very deep resonation, the sense of time slows down, the senses are intensified, and it becomes very easy to enter into deep rapport with other people. However, if the resonation has been prolonged and cumulative over a period of days, a natural reactive defensiveness sets in. People experience psychical irritability and a desire to close off or protect themselves from others. It is like having had too much sunlight and then stepping into a warm shower; it feels hot. The deeper energetic of the collective body begins to stress the individual boundary. At this point, we begin the remarkable exploration of the interface between individuality and collectivity. It is also an exploration of the discipline required to sustain higher and higher energy levels. Thus it is an acceleration of the phenomenon of universal heightening that is lifting mankind, and an opportunity to begin consciously to explore at the edge of an evolutionary process.

As a leader of conferences and a public speaker who is always conscious of uniting my being with the group energy (as opposed to didactic instruction), I am invariably in an energy level far higher than is natural to the egoic me. In fact, it was the enticement of this higher energy that initially caused me to build my life around the exploration of group energies. However, this has not been easy. It has required steady and ever-deepening disciplined awareness. I now look at everything I do in terms of its effect upon consciousness. Does this activity allow a natural balance with the prolonged exposure to the higher energies? My life is given over to a body that is far larger than my personal sphere and I find both bodies must be honored in different ways.

The collective body is inspirational, impersonal, visionary, able to transmute every personal concern, and gifted with exceptional powers of rapport both with people and the so-called inanimate environment. It is a high-frequency energy, a very high, fine note that burns the substance of the personal bodymind. In most traditions the spiritual body is valued over the ordinary man. In the work of Shankara, one of the great Vedantists, the body was regarded as "a sack of dung and bones." The orientation of the Christian saints was not dissimilar. In contrast, Walt Whitman's realization carried a very different quality. He sang the ordinary man just as eloquently as the higher counterpart. I find that my own orientation is more like Whitman's. The higher energy is always evoked in me when I am with people focused around some common interest. But I maintain balance by not valuing this over the ordinary experiences of life. By taking time to walk in the mountains, to do manual labor that brings a sweat and tones the muscles, and by accepting without complaint those periods that feel so grounded that there is no sense of ever having known the higher, I celebrate the ordinary man.

Yet few people would have any real way of appreciating either of these orientations without some direct experience of the different levels of energy involved. This can be invited by entering into resonance in a simple gathering of friends. By asking everyone to link hands and simultaneously turn toward the deeper sense of "I Am," the energy will accelerate and become coherent. All we have to do is meet in this way several times a week and we begin to fulfill our evolutionary potential. It is a process of mutual healing and empowerment of deeper intuition, increased sensitivity and At-Onement with people and our world, telepathic rapport and increased life force. We need not surround this relating with any kind of dogma. It is enough to let go of all personal concerns—that is, release our attention from the content of consciousness and make that radical gesture of intuition that carries us into the space of Consciousness itself.

Simply sit like this with your friends. If you get uncomfortable, shift your position or, if you are so inclined, begin to enter a creative relationship with the discomfort and use it as a doorway to deeper awareness. The resonation circle has no rules, no right way. It is an exploration that itself is a profound teacher if we can free expectations and, over a period of time, observe what happens.

THE SACRED MEDITATION

It is said that you can find the universe in a grain of sand if you know how to look.

In my unfoldment nothing has been of greater importance than a ritual of relating that I have come to call the Sacred Meditation. It is, to me, the quintessential process of inquiry, for it involves what in words sounds absurd: an equal relationship to oneself, God, and another person simultaneously. It is a process that so alters one's usual level of consciousness that it is virtually an exploration at the boundary where subject/object consciousness breaks down and the individual stands in a new dimension at the very edge of the Divine. Yet, like anything else, the depth of possibility depends on the availability and commitment with which the experience is embraced. I often say that a person who understands the extraordinarily vulnerable nature of transformational inquiry and practices the Sacred Meditation three or four times a week will be radically transformed. Yet there are no guarantees. There are potent spiritual channels and healers who enter into a similar space many times a day for years and years but are not awakened by these relationships. I suspect they do not grasp the process of conscious attention.

All expansion of consciousness, all spirituality, must ground in the human scene—in our capacity to live, touch, communicate and share together. In this sense, relationship is the beginning and the end of my work. But it is not simply relationship in the popular sense of fulfilling the need for companionship and intimacy. I am speaking of the domain of unobstructed relationship, relationship that literally reveals the universe in a grain of sand, or God in our neighbor. This is a level of relationship that changes the way we walk upon this earth. It humbles and at the same time hallows the very substance of our humanity.

From the moment I begin working with a group of people, it is my intent that together we will reach a level of energy where we touch this richness of relationship. I know of little else in life that is more inspiring, that turns our inner contemplation toward the miracle of life and our consecration toward the wholeness of ourselves and humanity. Usually this state is touched during the carefully choreographed ritual of energetic relationship that I have come to call the Sacred Meditation.

Visualize two people (it could be more); one is lying on a table, eyes closed, relaxed. The other(s) standing near the table are in deep concentration, their hands hovering over the supine person touching lightly or not at all. During a conference, each person experiences this first as a receiver and then is taught how to actively engage the consciousness in this way.

The evolution of the Sacred Meditation began for me in 1975 with Brugh Joy. Brugh had rediscovered the ancient process of energy sharing. He had taught himself to activate his consciousness in a particular way and allow an energy to flow from his hands. He had learned to become sensitive to the energy field around the body and began to share energy with people following a pattern that he called the Spiral. He taught this as a kind of therapy called energy balancing. The Spiral was a way to make consecutive contact with each of the chakras, starting from the heart at the center of the chest and progressing to the solar plexus, the high chest, the spleen, the lower abdomen, the throat, the base of the spine, the forehead, the knees, the top of the head (crown), the feet, and, finally, a space above the head representing transpersonal energies (see diagram). I have adapted this pat-

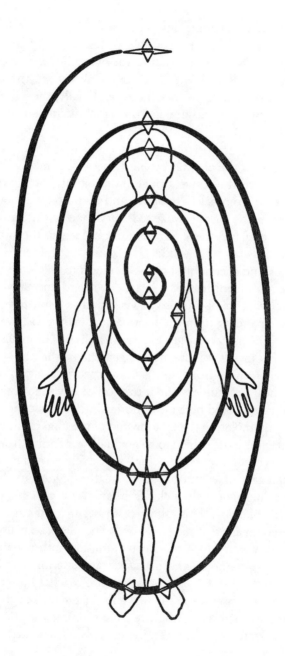

tern to include an opening, an intuitive sharing, and a closing. Once the spiral is opened according to this pattern, the hands are intuitively placed over specific areas of the body. The opening pattern can be considered a space of invocation, the intuitively guided time, a period of deepening. Finally, the pattern is reversed in a phase of closure and the ritual interaction is completed.

I consider the Spiral orientation a unique way to approach the subtle energies of the chakras primarily because it takes the emphasis away from the conventional understanding of Kundalini as a movement from below to above and then down. In fact, in my experience, the energy awakened everywhere at once and followed no particular pattern. Furthermore, as I regard the awakening process, it is far more valid to think in spherical terms than in the linear and hierarchical terms common to the older traditions. The movement from the heart downward and upward in an ever-widening spiral can also be visualized as a sphere of consciousness expanding from the heart. Some mystics believe that the heart is the primary origin and resting place of ultimate consciousness. For myself, it is important to emphasize that the "heart" is not the anatomical heart, nor is it any specific location in the body. The heart as I understand it transcends any such considerations and is only used here metaphorically, and as a conceptual focus for contemplating the relationship of the chakras in a new way. By imagining the sphere to be gradually expanding from the heart—the symbolic center of being—we can envision a far more dynamic process of evolution in which the higher and lower centers are simultaneously included in an ever-expanding realm of dynamic polarities. This allows us to begin contemplating a spiritual unfoldment that reconciles body and mind, sexuality and spirituality, power and love, reason and intuition, rather than forcing us to relegate one or another aspect to superior or inferior valuation. In this sense, and it is the essence of what I teach, the unfoldment of consciousness is not a linear progression but an expansion of the sphere, so that we are sustaining a relationship of dynamic equilibrium between increasingly more material and subtle universal forces.

Beyond these considerations, I find that the whole notion of an esoteric anatomy of subtle energies has little importance. Earlier it was important precisely because "I" needed the assurance that what I was doing had some rational basis. But today the notion of energetic relationship stands upon much more mystical ground. Why be concerned with an esoteric anatomy when it is not the doing, but the very *essence*, of relationship that is most sacred? Far too often, fascination with the chakras becomes a distraction for basic consciousness, which now begins to develop a diagnosis and pathology of the subtle body. Once again we have devised a new mental litany for separating ourselves from each other and from the immediacy of our experience. While understanding the subtle body has some value, ultimately no one really knows what a chakra is, or what is truly appropriate or healthy at this level. Thus I feel we are wiser to continue the exploration deeper into our own being and into life's ever-present wholeness, letting the understanding of the subtle dimensions arise as a consequence. Such understanding is wisdom and not a distraction. I am reminded of the injunction, "Seek first the Kingdom of Heaven and all else will be added unto you."

To this day I have never really varied from the spiral pattern in the outer form of the ritual because my medical background had already taught me the tremendous importance of consistency when learning to develop subtle sensitivity. We were taught to approach a patient from the same side and to progress through our examination in a specific pattern. The effect of this consistency was to eliminate some of the variables that our own body posture and vagaries of mood might impose upon the examination. For example, if impatience or self-importance goad one to randomly alter the process of examination, the possible alteration in observed data might originate from the patient or from one's own attitude. Consistency tends to counteract some of this. A retired surgeon, who had trained in South America and taught anatomy, told me something that I have never forgotten. He had trained before the advent of electro- and echo-cardiograms. Even stethoscopes then were just tapered tubes. The surgeon described to me how his cardiology professor insisted that he listen to the sounds of the heart in a specific pattern. He said his teacher would place his ear on the patient's chest and move it an inch at a time while remaining totally concentrated. Afterwards, the cardiologist would have a very accurate impression, not only of the heart, but also of the patient's kidneys and of his or her emotional life. Here, perhaps for the first time, I was hearing of a situation analogous to finding the universe in a grain of sand.

By remaining consistent in my approach, what began as a medically oriented interaction gradually transformed into the Sacred Meditation. When I maintained the ritual, more and more of my own internal reality, as well as the uniqueness of each person with whom I shared, would begin to stand out against the screen of consciousness. The rigidity of the form enabled the subtlety of the experience to appear against the underlying consecration of unconditional love.

The very presumption that the other individual *required* something, and that I might be the noble servant or channel, was the first ruse of the ego revealed. It became clear that the energy is always present and that the ritual was nothing but an excuse to engage a level of attention where this energy is more available to our awareness. To stand with another human being is to be the active pole of a Principle of Relationship for which they are the receptive pole. The valuing of relative identity was (is) simply meaningless. Gradually the whole process became worship.

Sacred Meditation as worship undoes our relative and somewhat illusory personal identities. It is this profound shift in context from interactions where the relative identities remain unquestioned (healer/healed, therapist/client) that is the leap of understanding of the Sacred Meditation. It is not therapy or energy balancing as much as it is worship. I believe it is an understanding crucial to our time. We keep accessing energy through the relativity of our roles, while all along there is an even deeper level of relationship ever awaiting us.

The Sacred Meditation is an inquiry into the illusion of oneself while in the presence of another, precisely because it is this illusion that makes the other person separate from us and limits the energy of relationship.

Gradually, each time I entered the Sacred Meditation I saw that there was really no person with whom "I" was sharing energy. How did I know they were there? I saw them, touched them, smelled them. But consider this: When you fall asleep, is the person next to you still there? Yes, you say. But how do you know? The answer is an inference. But, from another point of view, it may be more accurate to say that at precisely the moment we wake up and realize that we ourselves *are*, simultaneously the other is also there. In other words, the moment we enter subject/object consciousness, we experience the "I Am" of personal consciousness, and all the objects—whether purportedly material or psychical—come into existence (for us) at precisely the same time. The person with whom we are sharing energy is an object of our own relative consciousness, and when we trick ourselves into thinking that we are doing something to them, we delude ourselves. The only relationship we can really have is to the quality of our own attention to Consciousness Itself.

Thus we begin to see the door of the Sacred Meditation. It is a process of giving total attention to the immediacy of what we are experiencing—not spacing out into sensations, energetic phenomena or personal fantasies and thus losing the other person as an object of conscious attention. We enter into our experience, which includes this person, and as we sublime our own experience of being (turning our attention deeper and deeper to the infinite mystery that is God or the great Void), the very energy that unites us with the "other" sublimes them as well. They feel themselves being lifted into another dimension. In fact is is possible, if one is capable of tremendous attention, to become so At-One with the moment in the presence of another that they can be lifted to a state of temporary Realization (Samadhi). I have had this experience with quite a number of people.

But there is a further consideration before the Sacred Meditation can be fully appreciated. Just as the other person becomes an object at the moment we enter into subject/object consciousness, so too this is the way that we know God. Again ask the question, "Is God present when I am in deep sleep?" The answer, through inference, is yes. But it is a somewhat meaningless answer because it is not our experience. God becomes a Something of our immediate concern and attention at precisely the moment that we become something to ourselves. Thus, the Sacred Meditation calls for a radical jump of intuition wherein we simply engage the assumption that what we are experiencing (i.e. the totality of our awareness, which includes the person with whom we are sharing the ritual and all our sensations, hopes, thoughts and distractions) is none other than the living Divine. At that moment we are devotionally engaging our awareness in profound reverence while simultaneously embracing the other person as part of our field of consciousness. Going deeper, it is as though we are turning inside out. Rather than interacting with or reacting to what we are experiencing, we are simply falling deeper and deeper into it. There can come a moment when awareness is a single unified field of attention that seems charged with living presence. One's hands may seem to be on fire (for it is with the energy of the hands that we are creating a bridge of felt attention that links us to the other person).[1] The mind will be so still that a thought will flow through and we can observe it as though it were a two-dimensional comic strip balloon. The breath becomes so slowed and stilled and the very movement of the breath itself seems to transport the whole environment into a living flux. In reaching this state of unified awareness there may be periods of physical discomfort, but once the attention unifies, the body simply glows in a benediction of well-being.

Clearly the Sacred Meditation is precisely what its name implies, a state of deep meditation and worship. But it is a meditation grounded in relationship. The person with whom we are sharing is alive within us. Their slightest sigh causes explosions of sensation throughout our being. In the Sacred Meditation, there is no need to touch the person; in fact, touch can be an obstruction at first, for it so strongly cues consciousness to the sense of the other as separate and outside. Thus, without actual physical contact, we find ourselves standing in what for most people is the deepest state of meditation and simultaneously the deepest level of communion with another person that we have ever known. Not a word has outwardly passed, and yet here we are in profound communion. We notice that the slightest oscillation in at-

---

[1] See "The Energy Embrace" in my earlier book *How Shall I Live* (Celestial Arts, 1985), which includes a step-by-step exercise for entering this state. You can also obtain audio cassettes in which various inductions are shared.

tention causes an immediate effect on the energy field and our state of consciousness. We may have a sudden thought that deepens the sense of relationship and at precisely the same moment the person on the table trembles or begins to cry. The slightest turn of a hand can feel as if we are caressing the universe. The sense of aliveness in our body is immensely heightened and refined.

EXPLORING THE PRINCIPLE OF RELATIONSHIP

When I became aware of the enormous blessing I experienced by sharing with people in this way, I wanted others to have a similar opportunity. To make this state more readily available, I wait until a point in the conference when everyone has reached a higher energy. Then it is easier to free attention and move into the new mode. To convey this dimension, my voice and presence are more potent that any particular words. The breath is very important as part of the shift in attention. By breathing in and out of one's field of awareness in a relaxed but focused way, that field begins to be charged with subtle presence or feeling. Here it becomes possible to sense a connectedness with another that is beyond ordinary awareness. It is not unlike the sense of connectedness in the post-coital phase of lovemaking where lovers fall into each other and something far larger.

There are many ways to introduce this exploration. Ordinarily, people are taught how to share energy by imagining that the Higher Source simply awaits them. By calling upon the Source and visualizing it flowing into oneself and down the arms and out the hands into another person, anyone can learn to channel energy for healing or balancing. This can be combined with invocations of various colors or frequencies of energy. There is something so inspirational about any relationship entered into with the acknowledgement of a higher dimension, that with just a little preparation most people can be taught to touch this new level of experience. They can feel powerful currents of energy flowing through them or, occasionally, see the auric field around the body. However, to me the experience of the energy is not as important as the quality of attention in which we engage it and this depends on our consecration. The more subtle the consecration, the more "sacred" the relationship seems, and ultimately the more transformational is its effect on the meditator.

I found myself feeling uncomfortable when I first began to teach energy sharing. Who was I kidding? To share in this way with another human being was simply the greatest privilege of life. I was receiving the gift of giving while the other was giving the gift of receiving. To elevate myself to healer or teacher in order to enter this relationship was somehow dishonest. And to teach others to do the same is just as mistaken. Thus, while I am a teacher at one level, the Sacred Meditation is a gift, not a therapy. While healing may well come as a result of the energy that is generated, the real relationship is Lover to Beloved. The Sacred Meditation is teaching us the Principle of Relationship, the fact that when two or more are gathered and turn their attention to Consciousness Itself (or to any concept—God, the Christ—symbolizing the space out of which all experience arises), we are at once suffused with aliveness and we fill each other with a living benediction.

The Sacred Meditation as a ritual practiced regularly could change our ideas about what it means to be human. It brings us to the great adventure of consciousness grounded in relationship to all humanity. Unlike many Eastern meditative forms that turn toward the inner or subjective pole of consciousness and thus are very hard to integrate into outer life, the Sacred Meditation engages both inner and outer. The outer is symbolized by the other person (our neighbor who is ourself) and the inner is our whole field of awareness, the Divine, the Uncreated and Unknowable. There is something immensely empowering about a meditation that gathers people together in this way.

In fact, when we consider the ways in which awakening is being brought forward today, there are essentially three forms. The first is spontaneous, as was my own awakening in Lone Pine. But this is relatively rare and cannot be approached by any action of one's own. The second way is by induction from an awakened person to another. This is the way of the Guru, who bestows Shakti upon the disciple, but it has several intrinsic limitations. First of all, we are still involved in projecting a special ability upon the other and an acceptance of a subordinate position on oneself. This is not to deny the function of the awakened teacher and the value of true and mutual devotion between student and teacher. But see the exclusiveness in this, and the assumption that only special relationships can empower the higher energy. If this is so, then the few awakened beings in the world today have a lot of work to do. In point of fact, that an awakened individual should see himself or herself as having to do this would indicate a fairly circumscribed degree of realization.

But there is a third way that involves the Principle of Relationship (that quality of energy invoked by the clarity of our attention one to the other), and it is embodied in the Sacred Meditation. When we enter the Sacred Meditation, we sublime the very idea that we are or are not awakened. No longer is there a teacher or a student, a healer or healed. No longer are there only special circumstances when the higher energy is available. Now we see that it is the very quality of our relationships that have the potential to invite an awakening of consciousness. *Finally, there is nothing to give or receive except love.*

The Sacred Meditation generalizes to all relationships. It is a powerful tool with which we can explore at the edge of our being. It is a tool in which we are at once Lover and Beloved. We are not above/below, better/worse, than anyone else. The most improbable individual judged by outer consciousness may be the very one with whom we touch the most magnificent level of aliveness.

By exploring the Sacred Meditation we begin to enter into the grand adventure of the higher human possibilities. We are inviting the awakening of new dimensions of consciousness and new powers. But we are inviting them from the basis of a fundamental equality and in a gesture of true humility in which the highest energy does not come by claiming some special role or some special need that gives us power to do something to others. Why must we wait until someone is ill to give ourselves permission for deeper communion? There is a far finer energy that carries us closer to the real moment of aliveness when we are nothing and everything with our fellow human.

Lover and Beloved, this is the new humanity. I laugh when I think of how much we pay physicians and therapists when, in fact, every one of them acknowledges how enriching it can be to share with an open client. One might well ask those who are authentically drawn to healing and service to pay for the privilege of being able to enter into communion with so many people! Yet all of us have this opportunity. It should not be, and hopefully will not be, co-opted forever by therapists, healers, and spiritual servants. We can all awaken to the profundity that resides in our relationship to each other. It is not something that has to do with training or intelligence as we currently measure it. To develop attention and awareness is the free inheritance of all human beings. The Nobel Peace Prize could be given to the bus driver who maintains an open and unobstructed awareness equally as authentically as it is given to the saintly helpers who have become the symbols of goodness in our world. Humanity needs its symbols, but in the elevation of special people the image of service and holiness is co-opted by the sense of *doing*, rather than recognizing that *being* is the deeper service. We forget that relationship exists in everything, and that an open person is uplifted by the attention of others just as much as he or she uplifts. Any world we build, we will build together, and its greatest aliveness will occur when the leaders are servants and the servants, leaders.

15 ∗   SEXUAL ENERGY AND THE CHALLENGE OF INTIMACY

People who have not been in Narnia sometimes think that a thing cannot be good and terrible at the same time.

C.S. LEWIS

THROUGHOUT MUCH OF HUMAN HISTORY sex and childbearing were regarded as sacred functions, implying great responsibility to oneself, one's mate, and one's social group. People were brought up to approach these functions with maturity and sensitivity. Among the Mbuti tribe of Africa, sexual exploration is encouraged as a natural part of adolescence. Yet pregnancy is considered the responsibility of an adult. Thus, while a great deal of premarital sexual exploration occurs, it is always carefully and voluntarily controlled. Pregnancy before one is ready to assume adult responsibilities is very rare.[1] The dangers of sexual license as well as sexual repression were understood long before human beings evolved so-called modern psychological understandings. But imbuing each generation with the understanding of sex as a sacred function implies a highly coherent socialization process sensitive to the stages of individual human development. It also implies an understanding of the varieties of

---

[1] Turnbull, Colin, *The Human Cycle*, Simon and Schuster, 1983.

individual sensibility and wisdom about the needs and potentialities of society as a whole.

In our modern world, this overview is sketchy if it exists at all. At best, our approach to sexuality is splintered into the particular values and beliefs of distinct religious and ethnic subgroups. Ironically, in the midst of all this confusion we have somehow come to believe that there is a proper way to approach sex, with no real consensus as to what it might be. Our religious traditions suggest one direction, but their dogma often create more repression than understanding. This propels many people into rebellion. In our society we rarely have a genuine relationship to our own sexuality. We are always in reaction. We constantly evaluate ourselves against the customs of our particular social sphere and the shifting emphasis of media-created "reality." We refuse to face the psychological and existential ambiguity that has always surrounded sexuality and has deepened since the advent of religions grounded in man's transcendence. Never is the dilemma of sexuality placed in a broader transformational context where our individual capacity to regulate, heighten and refine our sexual expression is inseparable from the process of maturity and awakening consciousness.

In fact, when we look at the great lives, we see that virtually everyone has had to struggle with the issue of sexuality. This struggle is our birthright, but it requires far more than adherence to dogmatic beliefs. It demands intelligent and sensitive inquiry into oneself, one's relationships and, above all, one's consecration to life. In short, the profundity of sexuality has been unconsciously given away and we are energetically diminished because of it. Perhaps as a result of this, sexually transmitted diseases are becoming a primary force for the containment of the sexual impulse in our world today. This suggests the degree to which sexuality has lost its connection to the health and vitality of society.

As we try to understand what has happened to sexuality, our dominant impression is of fragmentation and disconnection. There is sexual pleasure, there is relationship, there is conception, there is family, and each of these has come to be regarded as a separate aspect of life that we can volitionally choose or inhibit. Through the use of chemicals and mechanical devices designed to prevent unwanted birth and overpopulation, we have unwittingly separated the sexual impulse from conception, from committed relationships, from family, and thus from society. With modern medicine, childbirth has also become routine, losing the great transformational force that it once carried for all people, and for women in particular. This means we have more or less separated sexuality from human nature. We can explore sexual energy in a way that it has never been explored before, but we have created a new kind of sexual intimacy, an intimacy in which the individual has no sense of relationship to a world beyond his or her own body.

*

The capacity to explore sexuality without the consequences of birth represents one of the greatest examples of humanity's ability to interfere with life force and perturb the human energy system both on an individual and a collective level. In this case, the perturbing does not obviously affect our health. While modern contraceptives have potent effects, we do not experience them in this way. We take the pill or injection, implant the device, cut the tubes, and go about our business with very little awareness that anything has changed. But something has been profoundly changed. It is a change in what can be, what can happen to us and through us. It is a change in our relationship to time and space and to future probabilities, and there is an implicit reordering in our energies. Most significantly, it is a change in how we establish interconnectedness with others, how the energies of our personal consciousness interact with our collective nature.

The generalized freeing of sexual energy from its natural consequences results in the capacity to claim sex as an aspect of one's individuality. This is commonly termed sexual "liberation." It is one of the most important changes in the human condition in the past hundred years, and it might be one of the greatest if it were accompanied by an equivalent awareness of life's wholeness.

Liberated sexuality, in my observation, often represents an exaggeration of genital sexuality. As such, the so-called liberated man or woman often represses the need and capacity for deeper relationship, thus inhibiting a higher potential of consciousness. The transient comfort of sexual release becomes a relief valve for lessening existential tensions that really require a deepened awareness and self-transcendence. By dissipating energy in this way, there is a diminished ability to enter a fuller consciousness. On the other hand, if sexual liberation refers to a greater sense of personal autonomy and the capacity to inquire into and take charge of one's own sexual destiny, it can be a valuable accompaniment to the adventure of consciousness.

SEX AND THE PLAY OF ATTENTION

As awareness grows, sexuality changes. It becomes richer and yet also more controversial. As energy is freed into radiant attention, the fantasies that surround the sexual process (and life in general) begin to lose their power to initiate behavior. Like the other contents of consciousness, these fantasies are simply witnessed. If we consciously decide to act on them, they can be pursued to sexual encounter, but we also clearly see that sex, while entirely natural, is no different from any other behavior. Sex becomes a choice, a profound choice, and how we make that choice tremendously influences our awareness. Only through awareness can we begin to master sexual energy, and this is neither a question of squeezing more pleasure from the experience nor of becoming celibate. It requires examining the whole arena of sexuality in relation to our consecration to life and then observing what we learn by entering the sexual space with alertness, openness, and honesty.

Consider. Is it possible to have genital sex when the mind is empty? Can we have sexual fantasies without simultaneously moving the energy into a sexual mode? Can there be personal intimacy that does not start as a fantasy? And if it does, at what point do we decide that the fantasy is to be incarnated into some form of behavior? From the opposite point of view, can we now observe the free energy of attention condensing into sexual, emotional or other dynamics?

For myself, I am constantly observing the play of attention. A sexual fantasy causes a condensing of the energy in the pelvis and a general excitation and tension within the body. It is as though I have moved from a spacious and more subtle body into a smaller, more intensely experienced, body. The focus is invariably upon the person who is the object of the fantasy. In contrast, when I am simply sitting in my natural attention or contemplating the life of an inspired person such as Lincoln, Martin Luther King, or Simone Weil, the energy becomes vast and silent. Sometimes there is an aching in the chest and the focus of thought is broadly abstracted toward life and humanity on a vaster level. There is no judgment or preference for either state, only an observation of how the energy moves as attention shifts.

There is a very interesting exploration for anyone who deeply appreciates sex, yet wonders if there is another way to find intimate communion with one's lover. Experiment with what happens as you come together with a partner and allow the sense of sexual energy to build. But before reaching the point of orgasm, allow all fantasies or thoughts about what comes next to dissolve away. Stay completely present for the sense of communion and energy, but as soon as your attention personalizes the energy (the sense of "my" body and "his" or "her" body indicates that one's attention is personalized), let the attention diffuse beyond this. We are highly—perhaps instinctively—conditioned to express the energy genitally once it becomes "sexual." But from another perspective what we call sexual energy is actually a mode of attention. If we free our attention out of the genital dynamic and remain present for the energy, something else begins to happen.

Exciting sexual energy and then freeing the attention so that it is no longer personalized is one of the ancient techniques of Taoist and tantric yoga. We can learn to touch in and out of arousal and then relax into an open quality of attention, a sense of consciousness-as-energy in which the I/you begins to dissolve. This is not a practice to be entered casually or aggressively, for it begins to break down age-old boundaries between states of consciousness. Traditionally, it has been the goal of yoga to gradually shed these boundaries in a highly disciplined way. To do so, yoga creates heightened energy through specific practices involving mental concentration, body posture, chanting, prayer, and selfless work.

Sex, obviously, is one of the natural conditions that excites energy. Therefore using sexual energy for this purpose has been an aspect of certain yogic practices. But, yogic practices removed from their larger context can be very dangerous. Only those who are seriously committed to transformation and have a deep commitment to relationship—a willingness to realize the other as Divine, and simultaneously to let go of the person as an object of need—should consider the exploration of this area. Power tripping with this exploration (for once one learns to enter this area, one can powerfully induct one's partner into whole new dimensions of sexual ecstasy) is dangerous. One must be prepared for the possible accelerated alteration of one's existing life pattern, including the relationship, the very basis of which may be threatened as the energy heightens. The heightening of sexual energy (energy in general) cannot be safely held in the crucible of ego-based power. Yet there is an intrinsic tendency to link egoic power (adequacy and inadequacy) with sex. If our underlying motive for heightening energy is personal power and inflation, the resulting deflation during a transformative opening can be terrible indeed. As with the transformational process in general, we must be prepared to carry the energy into a consecration large enough to give it full expression.

At a certain point in the early stages of opening, we translate energetic sensitivity into sexual attraction. I have often experienced how a woman who has opened energetically and is not even considering sex becomes immensely stimulating to many men who are unable to recognize the energy except as a sexual force. This is also true for men who, as they open, become very evocative for women. Thus there is an awkward phase where indulging sexuality can short-circuit the higher unfolding. Yet the call to sexual intimacy is stronger, more delightful, and often has deeper integrity than ever. As far as I am concerned, there is no formula for this phase. One must fully own his or her authority to say yes or no to sex and to remain present for the consequences. In a certain sense sex itself is not the problem; it is the romantic attachment that is often used to rationalize the encounter which once again makes the other the object of fundamental contemplation, thereby obscuring the deeper process.

Many individuals who begin to pursue higher consciousness become bogged down in emotional struggles because they are unable to keep from personalizing the energy or being seduced by someone else's attraction to them. There is an incredible loneliness and need for companionship pervading our society. Thus few individuals ever really examine their consecration to the depth where they can bring true authority to the issue of sexuality and relationship. Once they begin to open, they immediately want to ground the energy into intimacy. Almost every person faces this struggle. We need to focus on our unique capacity to face this dilemma. I cannot advise whether one should encourage or avoid personalizing the energy in the opening process. Rather I suggest that we learn to observe ourselves while continuously inquiring into the nature of our consecration. Only in this way can we have a conscious relationship to these universal ontogenic forces, so that they become the source through which we develop our own unique potential.

THE TRANSFORMATIVE TENSION OF SEXUALITY AND SPIRITUALITY

After my awakening, the capacity to commune in an entirely new way arose. Often I find that I am having "sex" merely by being in the presence of certain people. It no longer matters whether they are male or female, what they look like, how they live, what they do, or even whether I like them. If they are energetically available, our energies meld in a sense of presence and flow. I am always "making love" with those around me in accordance with their capacity to enter energetic rapport. It does not require words, or even knowing one another.

In certain moments, Existence itself is the Lover, and sex is "ceaseless relationship," the very essence of life. I do not attempt to enter these states volitionally. I am not directing myself toward any kind of experience, nor do I seek any. I surrender as I feel the energy intensifying. Just bringing the attention to the arising current makes it more pervasive; it is as though Life, the Beloved, takes me. In these states, through the very process of Being, consciousness (all that is, within and without) becomes a single aliveness. The birds outside the window call within me and the play of light on the leaves occurs in my very being. If one can accurately speak of a body, it is awareness that is continuous and inseparable from Existence.

When our attention no longer automatically personalizes the energy, and in the presence of another we are celebrating the wholeness of existence, sexuality transcends the body and particularly the genital dynamic. Intrinsic to such an experience is the release of the desire to possess another. When our sense of being and identity is predicated on the other's existence, and they become "our" husband, "our" lover, it is impossible to know them in a higher dimension. But as we reach into higher states of consciousness, the separation between "me" and the "other" begins to dissolve, and we realize that we share through Grace. No effort on our part has brought or holds the other to us. It is Grace that has brought this moment of sharing; it is also Grace that may end it. In this way, relationship becomes the mystery and undoing that it really can be and not just another fortress of the ego—another way to secure our identity. We are not lovers in reference to each other, but in reference to something far larger. Our relationship is an expression of devotion to That. This is the beginning of conscious relationship, or what I call *friendship*.

Yet the moment we choose to enter into friendship, with or without sexual intimacy, there is a personalizing of the energy; we cannot be detached or privately absorbed in the current. True friendship incarnates the highest degree of one's realization into the immediacy of human relationship. For this reason I have found true friendship one of the rarest, richest, and most difficult of life's gifts. It is entering a dynamic in which the other has the same claims over our being as does God. There is no longer the possibility of withdrawal and defense. It is to me a far higher level of relationship than that between Guru and disciple, student and teacher, healer and patient. In fact, it is far easier for me to be a teacher, inspirer, awakener, or healer than it is to be a friend. To be a friend is to incorporate these functions into ordinary relationship and at the very least acknowledge that they exist in the friend as well. One no longer has the safe harbor of lofty detachment and the potent sense of identity and purpose that the higher functions bestow.

For years I emphasized the aloofness of the teacher function, and it allowed a certain poise and balance that friendship rarely does. Yet I would call the emphasis on the teacher function a kind of developmental cowardice compared with conscious friendship. To be a friend is truly a holy dimension fraught with paradox, for we cannot pretend to the intimacy of personal sharing one minute and then withdraw into the impersonal detachment of the higher consciousness the next. We will be tried in the fires of our ability to accept the limitations and conflicts intrinsic to our humanness and no amount of wisdom available to us in the more transcendent state will matter, for that is not the sole state in which deep human friendship occurs. Nor do I believe it is the state in which the highest human potential is being incarnated.

In making the choice to move from the universal to the personal, we are entering, perhaps for the first time, conscious relationship. Before that we may have had all manner of relationships, but they were never really conscious because we did not have the capacity to stand outside the content of our own consciousness (outside the arising sexual feeling, the fantasies of need, aversion, affection, sharing). Unconsciously, we personalized the energy all the time; it is the very nature of subject/object consciousness to do so. But one who has touched the universal can stand outside these fantasies and simultaneously allow intimate relationship. From this vantage point, the choice to fully engage intimacy is an immense yet, I believe, inevitable sacrifice, for once again, we become vulnerable to the cacaphony of feeling, urge and passion. And this is particularly intensified when relationship becomes sexual. Sexual energy, by its very nature, requires and affirms the fundamental male/female, I/you polarity. At this level of energy, the sense of universal love, of sublime presence, is overshadowed, and the relationship invariably becomes more conditional and possessive. Thus, while genital sex can be a most profound expression of love, it can also addict us in a level of separation and dependency that is the blight of all love.

Traditional spirituality tends to obviate all this by rigidly regulating the arena of intimacy. It is as though we fear to get into the stables. Like Hercules, we would prefer to deliver one great flood of purification; or, more commonly, we would ignore intimacy, mark it forbidden territory. I feel that for full spiritual development we must not prematurely close off the risk and challenge of sexual intimacy to serve a supposedly spiritual aspiration. Even with the inevitability of losing clarity, incarnation does not occur at the level of the higher; it occurs where the higher and daily life consciously meet in an unending revelation of possibility.

The deeper we go into conscious friendship, the more profound the capacity to merge in oneness and the more compelling the force that creates separation and dependency. This is the transformative dilemma, the radical tension of conscious relationship. There must be distance and yet there is no distance. Every episode of genital sex becomes a sacrifice, a sacred giving-up of oneself, the "little death" it is sometimes called. (The big death is the yielding of the egoic identity into Oneness.) At this level of relationship, sexuality has become what it rightfully is in a conscious life, a transformational door. We are surrendering into separation (or there could be no sexual impulse) even as we honor our fundamental Oneness. It is no wonder that so many of us are afraid of profound intimacy that we have allowed our relationships to become regimented, mechanical, defined, and distanced. The more conscious we are—in the sense of our capacity to fuse with another, to know their essence, to suffer their pain and their joy— the more we ourselves are consumed and become a sacrifice into the moment. In fact, as we become more self-aware, this fear becomes even greater.

Yet we can be profoundly purified in this radical tension if we are willing gradually to yield completely into the mystery of relationship (friendship). Friendship can no longer be judged on the basis of whether it brings happiness or not. Compatibility or noncompatibility are issues of egoic self-definition, not conscious relationship, for in conscious relationship we are willingly releasing stances that rationalize the sacredness of any self-perceived identity. Whatever the relationship shows us to be, that cannot be what we are. Thus the great tension: For in order to meet in affection and sharing, we must make a stand in some level of personal identity ("This relationship is special; we were made for each other.") even while realizing that this is but a fiction, an equivalent fiction to the stance that would remain distant and reserved.

Paradoxically, the more whole we become in ourselves, the more we begin to surrender everything. It is not being surrendered to the other, per se; this would only be another way to safely define ourselves. Rather it is surrender to Existence in dynamic aliveness with every other being. When relationship has reached this depth, sex becomes more and more unfathomable; it may fall away or not. But, it is never something to be approached lightly. In such a relationship, we can use contraception and sidestep the transformative potential of birth, but we have not demeaned the transformative initiation of sexuality, nor of relationship. One transformational door (birth) has been closed, but a new door has been opened, and the vital energy of intimacy is being radiated into new aliveness and a larger understanding of life. To me, this is the true meaning of liberated sexuality; one has become profoundly relational to Life. Liberated sexuality produces friendship, and it is this, not any kind of sensual capacity alone, that is the highest expression of Eros.

THE DISEASES OF THE SEXUAL CYCLE

Sex, precisely because it is a door to greater energy, requires a great deal of conscious consideration, self-discipline, and social awareness—in other words, maturity. The energy liberated through sex is part of the great inheritance bequeathed to us by Life. It can radiate from us as our commitment to serve life, ourselves, and all people, or, if we are not mature, it can become a "toy" that we think we are entitled to because it is "natural." Then sex becomes a force without soul, and it may well invite the counterforce of disease.

The more we as a culture make sex readily available without transformative consequences, the more we potentially discharge energy into a limited dimension. It is the dimension where attention is focused in a fundamental dynamic of separation. In this dimension, individuality and material sensuality are exaggerated over our social nature and spirituality.

The counterforce of disease acts to provide limits to sexual indulgence. With the prevalence of genital infections, even a person who is not particularly promiscuous can still find himself or herself infected. Syphilis, gonorrhea, trichomonas, chlamydia and herpes are not inconsequential. Some are treatable with antibiotics and, while there are still significant risks (or discomfort) to these diseases, for the most part they have been minimized. I am tempted to say *unfortunately* minimized, for we have found a way to neutralize the balancing force of illness so that once again sex is on our terms. This is not quite true of herpes. Herpes is at such epidemic proportions that the chances of catching the disease are significant, particularly among certain populations. The herpes virus resides in the sacral ganglia, and an infected woman will potentially injure any child that she bears while the disease is active. We still await the long-term implications of herpes and other sexually transmitted viruses.

Interestingly, herpes tends to activate every time a person is stressed, whether physically or psychologically. And when we are stressed, the desire to take advantage of sex for releasing tension increases. Thus, in a situation where we might automatically turn to sex to release stress, we cannot safely do so. Perhaps this disease is saying, "Find some other way to resolve tension and create a sense of well-being."

Now there is AIDS, the newest and most destructive of sex-related diseases. Biologically, AIDS is a virus that causes a profound shutting down of the immune system. Metaphorically, the immune system is the bodily capacity to make specific discriminations and say no. The immune system says no to that which is not identified as a part of our wholeness. In this case, the immune system is either unable to say no or is indiscriminately saying yes. It is as though the boundary between Person as conscious entity and Person as elemental life is breaking down.

Some spiritual teachers claim that AIDS is one of the prophesied epidemics that foreshadow the advent of a higher human consciousness—that it is a purifying force necessary to uplift mankind. I find such thinking disturbing. Why is it so reassuring to think of life on earth as a school in which we are learning lessons that prepare us for a greater role in the universe? The underlying smugness and self-importance in such thinking, the sense of meaning and security it brings, should tip us off that this kind of ideation is born out of our own egos.

Surely it is in the very nature of consciousness that every experience is the soil of revelation. Every experience—depending on our awareness—offers new understanding. Lessons are learned, but it does not follow that they are the *reason* for any experience. Here again we see the error in ascribing a teleological significance to universal phenomena. Rationalizing life's profound difficulties as "lessons we need to learn," we create a place for ourselves in the universe, but we pay a price: We never learn to stand in faith before life's ineffable mystery. The effect is to limit our inquiry into the potential revelations of a tragic force like the AIDS epidemic.

Every experience, especially suffering, carries transformative potential, and AIDS is no exception. Already we are re-evalutating our sexual habits, as well as giving serious thought to related medical, social, ethical and legal issues—a process that represents our societal attempt to come to grips with deep-seated fears and basic conflicts about individual rights, privacy versus collective safety, and the responsibility of each person to the human whole. While much fear surrounds this disease, many people are meeting it with great courage and compassion. Every time we are given an opportunity to open our hearts and say yes when our deepest instincts recoil in fear, we stand at a potentially transformative threshhold.

Though we first became aware of AIDS when it surfaced in the gay communities of the United States, now it is clear that AIDS is not a disease of homosexuals, but a disease of all mankind. The question is whether we as humans are capable of deep, unobstructed intimacy that leads to spiritual wholeness and radiant aliveness. It is our capacity to love that marks our wholeness, and love is greatest when our separating self-definitions have been yielded into our larger humanness. Whether we define ourselves by our youth or old age, physical health or disability, skin color or sexual preference, at the moment when love and aliveness is greatest all such considerations become irrelevant. The courage it takes to release these self-definitions and risk the profound vulnerability of being unobstructedly open is reflected in the depth of aliveness we experience.

I am concerned about whether the gay persona—as a collective force—serves homosexuals or the society as a whole. Any collective persona limits the ability of individuals to express the full spectrum of their uniqueness. Like nationalism, the function of collective self-definition has value only to that point where it enhances aliveness. In the atmosphere of persecution that has surrounded homosexuality in our culture, the creation of a collective homosexual identity has allowed the leveraging of greater political and social freedom. But when that same identity becomes another form of repression and self-limitation, it obstructs the collective energetic. We must be very clear that the higher energy represents a greater truth than any relative identity, and have the integrity to release limiting self-definition.

The awakening process requires that again and again we face our inner ambiguities. Suppressing them, or labeling them as pathological, is no solution, and neither is the validation that comes through a collectively reinforced persona. Clearly, at the foundation of all our inner struggles there are forces universal to all humanity. We all have to face the elucidation and maturation of the feminine and masculine tension within consciousness. It can be very painful, depending on one's unique temperament as well as one's upbringing and cultural context. Yet rarely is the resolution of any psychic conflict to be found in the choice of one side to the exclusion of the other. From the point of view of realization and the awakening of a whole new potential in consciousness, no person is either male or female. It is precisely when this dichotomy briefly resolves in a state in which "male and female are a single one"[2] that the new consciousness is realized. I doubt that sexual preference has any influence upon the likelihood of realizing such a moment. However, the quality of our lives, particularly the depth and integrity of our relationships, may have an enormous influence on whether such an opening will bear good fruit or even be destructive.

Claiming, or having thrust on us, any kind of identity that separates us from the true oneness of humanity is at best developmental. When it becomes a thing-in-itself that one must defend, it

[2] *The Gospel According to Thomas*, Harper & Row, 1959.

can become destructive. One is now defined in a subculture that allows the accessing of certain psychical energies, but expressly or unconsciously rejects other aspects. At one time, some members of the gay community tended to exaggerate the limitations of the masculine psyche. It is an inclination of males in general to seek to express intimacy through sexuality. The masculine consciousness tends toward a certain kind of self-sufficiency or, more accurately, a need for autonomy that is often antithetical to intimacy. The exclusion of the feminine relational forces in some men leads to promiscuity in the very attempt to achieve intimacy. While promiscuity itself is not the cause of AIDS, it certainly increases the opportunity to contract and spread the disease.

Sexual expression throughout our culture often tends to represent a negation of a higher energetic possibility. This is implicit in the tendency to exploit sexuality for stimulation and sensation (a way of creating rudimentary identity) while refusing real intimacy. It is precisely this weakness in our capacity for genuine and deep intimacy and thus our unconscious imprisonment in a low-energy way of life that, I believe, makes us susceptible to venereal diseases. Perhaps the inability of our behavior to keep pace with the energy awakening within us is now being further challenged by AIDS.

It is said that if we could trace back fifty generations, we would find that every human being is a blood relative of every other human being. The physical link that unites all of us is the generative sexual act. There is a reciprocity of life force that transcends individuality and spans generations, past and future, when sexuality is naturally linked with the human cycle of procreation, intimacy, family, and social coherence and continuity, most especially when this cycle is felt as holy and bound in the fragrance of love. Sex need not always occur for the sake of procreation; sexual intimacy in the celebration of aliveness and friendship is truly one of life's greatest gifts. But then, knowing it as a gift, such sexuality is a cycling of energy throughout one's whole being that creates a link of integrity to the world around. We are heightened in such communion and made more At-One with life, not contracted and isolated.

If we sense the importance of our individual aliveness to the potential well-being of all humanity, do any of us have the right to dissipate our energies? It is the fineness of our individual energetic note, summated as the collective consciousness, that is the basis of intelligence and our capacity to be creative, to love and to relate fully to life. When any of life's great energetic doorways, such as sexuality, is not fully opened, when sexual activity remains stimulation and not full intimacy and communion, we are disempowering ourselves, squandering an opportunity to touch a higher energetic potential. Venereal disease is a testimony to how little we understand what it means to be human and how inadequately we are inviting ourselves into the adventure.

Looking at the sexually related diseases from the perspective of life-force energies and consciousness, it is as though the interconnected wholeness of life is being unconsciously or blatantly rejected. Such behavior reflects our inability to face the dilemma of personal freedom and the inherent enigmas of life that demand we learn to consciously (not dogmatically) limit our freedom if we are to know an even greater freedom. Self-mastery isn't repression. But because it is often hard to tell the difference, every movement toward real mastery is fraught with ambiguity and conflict. It is the willingness to engage this, to see the naturalness of it, that is in fact the very process of self-mastery. The illusion that sex is "safe" and a natural right must be carefully questioned. We do not consider it a natural right to give someone a weapon for harming others. Yet a person who is unconscious of the power hiding within the domain of the life-force energies, especially sexual energy, has picked up a gun and is shooting himself or herself, as well as society as a whole.

Unconscious sexual discharge has always represented a loss of discrimination between the centripetal forces of consciousness (our elemental, instinctual and physical nature) and the centrifugal forces (our rational, conscious, and Divine nature). In the past the natural outcome of genitality was inevitably linked with survival, personal power and wealth, esteem and social prominence, as well as creating the infrastructure of the society itself. Today with the rapid change in social structure, this cycling and reciprocity of energy has been radically altered. This liberated but unchanneled energy invites morbidity.

Yet if we seek to regulate sexual energy with moral injunctions we will fail. In fact, history shows that the attempt to impose moral values upon a society invariably results in repression and a resulting behavioral backlash. The reason for this is that behavior not clearly grounded in spiritual understanding (direct appreciation of the various levels of life force and other energetics) does not have universal meaning. Such behavior becomes dogmatic or worse, an unnatural violence and suppression of aliveness. What is needed is a direct experience of the awakening of higher consciousness and a commitment to self-mastery based on a growing sense of wonder at being human. Our behaviors must rest in direct experience, so that a personal sense of inspiration underlies our efforts to grow in aliveness. Education primarily oriented to the outer man will never adequately meet this need, and so we continually use our intelligence to fight illnesses, many of which would simply not exist in a more enlightened community.

Enlarging the Circle

He drew a circle that shut me out—
Heretic, rebel, a thing to flout.
But love and I had the wit to win:
We drew a circle that took him in.

EDWIN MARKHAM
OUTWITTED

The final word has not been written on what is "normal." The potential of an ever-growing complexity of human relatedness cannot even be guessed at. In this sense, the immensely increased visibility of homosexuality and sexuality in general can be seen as an important and creative awakening of humanity as a whole. Thus it is unfortunate that in looking at the challenge of AIDS, we turn our attention toward the seeming imbalance of homosexuality and thereby miss the larger picture in which the texture and possibility of human expression is growing ever more complex and consciously visible. But if we are to accept this larger picture and the inspiration and hope that it provides, we must also accept an equivalent responsibility and look at our own conflicts, ambiguities and (perhaps dangerous) indulgences as well.

Without passing judgment, we must seek to understand why the body behaves in certain ways under certain circumstances. Just as we study the human capacity to adapt to high altitude in order to learn more about the effects of oxygen deprivation, so too we must ask what is the effect of self-identifying in a powerful subculture.

The homosexual community has been the primary vector for the AIDS epidemic in the U.S., but it is not the source of the disease. I suspect that the particular expression of sexual energy within the male homosexual community has resulted in an unusually high vulnerability to AIDS that will not be quite as terrible within the general population. But I don't think the full source of this weakness rests only in the homosexual community. It is a mistake to separate "homosexuality" from the larger collective consciousness from which it emerges. I have no doubt that the very formation of the homosexual community in its current scope is a direct reflection of the larger society's sexual fragmentation and inability to integrate a wide variety of sensitivities and temperaments.

It is intrinsic to a rational and materialistically oriented society such as ours that the sacredness of life is no longer a central understanding. The effect of this is graphically demonstrated when we trace the meaning of certain words. For example, the original meaning of *wealth* is well-being. It comes from the same root as *whole*, from which also comes the word *health*. Yet the materialistic inclination that dominates in this historic epoch has transformed the meaning of *wealth*, so that it now refers to having the money to purchase well-being. Similarly, our rational and materialistic orientation tends to transform our appreciation of male and female. They become strongly separated and defined. Ironically, in the past, when the male and female roles were highly differentiated, the essences of *masculine* and *feminine* were not. In our society the opposite is true; the roles are blurring while the inner essence is becoming more and more polarized. The result is a tendency to exclude and even stigmatize many people for whom male and female essences are blended differently. It is the larger "we," as much as the individual homosexual, that creates the pattern of homosexuality we have today. There is only one consciousness; we are an interconnected whole. When the balance of energy begins to shift within the larger dynamic, sub-groups which already tend to be energetically one-sided may become even more so.

AIDS has spread like a cancer in the fertile soil of tremendously inbred sexual expression of a community that is showing us all our fear and distrust of differing sensibilities and, most especially, of intimacy and deep relationship. From this perspective, AIDS is part of the transformational impulse that is calling us responsibly to embrace the full spectrum of humanness to meet the challenge of our heightening collective energy. Here again we see that humanity has a choice to exclude or withdraw, rather than to try to integrate differing temperaments and sensitivities and thus breed a far richer and more deeply balanced humanity. Whenever exclusion and sub-speciation dominates and becomes exaggerated, this imbalance will sooner or later have its revenge in our physiology.

FROM CHILDBIRTH TO REBIRTH

The message is clear: The energy inadvertently liberated in our attempts to mitigate the "diseases" of the sexual cycle must not be squandered. I use the word *disease* in order to emphasize how we blindly tamper with life's natural transformative doors like sex, pregnancy, childbirth, and even illness. We are obsessed with the power to manipulate life in order to create our ideal of health, of physical and personal comfort and integrity. We rarely see how the spiritual integrity of every individual, and thus the whole of society, may be dependent on how these universal doors are met, how they are symbolized in consciousness and ritualized in life.

For example, let us look at childbirth. Just as sex is an initiation in itself, childbirth is the next level of initiation; it is a transformational moment, particularly for women, but also for men. Childbirth is a universal ritual of life, an experience that can lead to a brief transcendence of boundaries and an empowering into radiant aliveness for the mother. Women have repeatedly told me that during childbirth they experienced the expanded states we reach in the conferences, but had not consciously recognized them then. I have also heard midwives describe the sense of presence that happens at birth; this is one of the reasons they love their work. Another woman has told me how during labor she spontaneously began to make other-worldly sounds. She had no pain and celebrated a state of radical aliveness. Recently, a close friend of mine acknowledged the wonderful meditation it had been for him to assist his wife during labor. He said that the energetic exercises central to this work are very similar to the synergy he experienced with his wife.

In this more unified state, the process of birthing is also a process of uniting with a larger consciousness. There is, in this heightened consciousness, a space where separation and oneness are the same. A woman is at once united and freed from the child she births. Perhaps if this process is entered consciously, there will be less struggle later in life to release one's children, because deep within each mother at birth the sense of Oneness had been tapped that forever unites her to her offspring (and much more).

Although for the mother the transformative potential of labor and birthing cannot be denied, it must also be recognized that her radiant presence and level of consciousness can act as a subtle, yet profoundly integrative, context for the infant. It can mitigate the otherwise unavoidable trauma of the birth process. Birth is an archetypal process of radical transformation. It is a profound change in environment following a difficult period of severe unexplainable psychophysical stress for every infant. As in moments of fundamental transformation, one is simply overwhelmed and cannot know what, if anything, is guiding the experience.

In my own process of awakening, I reached a second key transition about one year after the initial opening. I knew that I had to go deeper, but I kept configuring the old control patterns. Thus I was traveling around the world alone seeking to lose myself, to see myself anew in the foreign contexts. Visiting an ashram in India, I was participating in a meditation intensive when I entered a state where I thought I would be utterly annihilated. I realized that if I made the decision to withdraw, I would be assuming that the circumstances leading to this particular moment had been wrong. I knew this was not the case. I had all along acted from the deepest level that I knew how to honor. Therefore there was nothing to do but surrender, even though my blood felt like fiery ice and I was sure that I would die or go mad. I was at this edge for only a moment before I was suddenly aware of recapitulating my own birth. It was not a memory of the birth canal.[3] It was preverbal, a state in which there were no words or concepts with which to identify where or what was happening. Yet I knew that this particular existential struggle and passage had been templated at birth: It was the archetypal process of radical change as seeming annihilation. The sense of annihilation gave way to exquisite peace and a sense of rising and falling on my mother's breast. Yet it was not my biological mother. It was a state in which I experienced Existence as the Mother. During my first experience of awakening, something seemingly came from without. There was a sense of God the Father and then becoming One (as in "I and the Father are One"). But in the second experience it was as though "I" had come from the inside out—out of myself into Existence, the Mother. Once again it is quite impossible for me to find words for this state. Imagine seeing a twig, a shadow, anything at all that enters your awareness. Know that, in the very act of perceiving, you Are. You are safe in Mother Consciousness, just as surely as when you were an infant in your mother's loving arms. It is a state in which we are ultimately confirmed, nourished, mothered by the phenomenon of Consciousness in all its infinite forms.

Because of this experience I realize how important it is that every woman be allowed to reach transcendent awareness whenever possible during the process of labor and delivery, and that the shock of birth be minimized for the infant. I believe this has important consequences for the child's capacity to individuate at other difficult transformational doors.

Of course, modern medicine holds that natural labor is too dan-

---

[3] Some people describe passing down the birth canal, coming into a delivery area and being held, etc. This level of memory presumes experiences and comprehension an infant doesn't have. Thus the state from which these reports are made seems to me to be a more superficial penetration. They are not truly recapitulating birth. Rather, while remaining in subject/object consciousness, they are putting words to a subtle memory. The memory in its essence may be authentic, but they have not returned to the original consciousness at birth. Such experiences can release a limited amount of energy but do not approach the mystical depth of actually reliving birth, and thus represent only a partial redemption of the archetypal birth trauma.

gerous to be allowed to be the initiation nature intended. The mother can die or be severely weakened; the infant can experience anoxia and die or be brain-damaged. The list of potential dangers grows as our capacity to define human fragility grows. But the strengths born in meeting the risks, in working with the pain— in preparing physically, psychologically, and spiritually with the support and participation of one's family and immediate social group—these benefits are immeasurable. If we meet birth as a transformative moment, there is invariably greater life force moving through us. I have no doubt that childbirth pursued in this way will progress with fewer complications. The anthropologist Colin Turnbull reports that in the years he lived with Mbuti Africans he never saw or heard of a single maternal or infant death or birth complication. As noted earlier, the Mbuti are a small tribal society in which every aspect of sexuality and the procreative functions of adulthood are thoroughly ritualized and integrated into life as a whole.[4] Where this integration is lost or has been unconsciously interrupted by modern labor and delivery techniques, we may suspect both a general increase in problems surrounding pregnancy and labor (which further rationalizes more medical intervention) and a stormier and perhaps neurotic process for both mother and child in subsequent years.

In our society it may no longer be possible to rely purely on natural labor. Medical science has carried us beyond natural selection and many people, the so-called high-risk groups, can only have children with medical assistance. However, we can enhance the consciousness with which all transformative doors are approached. We can employ our medical capability when it is necessary to sustain life if we also invite the maximum conscious participation of all concerned, and thus promote, as much as possible, the transformative potential of these moments.

The return to natural childbirth is an intuitive return to natural spiritual initiation. Unfortunately, to the degree that women select natural childbirth out of idealism or fear and rejection of traditional medicine, rather than acting from a genuine celebration of life, they are in a splitting process once again. They have

⁴ Turnbull, Colin, op. cit.

only partially begun the adventure of wholeness, and perhaps are already limiting the inherent mystical potential of childbirth.

THE GREAT CIRCLE OF LIFE

Human beings, in our elevation of life above the mystery of living, have unconsciously chosen body over soul, reason over spirit. The result is that we alleviate one form of suffering only to re-inflict it on ourselves in other ways. One wonders whether, setting aside the mystical potential of childbirth, we may be contributing to a growing spiritual bankruptcy. The "plague" of infant and mother mortality in birth has been significantly conquered, but now we have the plague of overpopulation. For overpopulation we have the remedy of birth control and abortion, but this makes sex easy to over-indulge; enter the plagues of sexually transmitted diseases, especially herpes and AIDS. All of these medical interventions are part of the overall consciousness that employs reason to conquer life's uncertainty, inconvenience and discomfort; enter the plague of M.A.D (Mutually Assured Destruction), before which all of our political, social, and traditional religious institutions lie helpless.

Sex, at the moment of orgasm, gives us a glimpse of Oneness, a moment of loss of boundary and expansion of consciousness. This is why it is so addictive. The degree of pleasure should give us some hint of the degree of maturity demanded by sex.

That a moment of sex can have ramifications over years and years of one's life suggests the incredible energy within the sexual space. The depth, intensity, and long-term impact of any moment is directly proportional to the degree in which time and space are forever potentially altered during that moment. Realization is such a moment, and its impact will forever affect every aspect of one's life (and the rest of the world as well). But, like sex, Realization doesn't just bring happiness and greater power. Both bring a profound understanding of power and powerlessness, and a profound capacity to embrace life's pain as well as its beauty. Both give us something entirely new and then demand incredible maturity and responsibility to that newness. While Realization unites subject and object, so that we experience Consciousness as a Whole, sex unites male and female to produce new life. We cannot just have this Divine nectar at our demand; we must give up something of ourselves.

What sex has asked, until modern times, is that we give up our childhood and become socially responsible. Pregnancy itself is a hope and a risk. It requires a certain personal preparation and hallowing. It generates a synergy of energy between man and woman, a deepening of relationship. Childbirth may mean the loss of one's life, or the death of the infant to whom one has grown profoundly attached. For the survivors, it means great loss and grief, a constant reminder that the greatest and the worst in life are closely tied. If all goes well, as it usually does, there is the wonderment and joy of new life, but there is also the added responsibility of supporting a family. Yet this responsibility is also a privilege that the magic of birth helps us to approach with greater selflessness than ever before.

Thus, the potential to bring life into the world must always be measured by one's capacity adequately to care for that life, and the ability of society at large to receive an additional person. This implies the development of self-control and self-mastery, not only of the sex drive, but also of all our creative drives. To face this challenge consciously is one of life's greatest gifts because it demands social awareness and prepares us for the larger adventure of the unfolding of spiritual awareness. It is this awareness fed back into society that is of the utmost importance for the health of any society. How could we ever regard this as something to be handled by a pill or an abortion?

Overpopulation is a by-product of many forces, not the least of which is *everything* we have done to prevent suffering, to elevate life over death without ever really looking into life's deeper balance. But overpopulation emerges from a humanity that is not spiritually aware enough to overcome fundamental issues of selfishness and self-interest in order to begin to act with a sense of the greater whole. It is the very relationship to death in any phase of life that we have tried to close with our rational knowhow. Yet this is life's natural way for inviting spiritual awareness and religiosity.

One of the reasons Depoprovera, a relatively long-term injectable contraceptive hormone, has been approved for use in the United States is that there has been little evidence of side effects in the Third World countries where it has been extensively used. I am willing to wager that in the West we will see a very different result. Here, where overpopulation is not really a threat, and conception is only a real hardship for the very poor—but where a desire for sex without consequence and without consciousness is the dominant motive for contraceptive use—I believe we will see far more complications: cancer, hormone imbalance, psychological problems, genital infections.

These side effects may not necessarily be directly attributable to Depoprovera. It is the near-sightedness of medicine that it likes tight cause/effect relationships. But in reality the side effects of the very consciousness of intervention are impossible to measure directly. In general, the recent impulse in medicine is to do less and less. We are seeing that many of our assumptions of value and benefit are fiction. I would take it a step further. Even when something is proven effective, I would suggest we weigh the implications for the whole human field. Extending our vision in this way, we may stop using so-called safe and effective methods because of their consequences in other spheres.

We are unbelievably unenlightened in our implementation of biological science. Human beings are energy systems, consciousness in dynamic equilibrium with the larger social and environmental consciousness. Use of a treatment in one context may have one result, and in another, a different result. True, a drug like Depoprovera may function more or less predictably from a biochemical point of view in all human beings, but the overall effect of the drug for each person cannot be evaluated so narrowly.

The best contraceptive, like the best medicine, is awareness. Developing awareness means that we no longer want easy answers or easy outs. When I was still practicing medicine, I began to see the immense confusion around birth control. Long before the Dalkon Shield IUD was found to be dangerous, I refused to use it because it created so much pain to implant. In fact, when it came to any form of IUD, I eventually became known as the doctor who would remove them. I saw that the effortlessness of sex was resulting in an epidemic of genital infections. I talked with my patients, and it seemed that these otherwise intelligent men and women were using sex as barter for acceptability and not demanding of themselves a real commitment to awareness. I began to suggest to my patients that a diaphragm or condoms were much healthier forms of contraception precisely because they are somewhat riskier. Using a diaphragm or condom means bringing self-awareness into sex. It means knowing even before we enter a potentially sexual exchange that we will stop in order to make the personal statement, "I care about myself and about you." I found myself spending more and more time counseling awareness, and by word of mouth my practice came to be predominately women, though people of both sexes were exploring consciousness with me.

To heighten awareness we cannot take easy roads. We do not have to go out of our way to find hard ones, but we must be willing to make choices consciously and be fully ready to accept all consequences. With regard to birth control, this may mean careful timing or abstinence if pregnancy is unacceptable. I know how old-fashioned this sounds, but I am not speaking of moral values. I speak merely of how we must approach life in order to marshall the fullest energy and aliveness. I am not speaking of self-mortification for the purpose of expiating sin. There is no self-mortification required, only an agreement to live life by Nature's rules and to hallow ourselves in the process. Abstinence honors the overriding sense of the sacredness of creation and is not deprivation, but rather conscious celebration of our real and ultimate potential as intimates. It means that we are assuming conscious responsibility for a basic biological process every day of our lives until Nature, Herself, frees us of these concerns. We flatter ourselves by thinking that our careers, worldly and spiritual, are more important than our sexuality. To this way of thinking, sexuality is our reward, a way of testing our desirability, a thing we can tap into for fun and refreshment, a needed break from the rigors of our busy, intense lives. This orientation is too easy; it must be re-examined. For most people, such an approach to life can only mean mediocrity and a lower energetic potential. We may shine superficially, but our depth of awareness will be modest at best. And the legacy of our self-serving mediocrity will ultimately mean greater suffering for the next generation.

Any way of living that attempts to make life acceptable or comfortable, so that we never build to the transformational moment, is the greatest kind of repression. Growth through effortlessness is only possible after we have deeply mastered the energies of consciousness, and this means having lived life fully with discipline and commitment. Thus those who favor restricting birth control and abortion, and thereby increasing the consequences of sexual intimacy, have a point. There will be more energy available to potentiate the shift to a higher level of awareness if we learn consciously to master the sexual forces. This is why these teachings are part of most religious doctrines in the first place. But these voices, raised so loud, often have no true concern for the social whole. Rather, they want to promulgate their belief systems and values, frequently in a prejudiced and inflexible manner. Religious beliefs that are followed without direct experience of the deeper energetic principles that govern their formulation repress the transformative potential. Invariably such beliefs lead to violence towards one's aliveness and towards the lives of others.

Most individuals are far healthier than we in our society ever credit them to be. The fact that many people have trouble just abandoning themselves sexually—thereby appearing sexually repressed, or dysfunctional—often reflects their intuitive recognition that the sexual space is sacred. Likewise, the generalized distrust of the behavioral laws imposed by traditional religions is evidence of wisdom. In any environment in which the enhancement of consciousness becomes the central meaning of life, sex automatically becomes sacred. In such a context, the overriding majority of individuals would find sex not only fulfilling, but also a door to a higher level of consciousness. They would also, spontaneously, find themselves voluntarily adhering to many of the traditional religious guidelines, for they would have reached the level of consciousness where such adherence is appropriate and not repressive of aliveness. On the contrary, the discovery in one's life of the truth of these values is a joyous event. It is like returning home to a long lost friend. In a world where such understanding is alive, overpopulation would cease to be a problem, because birth control would have been achieved in the only natural way, by the liberation of the sexual impulse into larger humanness. With this, I believe we would find a greater moderation and balance of all our creative energies.

16 * HIGHER ENERGIES AND CHILDREN

> *if everything happens that can't be done*
> *(and anything's righter*
> *than books*
> *could plan)*
> *the stupidest teacher will almost guess*
> *(with a run*
> *around we go yes)*
> *there's nothing as something as one*
>
> *now i love you and you love me*
> *(and books are shutter*
> *than books*
> *can be)*
> *and deep in the high that does nothing but fall*
> *(with a shout*
> *each*
> *around we go all)*
> *there's something calling who's we*
>
> e.e. cummings

FROM A DEVELOPMENTAL PERSPECTIVE on the transformation of consciousness, the child's task is to individuate into a self-determining adult and thereby function as a contributing force in society. To do so involves gradual mastery of various functions of consciousness. First, the sense of self vis à vis bodily control must be developed. This is accomplished through physical activities of gradually growing complexity. Overlapping physical mastery, and continuing well beyond the phase in which bodily consciousness is adequately developed, there is the recognition of sexual and role responsibilities in an expanding range of relationships. This simultaneously requires the maturation of emotional control and intellectual functions. With these functions operative, the possibilities for the expression of aliveness expand even further with the development of the capacity to set and fulfill self-imposed limits and thus achieve a sense of personal power. Personal power in turn requires the honing of will and intentionality. Eventually all of these capacities synergize, so that the undifferentiated and dependent child becomes a unique, self-determining being capable of virtually unlimited learning. This adult has the capacity to be inventive and thus create circumstances for learning that go beyond anything previously imagined to foster untapped capabilities for all humanity.

As human consciousness evolves from its relatively undifferentiated potential in the child, it does so through involvement in increasingly complex relationships to life and human endeavor. For example, games and sports are an excellent context for learning mastery of the body and basic social skills. For early physical coordination, the context can be a fairly simple activity provided by the family or the local school. For more complex levels of physical and social mastery, the context expands, and may even become global. An example would be the 1984 Olympic gold medalists in ice dancing. Here we witness a degree of physical mastery that literally extends human possibility. It is a mastery that stands upon the shoulders of previous generations of skaters, dancers, gymnasts and other athletes, combined with a rich musical and aesthetic awareness. Forged in the energy of global competition, the result was an expression that bordered on the transcendent. In another (far less dramatic) example, I regard my medical training primarily as a context in which I exercised a high order of mental and emotional discipline. Without such discipline, further development involving exploration at the edge of the new and unknown (i.e. fundamental creativity) would not have been possible.

To me it is odd that so many people regard their interests and careers as ends in themselves, rather than as scaffolds for the development, balancing, or expression of faculties of consciousness. This attitude reflects the absence in our culture of an integrative overview of the development of consciousness and, along with this, the absence of a real sense of what it means to be an adult.

What we call spiritual awareness underlies the whole process of individuation. This deeper continuum is the root of the sense of belonging, sharing, honesty, integrity, humility, and the capacity to love, to sacrifice, to see oneself in relationship to life and a servant to it. We often assume that the development of these attributes belongs to the latter phase of life, but this sense of relatedness, of connectedness, is very much alive and immediate in children.

When I was ten or eleven years old I walked a friend home from school who was in agony due to an illness called *shingles*. He was doubled over, trembling and moaning all the way. I cried with him and held him. My whole being hurt with him and I wanted with all my soul to help him. The point is that what we call spirituality—behaviorally, as well as in terms of subtle dimensions of perception—is active from earliest life. This must be recognized and allowed to remain alive in the developmental process if the achievement of adulthood is not to be a crystallization and endpoint in the flow of aliveness and discovery.

✸

Each stage of development rests in the ability to identify oneself as separate from, and yet participating in, an ever-expanding involvement with the world. Without this sense of separation, there can be no personal "I," and thus no structure upon which to build language and other forms of relationship. Unfortunately, participation with consciousness in a larger sense is often lost in the process of developing the restrictive subject/object consciousness that is the root of language and the egoic nature. In the West, the importance of a spiritual focus is often neglected in the developing child. While each infant must release undifferentiated consciousness to evolve the "I" of personal identity, and likewise each child must die to childhood identity at the transformative move into adulthood, this need not be at the cost of a suppression or even negation of spiritual awareness.

It is the availability of our spiritual awareness at every stage of development that is the basis of sensitive and appropriate social consciousness. Without a place for the expression of the spiritual nature, children gradually lose the sense of connectedness and belonging. They can meet all the requirements of the culture in terms of intellectual and vocational functioning and yet feel profoundly alienated. Often, in an attempt to find a sense of identity, such children create their own subculture with its own rites of passage into adulthood. The sometimes bizarre array of subcultures to which young people belong is actually a reflection of a deep spiritual impulse that is not being fulfilled by the larger culture.

Conformity to conventional social norms can fulfill the transformative impulse toward individuality and uniqueness only when the social norm is permeated with an alive spiritual value. Then conformity becomes a discovery of one's fullest capacities in and through a growing social relatedness and sense of responsibility. Such conformity is not suppression of one's uniqueness. On the contrary, in this way we each attain our highest potential in service to the good of the whole.

But conformity without the integrative presence of an alive spiritual consciousness becomes the submersion of one's uniqueness into a selfish, relatively lifeless and soulless mediocrity. Even the negative identity that comes from rejection of the soulless social norm is better than conformity to something that has no sense of deeper integrity. Sadly, in adolescence the search for identity often results in violent rejection of the norm and/or the self. Adolescents subconsciously recognize that the passage to adulthood represents dying to structures of the past—the end of childhood. But, without a social awareness that invites a meaningful participation in society and provides a base for understanding the transformation, it is easy to lash out against the world (the projection of the inner breakdown) or confuse this development with suicide. Suicide then becomes a ritual of transformation and an attempt to demonstrate potency before an inexorable inner force that the emerging adult has not been prepared to understand and welcome. To commit suicide fulfills the transformative impulse, but it is enacted in the wrong dimension. Instead of entering a process of change in which one level of identity is released and a new one taken on, one's physical existence is sacrificed. In recognition of this, some cultures provide a ritual death for their adolescents to symbolize the passage from childhood to adulthood.

SUPPORTING SPIRITUAL AWARENESS

Spiritual education can and must begin with early childhood. By education I am not referring to the imposition of our adult beliefs and values, and especially not the inculcation of the dogmatic religious moralism. Rather I refer to a recognition of the greater realm of sensitivity within the child and an effort to allow each child appropriate space to express this. Clearly, each child must learn boundaries for functional purposes, but their deeper awareness that perceives beyond these boundaries should not be ignored or suppressed in the process. Children are very sensitive to energy, and this sensitivity allows them to perceive directly in domains that have been lost to the average adult. They can perceive their interrelatedness to things apparent and nonapparent, and they have an innate sense of the appropriateness of these perceptions. While the degree of spiritual sensitivity is undoubtedly different in each individual, it is universally part of us from the earliest moments of life. Thus, when we attempt to dissuade a child of this level of experience or if we try to prematurely place their experience in a context more consistent with our own level of development, we succeed in alienating them from a vital base of their aliveness. When this happens, future transformational shifts will be highly disruptive, as is clearly the case with adolescence in Western society. And when adolescence is so disruptive, the awakening of mystical consciousness later in life may likewise be overwhelmingly disorienting, rather than the great blessing it can be.

The awakening process is not so traumatic in other cultures. In Tibetan Buddhist culture, spirituality is thoroughly integrated into the whole society. Spiritually advanced children are brought forth and honored by the time they are four or five. Levels of consciousness that the average Westerner would struggle years to achieve, or find highly disturbing if they awakened spontaneously, are welcomed and cultivated from childhood. To the degree that this awareness remains active in an individual, he or she can function with greater social integrity. Our survival literally rests upon the continuity of spiritual awareness during the process of egoic development.

However, support of the natural spiritual awareness of the child requires adults who are themselves awakening and sensitive to higher levels of consciousness. And here we have a problem, for cultivating the awakening process in the average, already highly suppressed, adult is an entirely different process from encouraging it in children. The adult already has a strongly configurated ego-boundary; the child does not. The sledge hammer of powerful energetic inductions that can awaken a deeper consciousness in an adult may overwhelm, and even be destructive, to a child whose system is far less defended and far less capable of handling high levels of energy. In short, the disciplines and practices of an adult pursuing the transformational process can be incompatible with the more delicate energetic capacities of their children.

My experiences suggest that, when an adult has reached a higher energy state, it is a mistake to impose the full extent of it on young children. A friend of mine, whose energy field had opened to a new level, used the process of hugging to induct others. He would hug people for a long time, heighten their energy systems, and carry them into a more open, meditative, undifferentiated awareness. One day he called me to discuss his work and mentioned that he was very disturbed because his five-year-old son's eye disease had reactivated.

Young Keith was born with moderately severe eye disease as a result of a uterine infection called *toxoplasmosis*. Most women are immune to this illness, so it does not affect the fetus. But occasionally a woman who does not have immunity contracts the illness while pregnant, and it affects the unborn child. Once the mother develops immunity, which is transferred to the child by crossing the placenta, the disease halts. Usually it will remain dormant unless the child's immune system is compromised by some kind of severe stress. Thus, it was a surprise when his existing eye disease suddenly began to worsen in an otherwise-healthy Keith.

On a hunch, I asked the father if he was doing anything energetically with his son. He said that for the past few months he had been hugging his son for an hour or more each day. This was not ordinary hugging. He was entering into a deep meditative focus and intentionally willing himself into a heightened energy. Sometimes he and his wife would hug Keith between them, thus intensifying the energetic effect. When I pursued my questioning further, it became clear that Keith resisted this practice. I have observed that children tend to avoid prolonged exposure to unmodulated high-energy states. But his father, in his enthusiasm for the awakening process, felt that heightened energies were good for everyone and insisted on Keith's participation. I suggested that they only hug for as long as Keith was comfortable and that he not activate his full energies while he was with his son. It turned out that Keith only wanted to hug briefly a few times each day. In a very short period of time, his disease became quiescent. This was fortunate, because the treatment used to prevent the ensuing blindness involved steroids that would have stunted his growth.

Perhaps it was coincidence that the disease quieted when the prolonged meditative hugging ceased, but I doubt it. The father's energy field was quite expanded. Sensitive adults often found themselves catapulted into altered states of consciousness just by being near him. However, he was not a master of these energies. Like many people who explore transformation, he had a blind sense of the value of staying in expanded energies. He unquestioningly gave tremendous significance to such states. For him, they attained the value of holiness. This is a perfectly understandable confusion for, when we first awaken to this dimension, it is as though God Himself has reached out and touched our lives and it is easy to lose perspective. The mistake is in separating the treasure of awakening consciousness from the larger field in which it exists. This field is the whole of life. Only an appreciation of timing and natural development makes it possible safely to integrate the higher mystical forces.

The higher states of consciousness are natural and appropriate when they are awakened in an individual who has thoroughly completed the development of the basic egoic structure. Even while this development is going on, it is still entirely appropriate to encourage—in a context of wisdom—the innate spirituality of children. Moderate encouragement of the subtle sensibilities such as sensing energy, or the capacity to transfer energy as in a healing ritual, can be shared with children without doing any harm to the fragile developmental process, as long as nothing is forced. Edith Sullwold, who has explored the transformational process with families, describes instances where very young children stand and whirl in the center of the room while adults sit in energetic resonation. The children were physically reflecting the energy vortex created by the meditating adults. This is a beautiful example of adults and children safely exploring consciousness together and learning from each other. Introducing children to such experiences encourages their innate sense of spirituality. It dramatically teaches that, even though we all seem to be separate, in fact we are all connected at a deeper dimension. Furthermore, a child who can share this with parents or other adults experiences approval of her or his deeper intuition and subtle sensibilities. Such dimensions are then seen as valid and appropriate to growing up.

Perhaps even more important than offering our children the kinds of spiritual experiences suggested above, we could learn to observe them more closely and allow their own natural spiritual expression. It is not only they who will be more whole as a result, but we also. As I reported in *The I That Is We*, I had the direct experience of being inducted into a marvelous state by a toddler. All that was needed was the setting aside of my well-intentioned desire to share my energy with him.

I wonder at the possibilities of relationship and natural creative expression of people reared in a way that allows them to develop their energetic sensitivity and sense of connectedness. We would have an entirely different regard for each other. Individuality would not imply separation to the degree that it does in our culture. We would have a far greater confidence in expressing and creating out of our uniqueness and with far less tendency for such expression to be at the expense of others.

THE CHILD'S NEED FOR ENERGETIC COHERENCE

Children are already multidimensionally open. They are highly conductive of energy and richly sensitive to everything happening around them. With children there is no need to overwhelm their newly forming sense of ego-boundary and personal self-definition with spiritual rituals designed for adults. Keith's experience suggests that higher energies can overwhelm not only the consciousness of the developing egoic self, but also the bodily expression of that self and its capacity to say no to that which is not self. As we saw in our discussion of AIDS, it is this very capacity that is the basis of immunity. Before this is possible, there has to be a recognized difference between the one who can say no and something to say no to. I suspect that the development of immunity and the development of identity are all part of an inseparable process.

The Soviets have reported that orphaned infants in large, poorly staffed clinics who received very little individual attention had retarded and inadequate development of their immune systems. One interpretation is that their immune systems were not being stimulated often enough by encounters with infections brought to them by human interaction. Others consider that the lack of breastfeeding might be a contributing factor. But, while breastfeeding is very important in activating healthy development, both immunologically and psychologically, non-breastfed children who receive adequate physical attention do not have the same immunity problems. Therefore, Ashley Montagu and other researchers have suggested that physical touch is necessary for healthy growth and development.

I have no doubt of the immense importance of physical touch for healthy development. Touch is perhaps the most basic sense. For example, we know that the sense of physical orientation in space is largely acquired as we move about the womb. It is even more highly developed in twins, probably due to the greater combinations of contact. And touch, in combination with a calming voice, may be the most direct way of helping to restore orientation to a highly disoriented person. However, I would go further than this. It is not physical touch alone, but energetic interactions that are necessary.

The egoic "I" is a coherent energy pattern. The differentiation of this pattern forms out of the contrast between the organized energy field of the parent and the relatively undifferentiated energy of the infant. It is communicated through a gradual process of induction that occurs between the two, but the parents' field is usually dominant because it tends to remain relatively consistent. Perhaps this helps to explain Bateson's assertion that schizophrenia is caused by a parent who is continuously giving a double message to the child. We can image this double message as a rapid phase changing without a truly consistent pattern. Each time the child's energy field begins to configure in accordance with the pattern in the parent, the pattern changes. Not only does it change, but the new pattern undermines the developing continuity of the emerging energy system in the child. Thus such children develop with large gaps in their energy structure. Behaviorally this translates as a weakened capacity to create a fixed sense of "I Am" that is the mark of schizophrenia.

The process of merging with and separating from the parental (adult) energetic creates the contrast out of which ego emerges. Of course, all the other aspects of physically based (sense-perceived) interactions are simultaneously at play here, but I believe it is the consciousness of the parents, the overall quality of energy they hold, and ultimately the collective social consciousness, that represents the crucial factor in the developmental possibilities for the child. This is not to say that infants arrive as empty slates that are completely programmed by the parent or the society. On the contrary, the child has immense innate potentiality which, rather than being determined by the parent, is more accurately *influenced* by the parent. Not every child who has a highly oscillating parent giving out a double message will end up schizophrenic. Likewise, not every highly conscious parent will imbue children with heightened capabilities. But such parents will influence them in that direction.

Gradually we interact consciously with larger and more complex energy systems, i.e. extended family, community, and society as a whole. It is our capacity to interact functionally with society that defines the state we call adulthood. Finally, if the egoic state has evolved through these increasing orders of complexity, it becomes possible to enter the awakened state that is a returning to a more universal awareness similar to (but also quite unlike) the undifferentiated awareness of the infant. The awakened state is both bound (has a locus of personal identity) and seemingly unbound at the same time. Thus it exists as a kind of door between dimensions. Now we are relating to energy patterns that are far more universal and thus more subtle in their nature. Realization can be considered a metaphor for consciousness At-One with movement on a cosmic scale. Unlike the basic consciousness that responds to immediate energetic stimuli—to daily cycles of earth rotation, monthly lunar cycles, and seasonal solar patterns—the realized consciousness cycles once in hundreds of thousands of years like the Milky Way (if at all). Ordinary consciousness swings in minutes or oscillates in monthly phases, whereas Realization occurs in a frequency that cannot be easily expressed by ordinary consciousness and thus appears timeless. As such, the awakened condition brings new energies and awareness into the world while simultaneously dissolving some of the basis of ordinary identity.

The gift that the parental consciousness bestows through its interaction with the developing child is a bounded, discrete, energetic state—in a word, a personality. Whether it is a good or bad personality, as convention regards it, is in this sense irrelevant, because we are more concerned with whether our personality "breathes" or not. That is, is it a highly separate sense of self (energetically) and thus relatively unperturbed by the larger world in which it is immersed, or is it partially open, conductive, available, and able to merge with a larger energetic milieu? It is this "breathability," this transparency of the egoic structure, that is more important as we try to understand whether our upbringing was healthy or not. We may have felt neglected, or overly controlled and suffocated, we may have felt miserable or happy, we may have liked or hated our parents, but from the perspective of transformation none of this is that important. If we have emerged with a strong, functional identity implying a well-developed self-consciousness, but are not so crystallized that we have lost the capacity to participate in dimensions beyond our personal awareness, this is, to me, a healthy development. It means that we are both individual and other-centered, both personal and spiritual beings. We can maintain a sense of self, and yet that sense is constantly being challenged in a creative and positive way by our capacity to respond to a larger reality.

I suggest that without a sufficiently developed self-consciousness existing simultaneously within a breathing, transparent egoic structure, one cannot evolve to a higher, more universal awareness. There is simply no way to bring back and integrate the experience of a higher dimension unless the faculty of self-consciousness has been well-developed. Thus it is precisely because the parental energy field is well differentiated, and in this sense bounded, relative to the larger dimensions, that an "I" that is the basis of self-consciousness can differentiate in the child. Yet, if the parental energetic is too crystallized, such a parent will inevitably, albeit unconsciously, suppress the multidimensionality of the child. The child will learn that breathing between ordinary subject/object consciousness and higher dimensions is not "right," and will gradually close off this channel. (As seen in our discussion of cancer and schizophrenia, too much transparency tends toward a schizophrenic dynamic while too much egoic structure and density perhaps tends toward the development of cancer when we are challenged to grow in a heightened energy.) Thus the energetic environment in which a child develops is very important and deserves our fullest commitment and attention. I suggest that this energetic differentiation process includes not only the egoic boundary, but also the physiological equivalents such as immunity.

✱

The awakened state is the final stage of human development, as least as far as we know now. It gives birth to a new identity within the collective body, a new level of aliveness that engages society as a whole, that makes available a new possibility in the consciousness of all humanity. Yet, the awakening process is in many ways the opposite of what parents do for a child. It is because the average parent is still essentially unawakened that he or she can act as a relatively consistent bounding force for the differentiation of an identity within the child. The child's un-formed psyche is continuously dissolving, continuously merging into many levels of relationship. That is why children are such excellent feedback systems for everything around them. One pediatrician told me that once he became aware of the depth to which infants and children reflect their environment, he began treating the parents' diets when presented with a "colicky" baby. Often the baby's digestion improved. It is precisely because the young child is so much a reflection of his or her subtle environment, that the parent must have a well-bounded energy field. The rare people who have awakened very young in life can be energetically too vast to provide appropriate boundary. Frequently they don't have children; those who do must modulate their energies carefully, perhaps allowing the child to find other adults against whom to contrast. Failing this, they can precipitate a terrible struggle in the child to develop a stable energy field (i.e. identity).

Does this mean that higher energy states are intrinsically bad for the developing child? No. In fact, I am sure that the contrary is the case. What could be better than to grow up in an environment where consciousness in all of its modes of expression is honored and every individual strives to evolve to his or her highest potential? But this implies two things. First, that the higher energies never be imposed on the children, and second, that the children aren't neglected while the adults pursue their spiritual processes.

Children have a rich, innately spiritual nature, but they cannot learn about being human without a great deal of trial and error. Spiritual unfoldment must include developing a creative relationship to all feelings. For children and young people, this means exploring anger, selfishness, possessiveness, self-centeredness, and so on. No one will arrive at peace and self-mastery without passing through the "nasty" stuff that so-called spiritual environments often try to expunge. Simultaneously, the myth of the cosmic child is so powerful in the present Western spiritual impulse that, rather than seeing this as a metaphor of infinite possibility for all humankind, it becomes the basis for "inspired neglect" of much that should be disciplined. The rationalization is that children are so pure and natural that they must not be overly confined or interfered with. In fact, even in spiritual communities, the line between neglect and too much control over the child's space is hard to determine.

Few spiritual communities are really well-prepared to raise children, especially if their focus is strongly transformational. In a transformational environment, the emphasis is on dissolution of the ego structures that prevent full energetic conductivity. The energy field of such a community is so intense and the disciplines so demanding that such a way of life is hardly compatible with rearing a family. Children are seen as peripheral, not a part of the central intent of the community. Space is often made for them and they may be well cared for, but the message is still clear: This spirituality is for adults. On the other hand, there are communities more socially idealistic and politically oriented that consciously incorporate their children into community living. But there is very little actual work on the transformation of consciousness in such groups.

To me, the integration of child-rearing into the high-energy transformational environment is a challenge for our future. In simpler societies, such as the Tibetan before the Chinese invasion, monasteries were transformational environments that also provided community services such as the rearing and education of children.[1] But there was the wisdom of tradition to guide them, and each monastery had elders well aware of the forces they were dealing with. The structure of the monastery functioned to ground the energies evoked by the meditative practices. The more mature aspirants were freed from worldly life and could thereby expand into higher energies so long as they continued to meet work and relational responsibilities. No attempt was made to initiate someone into the deeper energies until he or she had reached the appropriate stage of development. The young were part of the spiritual environment and had the immense benefit of contact with wise elders, but their youthfulness was honored. It is this kind of communication between generations and daily access to the deepest wisdom that is sorely missing in Western society.

Traditionally, spiritual awakening has waited until family life is complete, or it has been the vocation of those not drawn to hav-

[1] Turnbull, op. cit.

ing a family. But, this need not, and perhaps *must* not, be the case. A child who differentiates in a balanced high-energy environment has the greatest advantage of all. He or she will evolve the egoic structure throughout a broad spectrum of sensitivities and dimensions. Thus the potential for both individuality and compassion, separateness and inclusiveness, could be explored far beyond what would be possible if the unfolding were in a lower-energy environment. We must be aware that the child will naturally fight against the heightened energy and must be allowed to do so. As we have seen, it is not wise to face children with an energetic that is so vast and formless that it absorbs them. If they cannot successfully resist, they cannot adequately differentiate an ego.

It is precisely this struggle that will empower the depth and dimension of character. We must understand the forces we are dealing with and be willing to compromise towards balance and inclusiveness. Children can be exposed to a higher energy as long as it is occurring in an environment well grounded in ordinary living. Then rich and genuine growth, growth that fosters self-consciousness but does not suppress the multidimensional possibilities of consciousness, can begin in the home. It is the balanced quality of our energies, the integration of heaven and earth within our being, which, radiated as presence, is the greatest gift we can share with our children. It is the degree to which we ourselves remain open, uncrystallized, renewed by each day, deepened by each of life's challenges, and humbled to surrender in Grace (the real alchemist of change) that becomes the basis for a lifetime friendship with our children.

BECOMING MODELS FOR MATURITY

As more and more awakenings occur in people who have families, it will require great sensitivity, patience and wisdom to allow the process to unfold in the adult while respecting the equally wondrous but very different process occurring in the child. Few of us ever stop to consider the immensity of the fact that the first great achievement of human development is the capacity to go from raw sensory data to the process of speech. It helps to appreciate this achievement if we contemplate the life of Helen Keller. Here, without the benefit of sight or sound, a child was taught how to translate raw sensory impressions into language through consistent patterns of touch. For a young child's relatively open, unpatterned consciousness, oneness with experience is no great feat. It is only after we have made the great journey marked by the advent of language that the return to the unitive preverbal, presymbolic consciousness—the journey of enlightenment— becomes the ultimate adventure.

The demands on parents are great if they are to both pursue their own transformation and be a stable energy system for their children. The awakening process for an adult demands letting go; children require discipline, decisions, nurturance, structure, dependability. This is a challenge that many parents encounter as they begin to pursue transformation consciously. As their energy begins to open to new levels, the sense of their lives and their family involvement changes. Much of what they have lived may begin to lose its meaning or importance and there is a strong impulse to change lifestyle. The need to withdraw from the familiarity of old life habits is seen by children as a destabilizing of the family energetic, a loss of the consistent structure they require to create their identity. Children—not just the little ones, but the adolescents as well—sense the ungroundedness of the parents, especially in the early involvement with transformation, and often react, demanding a consistent energetic structure. They resist the changes, challenge the values, often act out rejection of these values by assuming even more vehement involvement in their own identity-defining activities and behavior. In my observation, if there are several children, usually only one becomes afraid and reactive.

It is a basic fact that, in order to perceive ourselves, we require contrast—something to measure against. Children will literally force their parents to take a stand, and conflict serves this purpose admirably. This is not just true when the parent has begun to become more unbounded, it is true of the parent/child relationship in general. It just becomes even more difficult if one has begun to awaken while still rearing children. I recall a good friend of mine who was rearing her daughter while at the same time working as a transformational teacher and therapist. She remarked to me one day how her work with students was becoming more and more effortless and natural, while her relationship with her daughter (then about eight) was getting more and more difficult. "Of course," I remarked, "the gift you give your students is the spaciousness of your energy, but the gift you are giving your daughter is a personality. Your students are being inducted into a larger space, being freed from the constriction of their all-too-crystallized personality dynamics. Your daughter, on the other hand, is working to configure her identity, and for that she requires that you become more dense for her to contrast with."

This can be quite disconcerting to the parent who feels that he or she is in a "damned if I do, damned if I don't" situation. She must continue her exploration, but is afraid that she will lose the closeness with her children, or even harm them. There is no simple answer; the parent must respect the child's fight for structure, even if it seems negative. With young children it is the consistency of one's love, even while administering discipline, that is crucial. With adolescents the problem is more complex, for the parent is often the last person who can offer spiritual meaning to them.

It is precisely the adolescent's need to separate from the parent and make the great passage to adulthood that creates the problem. Parents who are only first awakening often feel a rekindled identification with the struggle of their children. Many attempt to bring their own newly discovered aliveness home to their adolescents. But this often creates a double bind for the youngster. After all, Mom or Dad is suddenly more available just at the time when the young person needs and wants to break free. It is precisely at this time that wisdom and spiritual understanding must be conveyed to the adolescent by an elder or some other individual who is recognized as a model for wisdom. At best, this model is someone the parents respect but who is independent of the parents. And it is precisely this that has been lost in our culture. While not all the elderly are wise, few adolescents have access to them anyway. In fact, the heroes and heroines of our culture who are potent role models are athletes and charismatic performers. Unfortunately, these relationships are mostly imaginary and very superficial; they are stereotypical identities fostered through the media. At a time when adolescents are really quite open, their bodies flooded with new energies, they are naturally available and hungry for real wisdom and value. It is a time of great possibility, but there is little substance to these heroes and heroines of pop society that one could call spiritual or wise.

*

From the perspective of radical aliveness, the beginning of a resolution to the issues of higher energies and family life can be sensed when we realize the underlying conflict is between the self-centeredness of both the child and the parent. Once we as parents appreciate that our transformation is not some kind of personal achievement that we must strive for as something exclusively our own, but rather a process that offers greater aliveness to everyone, then the conflict between personal transformation and family life simply evaporates. We are left with a challenging process of discovery and an opportunity for deepening wisdom. We bring our awareness fully present to what is happening and examine everything against our deeper consecration. We recall that fundamental change is really Grace, and we voluntarily find the balance that serves our children as well as ourselves. It is a process of inclusiveness, but also of sacred renunciation and an embrace of ordinariness. We do not set aside the transformational impulse because of inconvenient timing, but we do not lock that impulse into some ancient stereotype that separates it from family life. This does not negate our deeper transformative and spiritual impulse, but rather serves it in the immediacy of our days. In this way, a reconciliation of the two different aspects of the transformational process appropriate to adults and children can be reached. We each must pursue our own wholeness into higher energy states without being seduced into thinking that high energy or spiritual life is separate from ordinary life. If the ordinary and the sublime are blended wholesomely, if the higher consciousness is radiant and inclusive and respects the development of others, then the young child can develop without being too energetically threatened. And older children can grow to respect the wealth of wisdom and radiant presence that emanates from a life committed to a full awareness. Thus, even as they prepare to make their way in the world, they are receiving spiritual substance for the journey.

17 ❖ BEYOND WAR

THE LAW THAT CONSCIOUSNESS WILL MOVE toward the highest level of energy capable of being supported by a system suggests that we will never move beyond war until we embrace a way of life that consistently generates more energy and serves the process of interconnecting humanity more effectively than war has done.

War, in this sense, is not a thing in itself; it represents the summation of all the capabilities available to mankind at the basic subject/object level of consciousness. It begins with the identification of self as separate. Once we give primacy to this separateness, the basic mechanism for activating energy involves setting up contests or competitions between the separate parts. For all the value we place on love and brotherhood, in my experience a world based on these principles is only genuinely possible for a very small number of people. War revolts us and we seek its counterpoint in peace and brotherhood. But in point of fact, while we say we want peace and we may exalt unitary values, the vast majority of people are more alive, more at the edge of their capacities, more creative, and able to celebrate the greatest unity with their compatriots, during times of contest and war. Thus, while I am no advocate of war, I know the futility and perhaps greater destructiveness of the ideals of peace and love when they spring from fear of war (and death) and not a radical capacity for life.

It would seem that the Law of Evolving Consciousness has little to do with humanity's reasonableness. It cares not what we think we want or what we deem to be reasonable, only what is necessary. The inevitability of transformation has its own agenda and timetable. If war as an activity is supreme in its ability to kindle humanity to fullest energetic potential, then war becomes the default option in the repertoire of dynamics available to spur human evolution. If our reasonableness is what underlies the effort to move beyond war, I suspect that such efforts are poorly grounded. It must be a *passion*, not reasonable at all. It must be a passion that arises out of a fundamental realization of truth and oneness so that one is actually *energetically* capable of uniting with a larger dimension and accessing energy from that dimension. It is not enough that it be a passion that comes from the power of a noble cause. To the extent that the peace movement derives its identity and purpose from having something to fight against, it does not introduce a new element or a new possibility in human consciousness. The people who support such a cause must be as totally enlivened through that cause as they would be if they were at war. We must be willing to die, and we must be involved in a dynamism of self-inquiry and innovative relationship as creative, intense and unconditionally committed as that which wartime might produce.

The aliveness represented by love versus that of competition, crisis and fighting can best be summarized by an experience I had some years ago. At a center devoted to working with dying children, the patients are taught to affirm sayings that emphasize love and peace. This is combined with visualizations to fight the disease, support groups for the families, and so on. I do not judge this work, because it does try to embody a deeper aspiration, but I wonder if it is not more for adults than for the children. My experience was with the brother of one of these patients and his parents. It seemed the more the parents tried to involve him in the program with his sick brother, the more he behaved violently at school. As I spent time with this young person, I noticed that whenever he spoke of his sick brother's program, explaining the ideas of love and reciting the affirmations, his aliveness went on hold. He was being obedient to adult expectations but not vital in himself. When he spoke of his pranks at school, his eyes were alight and his whole body throbbed with vitality. I got him to describe the program he and his brother were involved with at the center, and then to discuss what was happening back at school with his teachers and peers. Then I asked the parents to observe where his enthusiasm really was. It was clear to everyone that this little boy would start dying when asked to pursue the loving aphorisms and their values.

The psychology of siblings and families is complex. There were other factors, such as the boy's guilt that he was well and his resentment of the attention his brother was getting. But, on a deeper level, I believe this little boy was trying to heal his brother. He was unconsciously carrying a compensatory energy, an energy of contest, belligerence, egocentric stubbornness and potency. He was showing us that when he took on the spiritual values in order to accommodate the adult vision, he had less aliveness. But when he allowed his own authentic individuality to have expression (the expression of individuality in this case requiring an opponent, a barrier to push against), immediately there was greater aliveness and radiance. We can value spiritual teachings, but if we don't understand the dimension of aliveness in which such teachings are real and we impose them as the right way at an earlier level of development, we can very well short-circuit the life force.

With this understanding, we see that to move beyond war will never come only from a new way of thinking, if that thinking is just conception within the same untransformed energy system. To have outer peace, there must first be a realization of Wholeness and the difficult process of beginning to move toward inner peace. Peace itself may be an illusion like the myth of some past Golden Age, or more aptly that counterpole that arises in our imagination precisely so that we can judge or evaluate the endless ferment of change. The dynamism of war must not be underestimated. It demands an equivalent apocalyptic inner orientation, a level of discipline that arises without certainty of rightness or success, just as the soldier's discipline brings with it no guarantee of safety or freedom from injury.

We might well ask whether the movement beyond war can engender the necessary aliveness in a democracy as we currently live it. As it is, war has an inherent advantage. The immense psychical energy of war, which accelerates scientific and social progress, which catapults hundreds of thousands of individuals into actions where they are totally at the edge of themselves, risking all and moving with an aliveness that few had ever touched before, is only possible because the very apparatus of war is not democratic. It is autocratic. We give up our rights to disagree with a superior—or, even if allowed to disagree, we cannot refuse to cooperate without risk of losing life or freedom. We are told when to rise, what to wear, what to eat, what to do. We practice certain complex behaviors until they become reflex. We learn to rely on others to such a degree that the sense of camaraderie in war can exceed any former experience of love or friendship.

There is no intention here to romanticize or glorify warfare— only to underscore the level of energy involved. We must recall that this energy is not only occurring in the soldier, but also in the society that supports the war effort. In World War II, people working 12-hour shifts assembled Victory ships in less than 48 hours. In that same war, highly individualistic personalities came together in Los Alamos and other laboratories and in 26 months harnessed the atom to create the nuclear weapons that now, for the first time in history, may destroy our world or make war obsolete.

Consider that the level of energy of a nation unified in a war effort so accelerated science that we liberated a level of technology we still don't have the spiritual depth to regulate. Consider that much of the impulse toward liberalization that has occurred in the United States and other Western nations was a direct product of the reaffirmation of life and justice that resulted from witnessing the horrors of World War II. In the days following that war, Trappist and other spiritual groups grew faster than ever before or since. The war catalyzed spiritual opening and the mystical quest more effectively than peacetime generally does. Consider also, from a broader historical context, the way in which war has merged formerly separated cultures. Alexander the Great's march to India forever changed the face of the Middle East. With each new geopolitical ascendancy, larger and larger portions of humanity came under single rule and were gradually assimilated into a new cultural coherence. Then ask, what are we really looking at here? Is war really totally atavistic, destructive, negative, and evil? My answer is no. War has always been destructive but, given the level of realization of which humanity has been authentically capable, *warfare might well be considered our oldest religion.* Throughout history, no other institution, no other social or religious process, has ever mustered the levels of aliveness for such numbers that warfare has generated. Are we then to continue thinking that all this has been wrong, evidence of man's bestial nature or Original Sin? Paradoxically, warfare represents human civilization simultaneously at its nadir and zenith.

With great intelligence, not merely aspiration and idealistic thinking, we must ask the question: Is humanity now ready to move beyond war? There is a corollary to this question: Do we now have a new religion that has greater capability of unifying mankind and lifting us to a higher energetic potential than warfare? The answer I believe resides in whether we can generate as much transformative energy in our embrace of life as that engendered from our conquest of it.

Nuclear warfare, precisely because it cannot be won and because of the very real disaster it would represent, has changed our whole approach to conflict. Now for the first time the tendency to resolve disagreement through force of arms must be deeply tempered. Thus we must give a whole new level of attention, not only to smaller conflicts as they arise, but also to all the assumptions we have about personal interests that could eventuate in conflict. The result has been an immense acceleration of our recognition of the interconnectedness of all national interests. In fact, the very concept of *nation* is gradually becoming meaningless, to the degree that *nation* is a differentiation that cannot stand up against the far more natural unifying factors that bind humanity. All this is fairly obvious, and has led many to feel that the movement beyond war is inevitable. What is often lost in this understanding is the great value war has been, and the unanswered question whether human life can currently access equivalent and greater energy through a new *religion* other than war.

The religions of today are very young indeed when compared to the war dynamic. In fact, to the degree that these young religions became another way to identify differences rather than underlying commonality, they became the pawns of the war principle. More wars have been fought in the name of religion than any other factor. More people have died in the name of Christ or Allah than for any other reasons. The time has come for us to realize that traditional religion is the process whereby realization gradually spreads from the consciousness of one or a few individuals into the consciousness of many others. At present war is the epitome of subject/object consciousness. This consciousness is so ancient that it is the fundamental consciousness of all humanity. It is the basis of what I am calling the Religion of War and is far more than armed conflict. It rests in the power we derive from the manipulation and conquest of our planet, its resources, our psyches and our bodies. Even our medicine has a martial quality that fights disease to return the patient to the battlefield of life. Underlying in varying degrees all the new religions such as Christianity and Buddhism is an awakening sense of the whole, the realization of Oneness. This same realization is now being proclaimed by science in the study of the environment, and by systems theory and high-energy physics especially.

In fact, the Principle of Relationship first required differences to produce the heightened energy necessary for the realization of Oneness. Thus it is crucial for us not to blindly try to repress the Religion of War, to label it ugly and wrong and step nobly forward into our "right" understanding. We must stop condemning those for whom the Religion of War remains the path of greatest possible aliveness. From the perspective of wisdom, it would appear that the Religion of War grows from the primordial mist of emerging human consciousness. It has orchestrated the maximum level of energy available to humanity within the presumption of separation. It is precisely this energy that has helped lift us to the possibility of Oneness. And it is nuclear war, the final scenario of the presumption of separation, that most strongly marks the limits of our oldest religion and urges us to new awareness.

The new religion of life founded in Oneness also has war, but this war is the force of inner non-violence, self-mastery, that safely brings one to the moment of fundamental discontinuity and change. *As great as we imagine the physical destruction of nuclear war to be, it would be no greater than the psychic destruction if, in the same half-hour it takes to fight a nuclear war, all humanity (at our present level of maturity) were to suddenly awaken.*

There can be no hope of moving beyond war until more and more of us have faced the inner apocalypse of fundamental realization. But this statement should not be construed as rejection of the present peace efforts. On the contrary, the current beyond-war movement grows from the intellectual understanding of the commonality of all life. In presenting that vision, we are acknowledging a partial degree of incarnation of the realization of Oneness into the common human scene. However, it is incarnation only at the mental level; it is not full incarnation. In order for there to be full incarnation, the complete energetic reorganization of consciousness must occur, the new note of radical awakening must sound. Once there is the new note, simultaneously there will be the new capacity to access aliveness from the unity of life. This aliveness is greater than or equal to that which we can access through contest and war. It must be clear that we are not simply swinging from humanness grounded in individuality to a hive-like collective consciousness. Realization does not submerge the individual identity in any sense. On the contrary, it substantiates it in a way that one can only experience to appreciate. It is the uniqueness of self at such a level of openness that every other person is also perceived as fundamentally distinct in ways that were formerly imperceptible. Yet while each is unique, each is simultaneously a part of oneself. Thus for the first time we are able really to work in concert.

Currently, humanity can work in concert on a small scale without the Religion of War. The power of music and art has allowed orchestras and performers to work together for years at a time. Certain ashrams, religious groups and occasional social movements, such as those of Gandhi and Martin Luther King, have brought people together into unified function. In these latter movements, the heightened energy of nonviolent unity produces a degree of illumination in the opponent. This is the truth power of which Gandhi spoke. But it is more than the ascendancy of moral principle, it is the living demonstration that mankind can unite in higher possibility (selfless interest) and that the energy of such unity is actually greater than the energy of mankind united in the principle of war (self interest). But these efforts are not any kind of final demonstration. They are in fact intermediary states between war and the real capacity to move beyond war. Militant nonviolence and all efforts to create peace that are predicated on overcoming evil or injustice are still based on the principle of war (albeit held in a less violent manner). It would be an error to call Gandhi's work truly nonviolent, or to think that it has actually moved beyond war. It accesses energy in ways similar to the Religion of War. Yet it is a refinement of war, as it militates for a cause without violence in the usual sense. Thus it is wisdom, for, rather than repressing and rejecting the Religion of War, it lifts it to a higher octave.

Christ said that he had not come to topple the old laws but to fulfill them. It is the very nature of Realization that it grows out of the old consciousness even while it transcends it. To grow beyond war, we will need to take the best from it—the discipline, the selfless commitment, the profound cooperation and camaraderie, the clear goals—and still hold the sense of wonderment, mystery and unknowing that again and again aligns awareness to something beyond our own conceiving. We are reminded of Socrates during the Peloponnesian Wars, standing in a trance while the snow gathered on his shoulders and men died all around him. Perhaps he was so transported by the energy produced by the battling soldiers that, for him, it became Samadhi. Later he is reported as saying that there is more love on the battlefield than ever in home or temple. What he observed was the energy of humanity working in concert on a larger scale and, while it was destructive at one level, it was, from the level of realization, simultaneously creating the very fuel of transcendent consciousness.

It is this fuel that must not be lost in the process of moving beyond war. We must understand the tremendous difference between how a realized consciousness accesses energy and how the vast majority of human beings presently access energy. Fundamental to the Religion of War is contrast—an enemy to be overcome, a goal that must be reached. Against this, try to imagine a movement to higher energy that springs pre-eminently from the simple love of life (not the reactive embrace of life over death or against violence or evil). Can we imagine humanity consciously choosing to serve this? It is not possible consciously to choose this. It must spring from realization. To do so consciously would imply splitting life into a polarity of love and nonlove, and we are back to the Religion of War.

From the perspective of realization, humanity has never functioned except in harmony with life. It is only the quality and means of expressing the harmony that are changing. Humanity has never been lifted by the Laws and Commandments revealed by man, no matter to what source these revelations were ascribed. The revelations were simply expressions of realization describing a deeper essence of life. This understanding of the essential wholeness in all our activity throughout time *is* beyond war; the movement to create a world beyond war is not. This is the paradox, the radical dynamism of polarities that must be held as we dare to approach a hope of greater human wholeness. It is this understanding that is the wound of the peacemaker, for he or she sees that the very cause that is espoused arises from the lack of peace in one's heart. It is not the superficial lack of peace that is obvious when we find ourselves angry and in disagreement over procedural issues. Such disagreement simply means that we have differing levels of realization of what we think we serve and how we imagine it to go forward.

The health and beauty of the beyond-war movement is that it places every serious participant into the profound process of inquiry into his or her nature. The very aspect of being tricked into participation with the noble cause (the part of consciousness that is motivated by contest rather than love) leads inevitably to an encounter with oneself. This encounter is a wound; let us pray that it is a profound wound, a deep inner suffering that we cannot easily ignore. Let us pray that it is a wound of understanding that strips us to the deepest roots of the consciousness out of which we recognize our consecration to life. Let it be fraught with conflict and differences of opinion that drive us to humility, not righteousness. Let us pray that more and more of us will be brought to the deepest Dark Night within ourselves where we would die before we would deny that God's peace comes when we are made totally zero, and not because we have done a good day's work in a noble cause.

The peace movement is a natural expression of the force that brings us to see ourselves, our aspiration and the world we already live in, but have not had eyes to see. We will never intend, and then create, a world of peace; one day perhaps, if that is truly what we are in our deeper being, such a world will be. The possibility of such a world is clear to me, for I have known that realization and its peace, and can observe simultaneously those aspects of myself that thrive out of contest and those that, from the deeper peace, reflect creation. But I have no idea how we will get there. I can see the value in defining what we prefer. I can see the possibility of uniting a world community that is otherwise divided on so many issues. I can see the gathering of people with like beliefs and aspirations as the movement toward a unified energetic. Thus it is clear that the higher energy is being served in this way as it is in the battlefields of other parts of the world. I see that many who can never unite in the religions (Buddhism, Judaism, Christianity, Islam) because of the degree to which these have been claimed by the separatist self, will find a home in this new beyond-war movement. And I personally like it. The Religion of Beyond War rests squarely on the shoulders of each human being and not so much upon childish belief in a parental deity. It is a religion that values the aesthetic and sensual as well as the theoretic. Thus it will appeal to every variety of person—the feeling types, the intellectuals, the philosophers, the scientists, the artists and the children.

But, as with anything else, it will not (and cannot be expected to) be appropriate for all human beings. There are those who would turn beyond war into a battlefield of zealous activism in order to prop up their own identity. There are those, like the little boy, who cannot embrace such values yet without actually moving backward into a lower level of aliveness. They have a right to fight and die for their causes no matter what we in our quest for self-perfection would like to think. Those who would espouse the philosophy of beyond war must have love in their hearts for all of these even if they are terrorists or nuclear madmen. And if we are to truly appreciate the possibility of moving beyond war, then we must realize that the energy that comes from our capacity to work together in concert produces more energy. This energy feeds all human endeavor. Thus those who still pursue the religion of organized violence are going to be all the more empowered (perhaps briefly) by the heightening of energy that arises from those now able to enter authentically the religion of Oneness. If we were capable of growing into Oneness too fast (which fortunately we are not), the effect could be the very opposite of what we hope to accomplish. It could tilt the world into a violence greater than we have ever known.

To move beyond war, each person must hold, not only the appealing vision of peace, but also the wound of war, simultaneously within himself. It is like stepping out and in at the same time—like stepping toward peace and affliction at the same time. Thus the dynamic polarities find their wholeness within each of us. No side has been closed off, no aspect has been labeled and rejected, and each continues to work in concert to bring us to even greater availability and radiance. To the degree that we feel personal empowerment and value by belonging to something designated as rightful and noble, we must also be reduced towards real unknowing and openness—and this before God and each other.

18 ✳ RADICAL ALIVENESS

Dear camerado! I confess I have urged
you onward with me, and still urge you,
without the least idea what is our
destination,
Or whether we shall be victorious, or
utterly quell'd and defeated.

WALT WHITMAN

THERE IS A STORY in the Zen tradition of a famous Zen Master. In his youth he became terminally ill and was thought to have only a few weeks to live. According to the story, he entered his cloister vowing not to emerge until he was enlightened or dead. Nothing more is said about him beyond the implication that he became one of the most famous teachers of his time.

This is a story about transformation and about radical aliveness. I believe it tells us we can and must learn to die before we die. This is the heart of transformation, that we die into ourselves, into life. Perhaps we will be healed like Laura; perhaps we will experience realization; certainly we will tap a well of great wonderment. But closely akin to this wonderment will be a deep pain, a humbling uncertainty, a fertile unknowing. This is where life calls us to Her; this is where we live the ferment of change and the real potential to learn and be renewed.

This possibility of transformation stands forth as life's greatest adventure and also its greatest riddle. We are all, like the monk, terminally ill. We all will die. When I contemplate God's goodness, I see it in the beauty of the flowers, in the tears of caring people, in the simple gestures of concern and generosity with which we acknowledge each other. But in spite of all the richness and wonderment of life, for me the greatest proof of the wisdom that binds our existence is the gift of death. Finally, we all must let go. No matter how rich our lives, we all have maintained some control, have resisted the unknown in some way. The very quality of our doing this is the beauty of our lives. But now there is no longer any holding on. Death gives us that possibility of absolute freedom and renewal.

I do not know when I first understood this, but certainly when I was quite young. A friend recently reminded me that, one day when we were both about eleven or twelve, I turned to him and said, "Life is preparation for dying." It stunned him and stands out as one of the transformative memories of his life. I hadn't recalled this episode but I appreciate how, even as a child, the thrust toward life for me rested in the appreciation of the great doorway of death.

I knew Franklin Merrell-Wolff as a man who lived a full and rich life and approached his death as the greatest adventure of all. He believed it might be possible to make a conscious transition. He suspected that the falling away of the physical body would mean a falling away of all relative consciousness. He had no idea what the remaining consciousness might be like. I suggested to him that he had, perhaps, experienced a similar kind of consciousness at the time of his Realization. But in his closing years, undoubtedly due to aging, he had little or no capacity consciously to regain that exalted territory. It radiated from him as goodness, but otherwise for him it was only memory. Death was an entirely new adventure for him.

In making a conscious transition, he believed, like the Buddhists, that at the time of death it may be possible to merge relative consciousness with the Absolute Consciousness and in this way uplift all sentient life. To merge outer consciousness into the Absolute Consciousness is to radiate a unitive and bonding force across the breadth of manifest reality. Thus especially in death, when it is finally impossible to cling to the world of subject/object consciousness, there exists the possibility of great service.

Within an hour after his death, I, my wife, and a few of his close associates had the privilege of reading to him from *The Tibetan Book of the Dead.* We spent the night repeating "The First Bardo," which invites the departed to accept the Clear Light of Pure Unobstructed Consciousness, consciousness without characteristic of any kind. It was Dr. Wolff's belief that this reading might aid his conscious passage into the Absolute Consciousness. I cannot testify to what degree he was successful. But I can report the wonderful presence that radiated from the corpse in the first 24 hours after his passing. It was far stronger and vaster than anything I had formerly experienced with him (or had on the other occasions when I have been present at the time of death). This presence had the effect for me of rich meditative silence, and at the same time it empowered the sense of responsibility and commitment to the challenging road of sharing the light of consciousness with others.

But even to contemplate the possibility of conscious death means that we have approached life all along with radical aliveness, that we have not turned from the paradoxes, that the moments of great challenge have helped us step closer to that edge of "my will and Thy will." It is a blessing to know that there is death, that our inevitable tendency toward crystallization must finally cease. It is good to extend oneself out into life while gently superimposing the certainty of death. There is a muting of harsh edges, a gentling of the urges and the hidden absolutes, a subtle stirring and lifting in the hidden corners of our being. It is good that no matter how valid and courageous our lives, we each face one thing that is finally common to all people. It is good to know that the very best or worst of what we each create is but a temporary burst—that, like all life, it falls back into the soil of time. It is good to face the difficult feelings, to observe our aging, our changing function, as we consciously appreciate the wealth of experience offered to us in the full cycle of life. This is our full inheritance, this the stage upon which we enact the adventure of our transformation.

But while the possibility of transformation is always present, like death, there is no conventional process of education through which it can be grasped or attained. On the contrary, it is most likely when all our previous education fails us. When there are no longer any simple answers, when we must stand in our own light and learn to have a relationship to ourselves (whether or not it conforms to the values and expectations of the rest of the world), this is when our lives become true service, when our hearts open to embrace what had formerly been outside and separate from us. Yes, we must learn to be aware, learn that there is a possibility of inquiry and self-knowledge, and for this we do at first require teachers and tools. But eventually we must set these tools aside and have the courage to realize that there is no feeling, no doubt, no loneliness that is not itself proof of our humanness and our Divine Wholeness as well. Having a new relationship to ourselves, to anything that arises in our consciousness, leads to new possibility, new aliveness. Living out of oneself in this way is the mark of an awakened person. It is a kind of Virgin Birth.

"LET THERE BE LIGHT!"

We have come a long way in our understanding of ourselves. As God calls out in Genesis "Let there be light!" so too human consciousness brings light into *every* arena of the human adventure. All of our inquiry, whether religious, scientific, psychological or behavioral, is part of the basic impulse of Consciousness to know Itself. We search for proof of God in miracles and revelations. So many people want to be assured that there is Someone, Something that is looking out for us. We cannot answer the question of meaning for ourselves, so therefore there must be Something above that gives meaning to us. But when I look out and contemplate the Divine, I see It in the very phenomenon of our relationship to life. I see it in the call "Let there be light!" that we make every time we want or need to know what is beyond the next hill, inside the molecule, or underlying our feelings and behavior. And every time we ask, we are answered. Every time we reach out into our experience to see what it is, to make more of it, some new understanding emerges. At precisely this moment we have become larger. This is the action of the Divine, that in our ceaseless inquiry into life, whatever we discover never brings us to the end of ourselves. Thus, while we grow in understanding, it is actually Consciousness that has been carried one more step into incarnation through us, and simultaneously we have revealed an even larger context in which to appreciate ourselves. What greater miracle could we require than this, what greater proof that "we are made in the image of God," for wherever we turn our attention, there is creation.

At every point, when we have knocked upon the door of existence, we have been answered. There has not been one Virgin Birth; there have been billions wherever human beings have turned their attention. Throughout time we have knocked on the doors of experience, and the myriad openings are the very flowering of human culture. But we must stop taking this Principle of Life and attempting to make it a source of succor, a self-deception in which we believe that we will knock and get the answer we want and on our own terms. At no point have we knocked and received new possibility that did not simultaneously demand greater responsibility and maturity. At no point has the Divine given us light for our salvation within the narrow dimensions in which we can conceive of salvation. Every new illumination has shone into the darkness of ourselves and we have grown, but we never fully comprehend the meaning and consequences of each new burst of light. The darkness remains and calls us to even greater knowing. Thus, we knocked upon the door of matter, and eventually we found the atom. We knocked again and received atomic energy, and it gave us tools to save or to destroy. Invariably we knock when we are most confused, most in pain, or most intensely in need. We knock to try to close the door of death. And always we are answered; for a while life seems to get more secure, more wondrous. Yet death is present as before and comes toward us, once again in some new and seemingly larger and more hideous way.

For every person there is but one door that can be knocked upon. It is the greatest door of all and it is our self. It is upon this, and upon this only, that the body of humanity can build its future. But in standing before this door with wisdom, there is a great truth that has to be understood. Simply stated, it is the fact that we have never fully found ourselves and that we are in a ceaseless process of discovery. This is very important, because it frees our inquiry, so that we can once again knock with originality at the door of our being. Somehow we are always tricking ourselves into believing that we have found ourselves. It has never been true: Yet by some mysterious sleight of hand we think we know what is right and what is wrong, what we should feel and what we should not. These beliefs limit our free inquiry and our freedom to be infinitely renewed. We pause in conscious and unconscious assumptions of wholeness. But it is not true wholeness, it is conditioning. With this as the basis for evaluating ourselves, there can no longer be radical aliveness. We can no longer knock freely upon the door of our being to receive the Divine answer of the awakening self.

For example, we have knocked upon the doors of the mind and human behavior and have achieved wonderful psychological understanding. Yet the moment we proclaim that certain things are pathological (and thus presume a healthy psyche) we have fallen into error. In a given context and from a very specific point of view, there is validity in describing pathology, but then we must be very clear about understanding this specific context. At no point has our definition of pathology told us what we ourselves are in wholeness. From the point of view of Realization, we have never reached the bottom of any experience, never fathomed any feeling or behavior completely. Whatever answer we have found has only shown us a larger possibility, only expanded what we know ourselves to be. Along these lines, a priest I know recently observed that one of his greatest sources of hope came from the fact that the Supreme Court of the United States has so far been unable to agree on a definition of pornography.

If we begin our inquiry with the unchallenged presumption that we must figure out why we feel or think or act as we do, it limits the possibility. The question *why* presumes that whatever our experience, it should be something else. Now we have a problem to solve, and this orients us in psychological reality. It gives us a direction and a basis for knocking on the door of our self, but this is not free inquiry, not the application of an original mind, so that we may reveal ourselves anew.

Free transformational inquiry rests upon the radical understanding of Wholeness, not upon ideals that are themselves the counterpoles of what feels wrong, unhealthy or undesirable. Thus we are free to embrace all of ourselves, every moment of our experience, and let it be a springboard into our depths. We do not know (have never known) what a healthy psyche is, or a healthy body. We do not ultimately know what a healthy feeling is, or a healthy relationship, or a healthy marriage; neither are we *wrong*. Real discovery and originality never begins from an assumption of wrongness or pathology. On the contrary, it is seeing What Is in wholeness that yields the new and integrative understanding. Therefore we must not judge ourselves, not judge our experience. We must presume that our experience is the very truth of ourselves and our knocking begins with this presumption. This is what it means to be already whole.

If we truly hope to spiritualize our bodies or our relationships, it is not in asking ourselves to be a certain ideal way, rather it is in inviting God into each moment and thereby releasing every restraining assumption into a celebration of new possibility.

This freedom is so liberating. If our marriage is painful, if life does not flow as we want it to, if there are setbacks, if we awaken in the morning trembling with vulnerability bordering on pain, for a moment the door is open to a new relationship to this, a relationship in wholeness. Yet almost as fast as we recognize what it is we feel, we presume we are doing something wrong, and again the door is closed. Now we are imagining we should be some other way. We start knocking on the door of fantasized possibilities and calling upon something outside of ourselves for answers. Then we can begin to do something else, to rearrange our relationships and priorities and thus once again we have side-stepped ourselves.

The pain and uncertainty of life is not wrong. It is as right as the joy and wonder of life. The only thing we can do is knock upon all the doors. This is radical aliveness: We begin to face the little death of yielding ourselves more fully into life's immediacy. We knock upon the door of our own experience, and we can be sure that we will be answered. But we cannot be assured of what the answer will be. Then in our aloneness we can receive that answer and know it as wholeness, or, turning aside, relegate it to the junk pile of unacceptable experience where it continues as a force of destruction or negation. Thus we create the Shadow of which Carl Jung wrote.

MOVING BEYOND THE MIDDLE ZONE

As we awaken, the pursuit of wholeness based on incompletion subsides, and life becomes a process of radical aliveness. While the language of transformation seems to imply cause and effect, the process does not. Clearly, as we enter this process, we reach the moment when our efforts have no direct relationship to outcome. At this point, trying or not trying become the same thing, and there is no way to know whether what we do or don't do is healthy for us, whether or not we are growing. The ordinary guidelines for self-development and self-recognition are no longer meaningful. Thus begins the inner life of faith.

There is always a certain similarity between that which is higher and that which is lower. To be radically alive can at times look like apathy, passivity, or even giving up. One is fully present, but the forces acting within us have not resolved in a specific direction or focus. Any premature movement toward resolution is a subtle self-violation and we are constrained to wait in a difficult but tremendously alive tension. Yet it is possible to live in-between—not to give in to apathy or despair, but never to surrender fully into this radical tension either. In fact, most people live in this state. This middle ground occurs in many forms, but its key characteristic is an ideal view of life based on a desired good, a good that in itself is both a reaction against the lower possibility and an attempt to create the higher. In my opinion, most "spiritual" teachings focus or at least function at this level, somewhere between the higher and the lower, because their roots are never profoundly understood as arising out of a process in which what was lived and what came to be Realized are inseparable. We are always trying to distill the ideal out of the total process and so end up with codes and guidelines that trivialize the challenge of life.

For many, traditional religion has lost its ability to convey and induct the profound mystical aliveness that resides at its heart. Simultaneously, a whole new wave of churches oriented to a practical spirituality, a spirituality with *results,* has emerged to serve the need for a contemporary worship. But there is the danger of becoming caught within this middle zone. They create enthusiasm and vitality. This is essential, but we must not dilute religion and remove the paradox and mystery from it in order to help avert the apathy and despair of real life. In so doing, we also avert the sense of unknowing and radiant surrender from which new understanding and real depth is born. The result is a mass tendency to live in a kind of limbo, never going too low, never going high enough to kindle radical possibility.

This tendency is conveyed in virtually every arena of media-popularized life. It defines what is newsworthy, what can air on television or be publicly discussed. But we cannot really see our world or emphasize the real courage so many of us live when all that we present remains directed to that middle zone of life where stimulation and sensation is confused with substance. We are literally creating and sanctioning a mediocrity of aliveness on such a scale it is hard to imagine that the transformational impulse will not erupt to awaken us through terrible crisis and suffering.

We must be invited to move beyond simple answers or the feel-good ethos to a greater depth. Renewed social activity and participation with a community of other people searching for meaning and happiness is a beginning. A renewed sense of well-being and of personal fulfillment initiates us back into life on a larger scale and it seems as if we are accomplishing great things. Yet the journey has just begun, and on the road ahead lies more than the simple expression of our new enthusiasm. We cannot keep displacing our own pain and sickness on the needy of the world by becoming saviors, or prosyletizers for the next great truth. Certainly we can share our prosperity with others. But then we must be aware that we are accelerating their movement toward our own condition, and we are the ones who consume too much of the earth's resources; we are the ones who are most heavily polluting the environment; we are the ones who can end it all in minutes. Since we have not solved our own fierce problems, it is frightening to observe how easily we are seduced into trying to hurry others into the cauldron with us. And this in the guise of humanitarian interest.

I too want to see a world in which there is less suffering. But I see clearly that before this is possible we may have to learn to stop running from our own pain. I find no nobility in my own or anyone's suffering, but I have watched the games we play in our lives to subtly protect ourselves from fully tasting life. Suffering literally means "to bear up," not just to be miserable. To suffer consciously is to encompass more of life, its joys and its woes. Truly, many of the world's poor must stare into the darkness of starvation, but they are often closer to life and to the spiritual wealth of their own being than we in the West. Our deprivation is of a different sort. I offer no diagnosis, just an invitation to be transformed in it and thus bear witness to life's wholeness.

One day we may awaken to a glimpse of the Divine, and briefly the higher and lower will unite. Afterwards, understanding that both are inseparable, we will no longer know how to take a stand in relationship to either. Then also we will understand the Grace of transformation, for no matter how we prepare ourselves, the potential for full spiritual realization is not the direct result of our efforts. Likewise, we cannot save the world only through our efforts. Such efforts must be seen against our deepest understanding and consecration. There is no easy action for personal or global transformation that stands before us, and as we regard the various spiritual teachings and How To experiences that are being offered, we might well ask the question, "Am I running away from myself?"

Thus as we move beyond the middle stage, we enter a period of difficult tension, of the struggle between being and doing. We face fundamental aloneness in which we cannot know whether our efforts are madness or wisdom. It seems as though our very quest has invited greater darkness. Immediately we want to know what to do, how to be, and a part of consciousness will reach out for answers. Then once again we may turn for comfort to some spiritual process, but what worked before will no longer work to free us. Once we have come this far, the next step is radical aliveness.

If we can appreciate that this fundamental invitation to dance in the unknown is the very truth we must face, then we can let this process have its way. In this way humility evolves, and the self-importance that underlies so much of our need to know how to live right gradually erodes away. Simultaneously, we are slowly becoming more conductive, more available and more radiant. We are moving beyond the realm of egoic success into a spiritual reality.

How this is going to benefit us or the world with all its problems may not be obvious, but we will have grown in our capacity to love—ourselves and each other. At times such love may seem an insubstantial meal, and it feels as if we are losing everything and gaining nothing. The works of our former life were developmentally valid; now they can seem empty or just too small. Do we move on to other tasks or do our best to uplift the consciousness of those old environments? This very question and how we live the answer is radical aliveness.

THE PATH OF POSSIBILITY

Thus I find myself inviting us along the path of new possibility, a path that, if we have the strength, may allow us to give birth to new awareness and new aliveness. It is not simply a process of will and intent, whereby we make our world over in the image of what looks like wholeness to us. If our goals, our visions and our spiritual practices provide a way to substantiate our sense of self-importance, if they once again allow us to find a sense of enthusiasm and direction so that our purpose in life seems clearer, this is good for a while. But eventually, that which gives us a sense of strength and identity at the expense of our existential unknowing must return to undo us. We must face the unknowing, the fact that fundamental change is not something we control, and the risk of despair, helplessness, and the loss of self-worth this seems to imply, if we are to find the door to an even greater aliveness and wholeness.

This is radical aliveness: We are powerful and powerless simultaneously; we know and we don't know. It is a continuous process of balance, of falling too far in one direction or the other and then returning to balance once again. Energetically, we cannot build strength and clarity at the expense of our openness. It is not so much a conscious choice as a phenomenon of the energy itself. It will not let us rest for very long in self-importance or self-fulfillment. On the other hand, if we have become too open, so that we nearly cease to exist as individuals, the energy will demand that we enter the world. Our dreams, our fears scream, "Return to life, live it, give of yourself!" And no sooner do we do this, so that there is a sense of new vitality and purpose, once again an inner force calls us to openness, to undoing, and we begin to feel our newfound self-definition dissolving. The glimpses of Wholeness come, and when they do we realize how much more there is to life. We see how the mystery of life is more wondrous than we could ever imagine. And thus we become even more deeply committed to this process, which one moment feels like wisdom, privilege and Grace, and the next like the greatest foolishness or an unbearable vulnerability.

Gradually the swings between too much availability to the Divine and contraction away from It occur faster and faster. The potential loss of self-definition that causes paralysis and vulnerability becomes counterpoised by a sense of solidness and purpose. Out of this process a new consciousness develops. Form and formlessness, spiritual and worldly lose their distinctions. This consciousness is continuously radiant, continuously available. Yet it is grounded, ordinary, even practical. While we act with apparent certainty and strength, the door to the unknown remains ever open; a light shines forth and there is a sense of reverence and stillness. This is different from the light that radiates from powerful and accomplished people. Theirs is a light that warms those who need to see life lived with a sense of direction, purpose and achievement. Yet for the sensitive soul something is missing. It is the darkness, the undoing. The light of radical aliveness is dual. It will comfort and dismay in ways that are beyond rational understanding. For those who are already in the process of awakening, it will accelerate the swings, intensifying the beauty and the pain, the love and the fear. Yet because those who carry this light have passed through this fire and emerged in deep and functional relationship to life, their presence will also comfort. It acts as a living confirmation that one's quest is not futile; there is the sense of having been profoundly recognized.

The invitation of radical aliveness is more than a sense of direction, or a proper way to channel one's energies. On the contrary, as Whitman observed, it may lead to triumph or to being "utterly quell'd." One cannot respond rationally to this invitation for, in truth, it is not an invitation at all, but rather an ecstatic yes to life as it is. Then there is the birthing of understanding that formerly couldn't quite reach consciousness. Then comes a deeper appreciation of the underlying sensitivity, vulerability and uncertainty that most of us suppress, for we have never known how to accept its holy truth.

Radical aliveness is never an excuse to withdraw from meeting our day-to-day responsibilities maturely. In fact, it is primarily against the mirror of ordinary living that we are able to see the deeper process that is awakening. It is not an attitude of being above the moil, pettiness, or superficiality of ordinary life. It is not a reaction out of life's misery or suffering. On the contrary, it is a life that may be active or quiet, but it is always vibrant, always radiant. And its greatest gift is that, active or passive, it affirms life for life's sake.

Thus I have often pondered the phenomenon of the black butterfly landing upon my forehead. In the mating of light and dark, I see the intertwined helix of DNA, one spiral reaching upward while the other descends. It seems that the black butterfly brought to me a crucial piece of my own destiny. I had been a doctor, yet armed with knowledge and a protective role I somehow stood outside of life's pain. I was afraid of death, but without honoring and seeing the normalcy of the fear, I challenged vertical rock walls and towering mountains. I wanted to climb up into the light of a fulfilling life, but all along I was running away from an important part of myself. It was the dark side that completed the balance and allowed the Realization. Since then I have worked out of my experience of transformation, inviting full-bodied, vigorous aliveness, inviting profound human relationship through energetic rapport. As the energies build, there is always a process of undoing, always a period when to move to a fuller aliveness we automatically invite that which seems to represent the ruination and undoing of what we have been. It is precisely this part of our experience that we must somehow redeem. I am the black butterfly and, if I could, I would alight upon the foreheads of a hundred million people, so that we might embrace our undoing and come to wholeness.

✱

When discussing radical aliveness, I often question the notion of inner guidance and the implication that life can (almost mechanically) be led by following one's inner sense. Personally, I have never known any definitive inner voice that I could clearly discriminate from the voice of the ego. While I have often wanted to know "the answer," to feel sure about what's next, I rarely have. Instead, I maintain an open intuitive awareness that connects me to a sense of presence and energy. In addition, I have taken the path that required more of me—that asked for something new and so appeared to be the most uncertain.

To me, "inner guidance" is intuition that bestows a general sense of integrity and knowing in our lives. It refers to the process of self-awareness by which we learn to witness inner states and have more authority over our basic energy. But it does not guarantee wisdom or rightness. There is infinite interpretation of any state and infinite potential for distortion. The moment we say that we can tune in and discover a specific and detailed map that will show how to live in the immediate future or how to look at our experiences, we are playing the age-old game of self-deception. In making this personalization, we are imposing our own subjective, egoic requirement for order upon existence. This process is a way of trying to find an inner Mommy or Daddy, and in it we remain spiritually immature.

For all of us, one day there must come an end to a Mommy/Daddy relationship to life and to God. It is the price we must pay for maturity. For this to happen, our sense of existential unknowing and our sense of being, creating, and doing must finally merge. Thus, like the God of Genesis or the Kabbalah, we are always creating, always emerging out of the darkness, out of our own unknowing, each moment revealing the possibilities of the next in accordance with our consecration. The more our consecration embraces life as the Divine (really just a state of open, unobstructed attention) the less we judge life, the less we try to get it right, the less we search for hidden meaning, and the more irrelevant it becomes to try to see if we are on the right path. We gain "God" (as vibrant aliveness and new possibility which does not necessarily have to be pleasant) even as we lose control of ourselves. It is this process, and not the good or bad actions of conventional consciousness, that begins to show us our energetic stance in life. Thus "guidance," if we can rightfully speak of such a thing, is a tremendously dynamic process of awareness and profound understanding in relationship to every aspect of life. Distinguishing between inner and outer or right and wrong simply becomes meaningless. From this point of view, trying to reach inside for specific guidance reflects fear and distrust of life and being; it takes the subtle play of consciousness and imprisons it in a kind of psychic dictatorship.

It is clear that life has an integrity transcending ordinary understanding. Why do we want to believe that this integrity comes and goes, thus placing ourselves in the position of playing God and having to make it right? In my conference work, I have reached a space of immense freedom because I know I need not guide the experience to any particular place. I don't have any assumptions about where we are going. I know that just being present and attentive will allow us to reach a space that has its own intrinsic meaning and richness. Thus no two conferences are the same. They are a dynamic in which the combined and deepened attention of the participants eventually creates a vision of existence and states of being so profound that we all experience a whole new dimension of understanding. It is not my responsibility to make something special happen; I trust the essential nature of the experience itself. In this work we do not merely serve ourselves; something else is happening. We are creating space for possibility in our world.

Each time a group of people comes to those natural boundaries of energy where reactivity and defense seem to resist any further progress, and we appreciate that our worship in that moment is resistance, that resistance disappears. It is the same process that I have described for the individual in the singing exercises. The forces of Creative Relationship, Intensity and Unconditional Love are converging toward the transformational moment in a group dynamic and thus at tremendously enhanced energy levels. As we collectively learn to navigate this territory, I am certain that we are creating new doors (or lubricating old ones that are only rarely explored) so that others can more easily find their way into these depths. For days a new light of fineness and aliveness radiates from us because we have collectively reached the edge of the archetypal forces that define our existence. We explore it in our very cells, in the presence that envelops us, and in simple homage to the powers that make us human. Individually we cannot live this energy. It is born within us in preparation for our unobstructed relationship with each other. In this sense, the higher states of consciousness do not belong to one person, one messiah, but to all of us. If it takes humanity hundreds or thousands of years to reach the point where energies we briefly know today are our basic consciousness, we are even now opening the door that invites this possibility. It is as though our future is curving back to live with us for a while and calling us onward.

INNER DEATH/REBIRTH—AN INVITATION TO TRANSFORMATION

In the loneliness of certain nights, in the moments of deepest vulnerability and doubt, I wonder whether this call to radical aliveness is just my own pattern, whether it has brought me or anyone to greater light. I know that we must learn to face life's pain, but I wonder if perhaps there is not an easier way. Then in the morning comes the dawning of a deepened love and ordinariness and I remember how my own life has unfolded with its own wisdom and timing, and I trust this is true for all of us. It may not be easy, but when we are called in our hearts, we will be ready to face the challenges.

I think to myself how wonderful it would be if theories like the Hundredth Monkey story really do hold the answer, that all we need is enough people to move to a higher level, and the rest of humanity will follow suit. It is a compelling story and deserves a few moments of our consideration. The Hundredth Monkey story was reported by Lyall Watson in his fascinating book, *Supernature*.[1]

[1] Watson, Lyall. *Supernature* (Doubleday/Anchor, 1973).

It is speculative hearsay, not documented fact; yet I believe Watson is correct in asserting that it is a genuine phenomenon of the spread of consciousness. The story concerns how a particular new behavior appeared in a tribe of monkeys and spread beyond them. At the point where the last holdout (arbitrarily called the Hundredth Monkey) learned the behavior, the behavior jumped to other tribes that were separated by as much as thirty miles of ocean from the original tribe. The process of spreading within the original group is interesting in itself. The first monkey (Ima by name) developed the behavior of washing the sand off her food. She taught it to her mother and from there it quickly spread through the inner community of females and young. The behavior never spread to the older males, who had to die off, a time lapse of about four generations, before the behavior was generalized to the whole of Ima's group. Ima herself was obviously a genius monkey because she also learned to winnow rice from sand by tossing the mixture into the water and then scooping up the floating kernels. In this way she also learned to swim, and these behaviors (winnowing and swimming) slowly spread through the group. Watson only reports the jump of the original potato-washing behavior and not the others. The Hundredth Monkey supposition is that once a particular consciousness is shared by enough individuals, it then spreads automatically to everyone.

We are now generalizing this phenomenon to human behavior and our thinking is: If we can foster love and peace, it will spread like the Hundredth Monkey to all of humanity. Certainly, as with Realization, when there is a radical new leap in consciousness, the energy of that leap will gradually generalize to the rest of society. But when we are talking not of radical change, but rather of emphasizing the positive pole of our existing consciousness, then I suspect that as fast as we empower one side, the other side will also grow. I wonder, then, if we are not also spreading the fear, the judgment, the sense of wrongness that underlies much of our motivation to bring love and light into the world. The Hundredth Monkey phenomenon is happening all the time; it is the basic phenomenon whereby any moment of Wholeness changes the process of Becoming in our world. But understanding this does not make it a force we can wield on our terms. When we use this phenomenon as a rationalization to inspire more people to work for a better world, we are, I sense, meddling once again out of our very personalized fears and hopes. As medicine has done with childbirth, we too think that we can help birth a New Age in a better and safer way. Invariably our best efforts may only lead to new problems.

How can we think we know what is good for humanity? We argue that we do know, and a favorite example is that nuclear war is bad for everyone. Well certainly I have no disagreement. It is unimaginable to me that nuclear war in itself is any kind of answer. Yet the fact that it hovers over us suggests that radical aliveness is being invited now almost as a mandate for human survival. We must look deeper! It does not follow that because there is the threat of annihilation, we must become more loving. Love can never be the cure for war if the fear of war is what turns us toward that love. Love is born of radical aliveness, not hope for a better world.

The potential for nuclear war did not arise overnight. It has grown with human consciousness, and the forces involved are as ancient as time itself and as poorly understood. Throughout history, people have been concerned for the welfare of humanity. Many people, then as now, saw the time in which they lived as the darkest, the most terrible, the most corrupt. Like ourselves, all these people wanted to make a difference, wanted to find some cure, and they too consciously chose what they felt was right.

I suggest the same thing that has happened in the past is happening today. Now it is just apparent on a much larger scale, and with much graver consequences. That which saves also destroys; that which brings certainty does so by "killing" the uncertainty of a moment before; that which improves disease has "killed" the condition of illness. *Both the conscious intent (to create the good) and the unconscious motive (fear of destruction) create with equal force in this universe of wholeness.* Is it the survival instinct and the application of intelligence at the level of basic consciousness to improve the condition of life in every imaginable way that has also brought with it the capacity to eliminate all life? (We can use words like "survival instinct," but until we attempt the adventure of self-transcendence we really do not know what our words mean.)

Perhaps if we could have understood the great teachings that declared that life is already whole, and fundamental change is Grace, we would be more capable of facing our own survival as a process of radical aliveness rather than a ceaseless effort to gain security and peace born of the fear of being destroyed. Having deeply faced this, we would no doubt be much more capable of managing our own destructive potential. Perhaps we could have made a choice long ago to work to enhance awareness of our spiritual nature and thus keep pace with our reasoning capacity and our power to manipulate life. I don't know. I suspect that all along it has been a rightful process of unfoldment with no guarantees.

I doubt we have had any choice but to empower our "unawakened" consciousness through our efforts to secure life and thereby unconsciously refuse the inner Apocalypse that is the invitation of Transformation. But I don't think we can refuse it any longer. Like the legendary Zen monk, it is time for us to enter the cloister of our hearts and face our annihilation and our potential to transform.

Of course, at the level of daily life this seems ludicrous. What are we to do, allow illness, make suffering a great ideal? Are we never to try to improve life? No, this is cause/effect thinking again, reacting out of our lifelong pattern where doing something for wholeness is better than simply being whole. What I am suggesting is that our doing must become an undoing.

Let us meet life as it is. Let us penetrate into the very depths of ourselves by refusing to call wrong or unwhole that which frightens or discomforts us. Let us stop denying what our experience presents to us again and again, namely our ignorance, uncertainty, helplessness and death. Every time we rush to do something to fix ourselves or our world, let us recall that no action taken from our present consciousness to improve life ever does so without serious consequences. Therefore, let us undress ourselves as well. Let us see how naked we can become, how available to life.

This is radical aliveness, and out of it is born love. This love is emanation, a natural integrative force, that reflects our deeper balance, our resonance with Wholeness. This love grows as our awareness and our way of life refines to embrace more of what seem to be irreconcilable forces. It is not an ideal that must have its opposite. To become more loving is not something that we do, it is something life does to us as we live closer and closer to the unknown in each moment. To me this is the great gift and the great adventure of life. As the poet Kabir said long ago about love, "Those who seek to be reasonable about it fail." As love grows within us, so does our capacity to sustain the tension of conflicting or paradoxical understandings intrinsic to the multidimensional nature of human consciousness. It is love, born of radical aliveness, that may allow us to reconcile our immense creative and destructive capacity.

Our existing consciousness has probably taken thousands of millennia to become the dominant collective consciousness. The consciousness of Love and of Life's Wholeness may take many millennia more. The passage is a difficult process. Now we must see that there is no real remedy to nuclear holocaust as we presently look at the problem. War itself is not the issue. And consciously choosing not to have war is only the beginning. We must refuse nuclear war, but this will not lead to security. If we call for a peace that does not come from a realization of Wholeness, that does not invite the inner undoing of the Apocalypse of Awakening, I have no doubt that we will only generate some even more diabolical threat to our existence. And so a new tension starts, for we must develop ways to unify into higher energies through other means, through a way of being with life that is the most profound worship. The gifts of aliveness that we have gained by solving problems, by choosing sides, by transcending ourselves through crisis, will always be a part of us. But we will never place these into perspective until we can access life force in other ways. This possibility is the invitation to radical aliveness. We have seen what happened to Laura, and we know that this potential must also exist for humanity as a whole, and is unfolding even now.

TO YOU, MY LOVERS

The love of Life is the love of each other;
Our rebirth is our relationship, now and
    again now.

I bequeath to you, my brothers and
    sisters,
    something wonderful, something
    invisible.
I receive it from you,
    Woven of the depth with which we
    give ourselves over
    to each other, to life, to God. . .
    there arises silently in our midst and
    takes its place,
    a holy breath, our very flesh sublimed.
This friendship lifts me closer to Myself.
Possibility born, revealed, alive,
    completes my body, circulates my
    blood to infinity.

This is the power that we have.
Knowing this, we are freed and
    imprisoned,
    doomed to become Nothing and
    Everything,
    each to each other the living Source.

Who is the leader here?
Do we not hear the rhythm to which we
    must march,
    in the deepest, wordless intuitions of
    our souls?

RICHARD MOSS

✤ GLOSSARY

Aliveness: Vitality of the body, mind and spirit, a radiant quality of presence and alertness. This implies an ability to accommodate more energy. It reflects our capacity to allow undifferentiated beingness to be expressed through the bodymind in the same way that a well-tuned piano allows a musician to give fuller expression to a piece of music.

Apocalypse: A term used in Christian theology to designate the final showdown between the forces of good and evil. In the mystical sense, as it is used here, it means an inner confrontation, a discontinuity of consciousness in which identity shifts from the ego base of subject/object consciousness to a higher level.

Authentic spirituality: The challenge and impetus that comes from a way of life that honors the highest in ourselves while at the same time honoring the personal side of the nature.

Being and Becoming: Being is openness to what is, full acceptance of Life. Becoming is focusing, leveraging oneself to get a better view, a better vantage point on alternatives. Becoming is part of Being because the wholeness of life contains stillness and movement. This gives rise to an existential tension, awareness.

Centrifugal forces of consciousness: Rational, conscious and Divine nature, especially love. All these qualities tend to move us toward expansion or dissolution of self-boundary. Definition by inclusion, disincarnating.

Centripetal forces of consciousness: Our elemental, instinctual and emotional nature; also, will and intensity, which tend to concentrate and condense our energy and create self-boundary. Definition by exclusion, the incarnating force.

Thinking in terms of dynamic centrifugal and centripetal forces shifts us from a vertical, linear and hierarchical model (i.e. higher versus lower chakras, especially the sense of higher as better or more valid than lower) to a spherical and process model in which Being and Becoming, spirit and matter are seen as inseparable.

Commandment as Law: Commandment, as in the Great Commandment to love God and our neighbor as ourself, is not an injunction for behavior, but an expression of Law. Law can be understood as *prescriptive*, as in the human laws that tell people how to live, and *descriptive*, as in natural law, which is a portrayal of what already is. In the descriptive sense, the Great Commandment is law and is consistent with the fundamental premise that we are already whole. This view of Commandment recognizes the fundamental error of demanding its fulfillment by anyone who has not already attained a certain level of consciousness, for then law becomes dogma or repressive obedience. In life, every person's law is always determined by their level of consciousness. A person who is capable of loving God and his neighbor as himself will do this as a natural expression of being. Thus, for such an individual, it is a description of what occurs naturally, not a moral injunction.

Consecration: Our consecration reflects the underlying principle of our lives. It is not something we do; rather it is something we discover (or more truly, intuit) as we look at life from a deeper awareness. To intuit our consecration, we must let go of the judgmental mind and the setting of goals. This enables us to discern our life posture, to "see" ourselves more objectively. As we seek to intuit our consecration, we are simultaneously acknowledging that our lives have an origin and an existence that precedes our ideas and intents. This recognition, in itself, carries us into a growing harmony with the transformational impulse. The intuition of one's consecration is part of a radical self-awareness that constantly moves us toward a larger relationship to life.

Content of consciousness, psychic content: The entirety of organized and unorganized experience as it is presented in sense or thought. This includes both the ordinary content of consciousness (i.e. feelings, ideas, sensations) and the subtle content (clairsentience, clairvoyance). As we mature in the transformational process, the content of consciousness ceases to be the principal determiner of how we approach life because it is based on a limited sense of identity. Consecration to life becomes more and more important.

Creative involvment, the vector of: An *a priori* quality of spontaneity and originality with which we meet an experience. It is the extent to which we are able to engage life without the usual filters of the judgmental, comparative, and evaluative faculties of mind.

Discontinuity of consciousness: A break with the familiar and the known, allowing a jump to a different dimension of consciousness. In a certain sense, a death. The point of discontinuity in consciousness represents a "corner" around which the ordinary mind is incapable of projecting. In daily life, major discontinuities leading to Realization or Enlightenment are rare, but minor discontinuities are more common (as in so-called clinical death or the moment of impact in an auto accident). It is interesting that the few individuals who survive leaping from the Golden Gate Bridge frequently show a remarkable transformation of consciousness and return to happy, productive lives. Likewise those who have near-death experiences (clinically die and are resuscitated) often demonstrate profound transformation. On a clinical note, chronic pain initiated by an accident can often be released by inducting the person to the same level of energy that occurred during the discontinuity at the moment of impact (often a very high level of energy). It is as though the pain is bound at this level of energy and not merely in the physical structure alone.

Divine body: A perfect state of unobstructed being. In this state, the egoic body has been transcended and one's physical structure is infinitely more conductive. The same level of energy that would cause intensified psychic content and physical manifestations of every kind in the egoic body is now radiant aliveness. These two terms (egoic body and divine body) must not be seen as absolutes, but as expressions along a continuum. We are constantly shifting along this continuum at moments of discontinuity depending on the focus of attention and the action of Grace. Even a few moments at the level of the divine body can produce profound physical healing.

Door of aloneness and devotion: The door of aloneness has nothing to do with singularity or separateness, even though at times we may find ourselves without companions. It is a dynamic of ceaseless attention and ever deepening relationship to the immediacy of life. One cannot depend on external authority. Approval becomes irrelevant, and one becomes a light unto oneself. This is when we experience all as the Living God. It is the point when our understanding has surpassed our capacity to choose for or against.

Egoic body: Our egoic body is a reflection of whatever it is that circumscribes the limits of our concerns. It is a field of sensations that reinforce our self-definition. It is our conditioned way of accessing, holding and expressing energy and aliveness. It is the way of being in our bodies that we have learned by emulation of parents and societal norms and that at a deeper level has been inducted as the energetic template through which we hold life force. The egoic body can only sustain a circumscribed range of energy before it manifests exhaustion or illness. When we encounter a new level of energy at any change point or meet an awakened person who carries a higher energy, the egoic body may conduct this energy in a constellation of psychosomatic response (i.e. anxiety, bliss, asthma, constipation, diarrhea, palpitations, sleepiness, and so on).

Energetic: Having to do with energy (see **Energy**). Also the quality of consciousness that, itself, determines or influences our subjective experience.

Energetic conductivity: The capacity to accommodate more energy—other people, other aspects of reality—in one's definition of self. In a sense, one's energetic conductivity can be regarded as the ability to remain open and available in circumstances that provoke a tendency toward self-definition and reaction.

Energetic saturation: The psychic condition of transformational readiness where the container of one's life (i.e. belief structures, lifestyle, habit patterns) is no longer large enough for the energies one is capable of accessing. Energetic saturation may precipitate a fundamental or radical change of aliveness.

Energetic shift: A change in the content of consciousness, in the relationship between oneself and everything else. It is accompanied by a change in the sense of identity. Energetic shift can be provoked by almost anything that catalyzes us into the present moment and is as ordinary as the euphoria of skiing to the extraordinariness of mystical awakening.

Energetic template: Archetypal forces that define possibility, or an individual, living or departed, who has accessed and carries a higher energy providing a source of inspiration and object of affection for another. This also defines the function of the parent for the child, or teacher for the student. The Guru functions as a template by providing an individual with a model embodying a higher energy (usually perceived as love). To the degree that this relationship enables the individual to see higher human possibilities in another, one receives an "energetic impress." Subsequently, the next step of finding the higher possibilities is facilitated.

Energy: We can think of energy as occupying a range of expressions across a spectrum. At one end of the spectrum is Pure Energy or Consciousness. This is energy not yet particularized into the familiar and identifiable. It is unconstrained beingness, a primordial field of being out of which particular forms emerge. At the other end of the spectrum, energy becomes crystallized or held captive by the rigid boundaries with which we perceive aspects of reality.

Because energy is the basis for life, it is also experienced directly.

Most basically, energy is vitality, sexuality, feeling, intensity, but it is also a felt presence or current in and around the body. It is important to be able to directly sense and move energy as a stage in developing awareness. To be able consciously to shift our level of energy allows us to move from focusing only on the content of consciousness to appreciating more subtle dimensions that tend to determine the quality and type of psychic content. Higher energy refers to a more inclusive, universal awareness, while lower energy refers to a denser, more personalized consciousness. Higher energy is increased sensitivity. At higher energies, more formlessness and ambiguity can be accommodated in an individual's consciousness, and there is more fluidity between subject and object, less rigidity between what is habitually considered to be self and not-self.

Field attention: The capacity to extend a sense of attention as a felt presence or palpable stillness that is both internal and external. It transcends yet includes the ordinary content of consciousness. This is taught first as energetic embrace and then deepened through the Sacred Meditation. Field attention can be thought of as the consciousness sometimes referred as I AM. This consciousness is not a concept or belief, but rather is a palpable attention that allows bodily as well as cognitive and subtle sensibilities to register or interact with a larger sense of being. This attention is the basis for both inner silence and profoundly heightened sensitivity.

Freed attention: A sense of clarity that occurs when we are no longer immersed in our subjective reactions to people or events. Energy is released to new creative potential when we free attention from a particular pattern of belief. As we grow in consciousness, freed attention is the means by which we are able to realize our own innate power to allow (not create) new possibility.

Fundamental transformation vs. energetic perturbation: Fundamental transformation is a radical shift in one's psychic structure, a shift in one's capacity to access and hold higher energies. Energetic perturbation is the application of a "shock" to the being that results in a temporary expansion of egoic boundaries— often with a feeling of well being and new possibility. While the effects of such a shock may be similar to effects observed with fundamental transformation, they are always transient. In contrast, the effects of fundamental transformation are permanent, since they result from a change in the capacity of the being.

Gravity and Grace: Gravity is the pull towards the habitual consciousness which is reinforced by the structures (i.e. roles) of that consciousness. Grace is the constant pull to the higher consciousness. The effect of Grace enhances as we learn to free attention and re-enter our relationship with life with a new degree of connectedness.

Higher intention: A conscious resolve to live according to certain values and ideals, creating a standard for self-critical spiritual discrimination. Such a resolve is based on goal setting, thus at first it arises from a hidden assumption (consecration) that we are less than whole. Realizing this, we eventually release higher intentions, thus acknowledging our new consecration in wholeness.

Incarnation or embodiment: The process of living the transcendental principle in time and space. One's whole being is conducting a higher energy into the manifest plane. For example, the principle of Oneness is given expression at the everyday, physical level as sensitivity and radiance. Incarnating implies a profound and ongoing purification of one's whole nature and the freeing of all creative modes of expression. Thus it is far more than a passive capacity to reach higher states of consciousness (as in meditation) or to express the higher as concepts or belief. It is a cellular transformation with accompanying expression in vital physical aliveness, enhanced intelligence and voice resonance, so that one literally creates spaciousness of being throughout the *whole range* of ordinary living.

Intensity, the vector of: A certain quality of attention to the immediacy of the present moment that involves our whole being, resulting in the unification of self and experience. Intensity accesses will and therefore enables us to derive a greater degree of command over factors that tend to dissipate our energy.

Intention: A desire to achieve an identifiable goal. Intention ordinarily has its foundation in a sense of lack and a wish to improve oneself. To the extent intention is a reflection of desire, it is restricted to conscious knowing. Intention, in itself, is therefore not sufficient to empower the deeper transformational spaces, since transformation takes us into the unknown. As long as intention is based on what we think is "right" for us, it is confined to the known. In this sense, all intention is ego-based.

New Age Fundamentalism: Any of the current spiritual teachings that offer one-sided formulas or recipes for living. The student is thus replacing one set of beliefs for another, rather than inquiring into the nature of being.

Obedience and choicelessness: Obedience occurs when we recognize the illusion of alternatives, and we consciously yield to the deeper call of Consciousness. This is not capitulation to an outside authority, but the recognition that we can no longer have life on our own terms.

Psychic dictatorship: The capitulation of our birthright as beings of infinite potential to some form of inner guidance rather than the ability to distill wisdom from the ferment of human experience. This can take the form of always wanting to get specific directions to ordinary decisions. This presupposes that there exist fixed answers and some shortcut to wisdom.

Religion of War, the: Religion comes from *religio* meaning "to bind back," that is, to access one's fullest energies and aliveness. To the extent that war offers the present subject/object consciousness (the presumption of separation affirmed by ordinary consciousness) its most intense level of energy, warfare is a religious phenomenon.

Ritual consecration: A conscious invocation expressing the truth of the wholeness of life. It creates a spiritual context of trust as one enters new dimensions of experience.

Sacrament of Ignorance, the: This is when we come to regard our limited capacity to know Reality not as defeat, but as an occasion and opportunity for wonder. Implicit in the Sacrament of Ignorance is an intuitive recognition that the reality we experience is as much an aspect of our own subjectivity as so-called objective data. This creates the condition for an inner mental silence and openness, which is the true temple of being. In this temple of silence, we are taught by Existence.

Spirituality without a body: Spiritual teachings of the channeled variety. Such teachings are "spirituality without a body," since they are incapable of providing the same kind of relationship or role model as a living teacher. These teachings fail to deal with the fundamental paradox of balancing the higher dimensions with the needs and reality of the physical body and material timespace. In effect, they purport to give clearcut and precise answers free of the ambiguities and paradoxes of lived spirituality. Channeled teachings represent a step in the embodiment of higher energy beyond everyday consciousness, but do not transcend the basic dichotomies of subject/object consciousness and are not representative of an embodied state of realization. Inevitably such teachings tend to create fear and dependency because they involve a level of polarized consciousness that deals with good and evil, disasters, punishments, and so forth.

Transformation is not "on our terms": Transformation is the inevitable process of maturing as we dive deeper into life. Genuine transformation is rarely if ever available within the familiar context wherein we seem to have control or where we choose to do things because they will make us happy or better people. We do not have final control over the timing, nor can we be assured of the smoothness or dignity of the transformational moment. After a profound energetic shift that may characterize a transformational breakthrough, there is every likelihood that the subsequent life will bear little resemblance to what was previously imagined. Truly transformative breakthroughs usually catapult one into uncharted waters.

Transformational imperative: An innate law of spiritual reality wherein life in its totality is perceived as ever fostering higher and more coherent levels of consciousness. Even as the energy of the physical universe dissipates from the ultimate of the Big Bang theory toward entropy (The Second Law of Thermodynamics), the transformational imperative states that the diversity of life is growing and gradually expressing the capacity for movement to more unified and inclusive states of consciousness. In the human realm, there is a dis-identification with roles and definitions to facilitate the liberation of consciousness from fixed forms.

Transformational vector: Any collection of forces, energies, objects or characteristics that taken together produce some particular result. For example, a disease vector consists of all the factors producing a particular disease. The vectors of the singing exercise each bring a particular set of energies and awarenesses to bear on the processes of "singing until the song sings you." A vector in the transformational sense is a spiritual "mechanism" or psychological posture through which we access another level of consciousness. It can also be considered as a way to connect with a larger reality.

Unconditional Love, the vector of: Unconditional Love can be thought of as the principle of inclusivity in which Existence is wholeness and everything is exactly what it is. As a transformational vector in the exercises, it is a field attention through which the wholeness of oneself and all that one perceives (including the other) is affirmed in sustained energetic embrace. And through this affirmation, the other experiences energetic resonance and upliftment.

The transformational vectors (Creative Involvement, Intensity, Unconditional Love) cannot really be separated. For example, if Unconditional Love weren't already present, spontaneous Creative Involvement would not be possible. We would continuously distance ourselves from the immediacy of our experience through judgment, reaction, analysis; in short, be forever locked in subject/object consciousness. In this sense, transformational vectors are like the threefold nature of the Godhead in Christian theology (Father, Son, Holy Ghost). When the vectors converge in the transformational moment, we are living in the state where "I and the Father are One."

Unconscious normalizing: Normalizing in its scientific application is the process of settling for approximations through simplification and "rounding." Its natural consequence is the sacrifice of integrity for practicality. In a psychological sense, it is a process of selecting only that information which figures directly in reinforcing the dominant reality structure we have selected for ourselves. Reciprocally, normalizing results in repression of all that does not figure directly in supporting our relative models of the universe.

Unobstructed relationship: A quality of free attention between two or more persons. Here the individuals are able to see the other as whole, as divine, as if they are two mirrors facing. This occurs when all self-involvement by those persons is absent.

Virgin birth: Having a truly new relationship to oneself, so that anything that arises in consciousness leads to new possibility, new aliveness. When all that we have learned in the conventional sense is no longer adequate, prompting us to stand in our own light and learn to have a relationship to ourselves independent of the values and expectations of the rest of the world. It is the freedom to embrace all aspects of ourselves, every moment of our experience, and let it be a springboard into our depths.

Wisdom of Ignorance, the: This does not refer to ordinary ignorance, as in lack of information. This is the wisdom that suffuses us when we come to the limit of the known and are able to acknowledge that. It is the intuitive insight that comes from an acknowledgment of the limitation of the mind and of conventional ways of knowing and applying knowledge. It is a door to infinite possibility. This is a new kind of attention focused on the vast background against which conditioned forms of knowing are continuously seen for their relativity.

THREE MOUNTAIN FOUNDATION

Three Mountain Foundation, a tax-exempt organization inspired by the work of Richard Moss, is dedicated to providing new vision and language for the expression of the evolutionary impulse occurring throughout the world. It sponsors transformational workshops for individuals, youths, organizations, hospitals led by Richard Moss and his associates. Its books, tapes, publications and programs explore the integration of the ongoing adventure of transformation into the practical realities of daily life.

HOW SHALL I LIVE

Transforming Health Crisis into Greater Aliveness
Book and Tape Series

Using health crisis as a metaphor, this book and tape series guide us into a new understanding of the healing process by exploring the potential for growth inherent in all crisis. *How Shall I Live* does not reject modern medicine, but increases its scope and effectiveness by broadening its vision. Dr. Moss shows how his own experience of surgery changed his life and discusses several remarkable case histories where the patients experienced faster recovery rates, fewer transfusions, and a long-lasting sense of well-being by learning to tap into the ever-present energy of wholeness and health. Both the book and tape series present specific energetic exercises and meditations which have proven exceedingly valuable for health care personnel, patients, family and friends. (Book, Celestial Arts, 1985) (Tape Series, Three Mountain Foundation, 1985.)

THE I THAT IS WE

Awakening to Higher Energies Through Unconditional Love

Richard Moss's first book has become a classic work on the transformational process. People from all over the world have been deeply moved by *The I That Is We* because of its clear expression of mystical states of consciousness and ability to induct the reader into new dimensions of being. In this book Dr. Moss delves into such areas as the illusion of separateness, living at the edge of formlessness, the transformative value of travel and disease, and the heightening of energy that occurs through group interaction. *The I That Is We* is a profound statement of the dynamic, ongoing challenge of living with expanded awareness. (Celestial Arts, 1981).

AUDIO TAPES by RICHARD MOSS

Talks covering all aspects of the transformational process are available on cassette tapes. These tapes have been heard throughout the world and are recommended by doctors, therapists, and ministers to assist individuals who are in crisis or transition. Dr. Moss's vibrant voice quality and presence are communicated through the taped medium to allow the listener to experience new levels of consciousness.

THE THIRD MOUNTAIN

THE THIRD MOUNTAIN, a tape and magazine published twice a year by Three Mountain Foundation, present an ongoing forum on consciousness exploration. Articles, interviews, and talks by Richard Moss and his associates present the subscriber with a current and timely view of the transformational process.

For an updated tape list and further informaton on conferences, books, tapes, and magazines, contact:

THREE MOUNTAIN FOUNDATION
P.O. BOX 1180
LONE PINE, CA 93545
(619) 876-4702

Richard Moss, M.D. released the practice of medicine in 1976 and has since led workshops throughout the world. He is widely regarded as an inspirational teacher and master of awakening individuals into new dimensions of consciousness. His work bridges traditional medical, psychological and spiritual thinking and moves into the direct experience of higher consciousness.

He enjoys rock climbing, sculpting, writing poetry, and tending the orchards of his home at the base of the eastern Sierras. He founded and directed the transformational community at Sky Hi Ranch for three years before moving to Lone Pine, California in 1984. Three Mountain Foundation, a tax-exempt organization, provides workshops, lectures, tapes and other writings based on Dr. Moss's work.